The Witching Hour

SILVER RAVENWOLF is perhaps best known as one of the most widely published authors of her time, including bestsellers *Solitary Witch*, *Teen Witch*, and *To Ride a Silver Broomstick*. Artist, doll maker, chandler, photographer, and internet entrepreneur, she also heads the Black Forest Clan Circle and Seminary, a Wiccan organization that consists of over sixty covens in thirty states with three international groups. Wife of thirty-five years, mother of four grown children, and grandmother, Silver has been interviewed by the *New York Times*, the *Wall Street Journal*, *US News & World Report*, and A&E *Biography*. You can find Silver on Twitter, Instagram, Facebook, and WordPress (silverravenwolf.wordpress.com) or visit her at silverravenwolf.info.

SPELLS, POWDERS, FORMULAS
AND WITCHY TECHNIQUES THAT WORK

The WITCHING HOUR

SILVER RAVENWOLF

LLEWELLYN PUBLICATIONS
WOODBURY, MINNESOTA

FIRST EDITION
Third Printing, 2018

Book design by Rebecca Zins
Cover design by Ellen Lawson

Llewellyn Publications is a registered trademark
of Llewellyn Worldwide Ltd.

Library of Congress Cataloging-in-Publication Data
Names: RavenWolf, Silver, author.
Title: The witching hour : spells, powders, formulas, and witchy
    techniques that work / Silver RavenWolf.
Description: First edition. | Woodbury, Minnesota : Llewellyn
    Publications, [2017] | Includes bibliographical references and index.
Identifiers: LCCN 2017024204 (print) | LCCN 2017031512 (ebook) | ISBN
    9780738753980 (ebook) | ISBN 9780738753423 (paper)
Subjects: LCSH: Witchcraft. | Magic.
Classification: LCC BF1566 (ebook) | LCC BF1566.R338 2017 (print) |
    DDC 133.4/3—dc23
LC record available at https://lccn.loc.gov/2017024204

Llewellyn Worldwide Ltd. does not participate in, endorse, or have any authority or responsibility concerning private business transactions between our authors and the public.

All mail addressed to the author is forwarded, but the publisher cannot, unless specifically instructed by the author, give out an address or phone number.

Any internet references contained in this work are current at publication time, but the publisher cannot guarantee that a specific location will continue to be maintained. Please refer to the publisher's website for links to authors' websites and other sources.

Llewellyn Publications
A Division of Llewellyn Worldwide Ltd.
2143 Wooddale Drive
Woodbury, MN 55125-2989
www.llewellyn.com
Printed in the United States of America

This book is dedicated to Thorn Nightwind,
whose support and assistance has been invaluable.

The intuitive mind is a sacred gift, and the rational mind is a faithful servant. We have created a society that honors the servant and has forgotten the gift.

• • •

ALBERT EINSTEIN

CONTENTS

CHAPTER SIX:
Magickal Powders
and Herbal Blends 197

CONTENTS

INTRODUCTION

The witching hour…that moment when every fiber of your being says, "This is the time to do the magick…the ritual…the enchantment for what I need!" It is a feeling like no other; perhaps your hands tingle, there is a quickening in the heart, a shiver in the shoulders. It could be dawn, a misty twilight, or the deepest, darkest inky night. It is a time when all of your being urges you to get up, get moving, and get working! Confidence that you can easily step from the problem at hand to the success that you desire seethes around you. And you know, to the depths of your soul, it is time for magick: the moment your power has matured.

Your witching hour.

Will you forge ahead? Follow your instincts? Flow with the universe to achieve?

Will you be brave?

Will you be clear of mind?

Will you take the risk of change?

Will you throw the golden lasso of accomplishment and draw your success to you?

Will you *believe*?

This book you hold in your hands is the result of the purest, most honest, most dedicated collection of interesting secrets of the magickal arts. It has been nine years since my last book and much has transpired in my life—some of it so marvelous I can't even begin to express my delight, and some so dark that the pain was almost too much to bear. I spent many of those years learning, studying, trying to grow as a person and as an author. My goal in my writing career has always been to gather experience, assimilate, learn, create, and develop a clearer, stronger platform for success for all. I kept that goal in spirit, whether I was able to write or not through these many years. I felt that I could not give you a book without giving you good, solid techniques to use, and for that I had to practice, practice, practice.

Some saw my drawing back from publishing as a weakness.

Some gossiped that I had no more to give my brothers and sisters.

During this time I realized something very important: who had the magick…and who didn't.

Words tell you much, if you observe.

Break out of the box, my little muse said.

Break out of the mold, whispered my mind.

Rise above. Think differently! Find the way! See the future!

My focus is always on the reader, my partner, my friend. My words are links between us as we raise each other up, as we try to walk the high road, as we try to succeed together. This is not a book of "let's throw something together to make a sale."

No. No. No.

This is a book of magickal power, sweat, tears, and triumphs—nine glorious years of it.

No matter what is going on in your life right now, I am here to tell you that there is a lot of power on this side of the grass. You just have to reach out, acknowledge that power, have confidence, and use it.

It isn't difficult.

It isn't so mystical that you can't comprehend it.

It isn't a secret just for the few.

Have faith in yourself! Conjure it!

I did, and so can you.

CHAPTER ONE

The Magickal You and the Work That You Do

Nothing is concrete. Everything is limitless. The universe acts upon the seeds you plant in it.

You are exclusive.

You are unique.

You are exceptional.

Step out and step strong! If you are ready to believe in the power of yourself and your ability to connect with the oneness of the universe, this book is for you.

There will be techniques in this book that you already know; you just needed to be reminded. There are ideas here that are new, goodies to work with, fun things to do. A switch in perception, a light in the dark, a different way or method of enchantment—all this and more.

The only thing you absolutely must do?

Believe.

The Preparation of Your Mind

I have learned that the best enchantments are done by those who have acknowledged the power within themselves and realized it is okay to have a unique way of working with the mental, emotional, and physical aspects of magick and ritual that best suit their style and personality. These people may have a favorite set of charms or chants, gestures, or blended practices that have proven, over time, to render excellent results. They have managed to overcome those who make fun of their activities because they know that what they are utilizing works—and works well even though they don't have whatever some pressuring soul online thinks they need to be official. These people are always building, constantly learning, and are willing to embrace new ideas and experiment, striving not to do what the masses tell them but, instead, practice what will bring fulfillment in a positive way to themselves and others without doing harm.

These are the people of Spirit.

Working with Mother Nature's gifts is a very shamanic practice. It is one of blending with the earth and her bounty—of allowing yourself to go beyond what most individuals see, hear, or feel and to commune with the living energies of the land, sea, and sky. The more you work with these energies, daily stressors slip away. They don't bother you as much. You'd rather listen to the crickets, the coyote in the woods, or the cardinals in the tree than the politics on the television. Their messages are far more important than the warbling of a social media personality contest.

By celebrating and embracing nature, harmony becomes a more constant companion. Balance is easier.

This is the gift of Earth Mother.

In my experience, your state of mind is the highest priority when practicing any type of enchantment, whether you are beginning to formulate a magickal powder or herbal blend, casting a spell for wisdom and healing, or taking the time to honor Spirit in ritual. Daily meditation and learning to walk outside and blend with nature can bring you mental, emotional, and physical health. It is also how you learn about the plant life in your area. The collection around you tells you what endures, and if you study what you see and hear, nature explains her survival tactics. In the shamanic world of plants, animals, trees, and insects, every being is of great importance. Each has its own power. All are willing to share—even the rocks! But...

Only if you listen.

The Spirit Walk

I first introduced the Spirit Walk in my online Braucherei classes and blog. (Braucherei, or Pow-Wow, is a Pennsylvania Dutch system of traditional folk medicine.) This is a short (or long, up to you) walk outside with the specific intent of observing. Rather than a game plan, you allow Spirit to guide you. Before you go on the walk, quietly ask Spirit to guide you and show you what you need to learn. It is okay to ask for a natural gift to place on your altar or sacred area in your workroom. You may find a feather, an unusual stone, a beautiful flower, or another object of nature. You may not find anything at all! Indeed, your gift may be your experience of meeting a unique form of nature up front and personal. I remember that one individual found an unusual manmade object that was of significance to his private history, and he believed it was a sign that his ancestors approved of what he was doing and were assuring him that they were always watching, ready to help when he needed it. What matters is that the walk is taken with joy and the willingness to learn something new. The more you practice the Spirit Walk, the more information will come to you. In fact, there will be days when you are flooded with incredible energy! There will also be times when the only gift will be peace in the heart; perhaps this is the greatest gift of all.

As you go on your various Spirit Walks, make a list of what plants, trees, and animals reside around your home and your workplace; you will find distinct differences even though, on the surface, they all seem the same. These signs of nature tell you about the energy of the place, whether it is sick, healthy, or in between. Don't assume just because you live in an area that appears stark that the environment is sick. What is there has learned to adapt. How did the plants and animals change to survive in that habitat? What are those plants and animals best known for? Do your own research because the messages you receive will be tailored just for you. Yes, there are generalizations, but only you and the way you process information can unlock the information that is meant for your circumstances. If you maintain a garden, you learn that each year there is something different to deal with in the care of your plants. Some years will be bad for certain kinds of bugs or fungus. Yes, weather conditions are a factor, but go deeper. What does that fungus do? What is going on in your life at that moment? Do your circumstances in any way match the function of that disease, blight, weed, or bug? Then work to fix it—not only in your garden, but in yourself as well. That is the shamanic way of healing. Just remember, weeds are not always a problem; many times they carry the healing message you need.

I have lived in the city, in the suburbs, and in rural areas. Each is unique. Each has its own special energy. You will not lack the experience of nature because of where you reside. Nature is everywhere. Each time you return home from your Spirit Walk, take the time to look up the general function of plants, animals, or insects. It won't take you long to realize and relish the wonder of it all!

The Mindset of Magick

All magickal operations, regardless of limited tools or all the rattles, crystals, or wands on the planet, work on what you know to be true. The keyword here is not "true," as you might think, but a set of words: "what you know." If you believe that the universe is a sea of potential within and without, above and below, then you have the secret to all power, all magick, all success. If, of course, you know this to be true within you, then your perception of the world around you changes and all things you desire are absolutely within your reach. You must only choose to accept or decline what your thoughts have created.

You have to believe it to receive it. You have to acknowledge it to get it. You have to affirm that it is yours and so shall it be if, and only if, you agree that the field of unlimited potential is around you and within you—that because this sea exists, anything is possible. Think of it as a sea you can breathe, and as you breathe slowly in and out, your thoughts attach themselves to this sea. These thoughts and your emotions control how you manipulate this sea within yourself and what you send out to manifest into the world around you. Your thoughts and feelings are conduits, pipelines, to manifestation. Some folks visualize this sea of potential as waves that turn into particles as you focus your thoughts on the specifications of what you wish to manifest. These particles, in turn, condense

6

into events, situations, pathways, or physical objects. Your belief creates the quantum lock necessary for your desires to manifest. The repetition of positive, clear thoughts collapse pockets of energy in the sea, creating a pattern that is then energized to bring you what you want. Conflicting thoughts and emotions can completely block or destroy your goals and desires.

Magick is all about the mind and how you use it, and know this: magick is all about either "bonding" or "releasing" within your personal field, which is nested in the network of energy that encompasses all things. I often call this field, the nervous system of all that is, the "sea of potential."

When trying to explain definitions in magick, wording is confusing. Some people are very literal, whereas others are figurative in their mental process. Almost every word in our language can have a variety of meanings and associations that are unique to the person hearing and using it, and even if you think the word is straightforward, it probably isn't. For example, let's take the word *air*—okay, so it is what we breathe, and most of us agree on that definition, but when we say "she had such a snotty air about her," now we are in a different area of understanding. If I say "air" to one person, she may think of sweet summer breezes—but the guy listening in on the conversation may think of a tornado that has just launched a cow across the road. A third person immediately jumps into how dirty our air actually is due to pollution and do you really know what the heck you are breathing and we must fight to stop the outrage of what is going into our lungs.

None of these visualizations are wrong considering the topic of air, but all three of them could be way off the mark of what you are trying to express by using that word. Attempting to share a concept that cannot be seen, that relies on your perception of the world versus that of someone else, isn't easy. Frequently, I've witnessed fussing over a definition in our community based on opinions that are not compatible, sharing only the word or words as the common denominator. I have also found that those individuals who argue the most, using condemnation and hatred as a tool, are actually fighting within themselves because they fear they may be ultimately wrong. As practitioners become more knowledgeable, definitions of words within ourselves may change so that we have a better grasp or connection in our personal magickal operations. The cleaner we make the image for ourselves, the better our work. It is possible, without damaging the core of what we are trying to accomplish, to discard old words in place of new ones that help us create a better, stronger, faster link to our ultimate goal. Our new perception (although better for us personally) may not be accepted or understood by our community as a whole. That's okay. Concentrate on your own ultimate understanding in the matter because that is the end game in any issue you are working with.

For years I have studied, written, contemplated, and experimented, trying to find my own understanding of magick and its relation to real science and the world around us. I have read old grimoires black and white, dug into the writings of magicians long deceased and out of print, and looked for commonalities in techniques from different cultures, always asking myself *what is the base, the bones, the bare structure from which they worked*? Therein lies the key. To most of society, magick is this superstitious entity that doesn't really exist but wouldn't it be great if it did. In my world, magick and science are the same thing and quite real; it is just that our society hasn't caught up with it because so much science is still unexplained in laymen's terms. And if people did understand it, what an interesting world that would be. What if children were taught about the power of the mind? What if we opened the door to quantum physics in a way that folks could understand and *use* it? But what can heal can harm, and for many the fear of destruction is greater than the desire for wholeness.

And so the blindness continues. Even in our own magickal community if you allude that science is what we are actually practicing, we are called New Age or some other set of words in a derisive tone, indicating that we know nothing. Well, they can just believe that. It works for me. It heals the sick. It defeats the foes. Yeah, it may sometimes take a while; but it happens. In fact, you are reading this book because of the success of the techniques presented in it. So be it.

The Power of Release

For seven years I ran an online release program during the month of December on my WordPress blog (silverravenwolf.wordpress.com) to help people easily combine acts of magick and ritual with everyday tasks. This was a free program that lasted for thirty days, designed to help the magickal practitioner deal with the stress of the calendar year closure in combination with the holidays the world celebrates. The main theme of the release program was this: let go of one thing, just one, every single day. Over the years I added challenges for the truly industrious or fun things to do to take the edge off this high-stress period. Writing the blog taught me many things, from the practical to the creative to the magickal. I also learned a great deal about my readers and the issues they were dealing with. The premise of the program was that each year we were all in this together. I worked the program right along with the readers; that way I was not telling them what to do and standing back with no vested interest in what they were actually doing. I was right in there with them, from start to finish.

One of the most important observations I have learned through all those years is that *release* is vital for a healthy individual, whether you practice magick or not. If you don't let go of all the past garbage in your life, it will eventually build to a point where it will suck you into the tar pit of your own subconscious waste. This mess will bubble out in a variety of health issues or in negative behavior that affects not only yourself but the world around you. By systematically letting go of as much emotional detritus as possible, you can enjoy some mental and physical benefits that carry over into your everyday life.

It was the continued success of the program that taught me this release process should be incorporated in daily activities such as house blessings, cleansings of the environment on a cyclical basis, spiritual cleansings of the body and mind, meditation that focuses on the release of negative thoughts and emotions, and regular release ritual, spells, and rites. Release work flows extremely well through the third and fourth quarter moons; however, releasing negativity, worry, and fear through some type of symbolic act each day helps to build a stronger spiritual base within the self. The release program I spoke of earlier works on the idea that by releasing something in the physical world that is no longer of use, broken, or carries nasty memories, at the same time you also are releasing negative thought patterns. You get a twofer.

When people write to me telling me that their lives are horrible, that their finances are in the toilet, that their emotional state is beyond horrible, I aways give them the following advice: *put it in your mind that you are on a magickal mission.* Some people like to think of it as a challenge; others choose to believe that the tasks are a group of sacred activities. It doesn't matter how you jump into it; the point is you have to make the conscious choice for change, supported by a physical act that you mean business!

Secondly, acknowledge that all upsets in life are a process. Such difficulties are not the end of the matter. They impact your life because you need to get moving, not sink into the grave of despair. Where to go from here is what counseling, study, and divination are for. *Problems are beginnings.* Too often we think of negative issues as endings, and so we hug those difficulties dearly like they represent our favorite toy of fifty years ago. I don't know why we do this, we just do. And at that moment we think that if we let go of the battered, smelly toy, we lose. It never occurs to us that we have to release the initial mental shock of the problem and move forward in the direction best spiritually suited for us, not pick at it like a buzzard over a dead carcass. The other interesting thing I have learned is that "it ain't over until you say it is." Even if the issue seems to be a solid decision made about you that is hurtful and wrong, and you have been told there is no other recourse, it isn't the end game. I have learned that *you* are the one that closes the stadium and turns out the lights. Nobody but you. The question then becomes: What will my choices be? Will I choose wisely? You can still move on, move away from the pain and unfortunate circumstances, and let go of the junk, yet win in the end. You don't have to eat, drink, sleep, and talk about the problem ad nauseum to win; in fact, those activities will probably ensure you lose because you've gotten mentally stuck at the beginning of the process. Don't stalk your problems.

You can move on. Find another job. Meet new people. Discover new talents. Learn how to mentally manage things differently that will improve not only your lifestyle, but those of your family as well. There is always an open door *somewhere*. Sure, it might take a little time. So what? You can say to yourself, "How can I change things to make sure that the negative experience never happens to me again? How can I turn this situation or experience to my benefit? How can I help others with what I have learned?" You are not a single canoe, cut off from the universe, drifting upon a sea of gunk all by your lonesome, singing a tune of wanton despair. That is your perception, and it isn't right. It is narcissistic. You are not cut off from anything; you just aren't seeing the connections that are oh so there! It is the understanding that these links exist that turns on the light of realization within ourselves. You see that what you thought was this rickety, itty bitty boat is actually a pathway that leads everywhere to everything; you just thought it was a boat because the light on your cell phone was out. Your own illusions are your worst enemy.

Releasing negativity and performing cleansings of all types help to barrel through those predatory, self-inflicted personal myths, allowing us to move forward in a joy-filled, positive way. So, when the bad stuff happens or you want to change your life because you don't like how it is playing out, I have a few simple recommendations that work.

First, do a complete spiritual cleansing with blessed herbs, blessed water, etc. (see chapter 5) to set your mind in the new direction.

Then rearrange one large piece of furniture in your home. Yes, move it. If you can't physically do this, have someone else do it. There is always a big piece of furniture that seems to be a problem in any home: it is there, you wish you'd put it over there, but, oh well, just leave it. By moving a large piece of furniture, you are revitalizing the chi (energy flow) of your living environment. This is particularly important if you are immersed in financial problems or if someone in your home is extremely aggressive or negative.

Clean all clutter in the house. All of it. Every little bit of it. No more piles of books and papers in the corner. No more pieces of dried banana peel under the sofa. No more clothing all over the floor. Just keep singing to yourself, "No more, no more, no more, no more!" Use a three-pass technique—that way, you don't get depressed even before you've begun. You can do this on successive days if the mess has gotten ahead of you. Make the process as magickal as possible, adding as many magickal goodies as you like—herbal room sprays, floor washes, incense, whatever lifts your spirits as you work.

The three-pass technique embraces the vibration of the number three, where each acknowledgment ramps up or tones down the energy targeted by the intent. In clearing an area, first remove all things that have no emotion attached to them the first time you work on a place, cupboard, or drawer. Getting rid of those things—objects without emotional energy clinging to them—lightens the task. Because you will be looking at the area three separate times, it is easier to move forward. You are giving yourself time to emotionally let go of items that hold more tangled energies, and you are also giving yourself time to make this choice during the second pass. During the last pass ask yourself the following questions as you hold the object in your hands: *Have I used this in the past six months? Do I even know what this object is for? How does this object make me feel?* If I am emotionally distraught over an object, I get rid of it. Realistically, I can't take anything with me from this life to the next, so why (I ask myself) am I holding on to this ratty old thing? That's my way of talking to myself—you will have your own inner dialogue.

Throw out or give away the oldest object in the house that has no value.

These three activities—moving furniture, clearing clutter, and removing one old object—are physical statements to yourself that you are working through a problem, not hanging onto it for dear life. If you try to rationalize why you are not doing these three activities, then this is a sure signal to yourself that you are mentally, for whatever reason, not ready to move through the difficulty. There is no excuse. There is always a way. Go with that and things will absolutely begin to change.

The last step is to list ten things that you absolutely love, and focus on as many activities as possible that involve items on that list for a thirty-day period. Use the symbolism of one of those favorites on your altar as an "open the way" focus. One person I know uses a statue of an elephant

(Ganesh); another uses a model of the starship *Enterprise*. Other focus objects have been an antique car, a ship, a surfboard, a Pokémon, etc. The object doesn't have to be considered magickal (like a statue of a fairy)—in fact, we've found that the more mundane the image, the better.

What if you don't have any pressing problems? Will these activities still be useful? Absolutely! The release program blog showed a significant improvement in all the lives of the individuals who posted their comments as they worked through the process. Some started with problems, some didn't. There were those who were moving through illness, loss of loved ones or pets, and loss of job or home, and there were people whose lives were stable and just wanted a delightful boost. The beautiful thing about this information is that I'm not just telling you; you are able to read the information for yourself, as the blog is open to the public.

Release Before a Working

All magick begins with release and ends with release.

In the old days, the mechanism of beginning with release was called "sacrifice," and like many words it has a variety of meanings. Too often, the mind goes to the worst possible connotation, giving up something you love in a violent way. That is *not* what it means in magick! Here, you must be willing to let go of past negative behavior and thoughts, free yourself of worry and fear, and dispense with broken beliefs that are actually harming your positive life path. You can do a super big ritual, go to therapy, or vent to your friends; all these things are a good form of release. However, we are human, and "once and done" just doesn't work. As we move through life we have a variety of experiences, and each one of those situations has emotional energy attached to it. You never stop collecting emotional garbage; however, you can limit the barrage by right action, right thought, and continued spiritual practices. Because we are such excellent collectors of energy, each and every day we need to do some sort of balance training to easily let go of negative thoughts and feelings. Likewise, we should be sure we stand firm in the best possible mental place before each and every magickal working.

There are a variety of practices that are employed to embrace the idea of release: creating sacred space, taking a ritual bath, house and ritual room cleansings, personal cleansing ceremonies, etc. However, although we have done all those things on a regular basis, doing it every single time we want to do a working can present a problem. You are busy. You have a full life. Locking yourself in your bedroom for even a half hour (or running into the woods for forty-five minutes) presents a real scheduling problem. If no one in your house lets you shower in peace or sit on the toilet for five minutes without an interruption, they certainly aren't going to let you get away for an hour to commune with the gods.

Mental Release Techniques

Face the east and breathe deeply several times. Allow your mind to shift and blend into your surroundings. Touch the peace of the universe, then pull back. Breathe deeply. Touch it again. Pull back. Then try this short charm as your final release mechanism so that you can firmly "lock in" to that spiritual energy. As you say the charm, envision exactly the images that are being invoked.

"The pungent smoke of burning sage." Breathe in deeply, imagining you are smelling the smoking sage. As you exhale, envision that the smoke is carrying off any negativity around you.

"The burst of liquid sparks." Breathe in deeply, imagining that tiny lava-like sparks are burning away all negativity around you.

"The rush of salted air." Breathe in deeply and imagine you are at the beach: hear the pounding of the surf, smell the sea water vapor. Imagine that a quick yet gentle breeze filled with that vapor envelops you and cleanses your body, mind, and soul of all fear, worry, and doubt.

"The crumble of pungent black earth." Breathe in the sweet aroma of fresh, warm earth, the type from a rich garden bed. Imagine that as you crumble the dirt in your fingers, you are physically releasing and letting go of any negative energy that is attached to your body.

Take another deep breath and say, "I *am free.*" Then reach out with your mind and accept a flood of white or golden light that unites you with the positivity of the universe. Or you can let that feeling of peace unfold within you like a flower, and as its petals open, each one vibrates and touches the white or golden light of the spirit of One. You can intone a blending chant of some sort, if you like, or fill yourself with a favorite prayer.

Try this release technique for at least a week each morning, each evening, and before you do any working. If you don't like the way I've presented the elements to you, feel free to write your own prose. The idea is to experience the elements within yourself. Mixing them is acceptable, as "the rush of salted air" is really air, water, and earth, etc. The idea is internalizing the cleansing with visualization that pops within the mind and combines words, thoughts, and emotions into one. This technique works well for the projects in this book as well as many other magickal applications. I encourage you to spend some time writing what will most speak to you. Trial and error isn't a bad thing.

Mental Release and the Power of Water

One of my favorite Braucherei techniques is the use of running water combined with sacred chanting. Water vibrates well to your thoughts. Its flowing movement not only helps you release negative thoughts, but also absorbs your intent and moves that energy to the conclusion you desire. All you need is a running tap and yourself.

To release, hold your hands under cool running water. Breathe deeply, allowing the experience of the cool water rushing over your hands to permeate your entire being. Think of nothing but the feel and the aroma of the rushing water. *Be* the water.

Do this for as long as it takes for you to feel that you *are* the water. Continue to breathe deeply, and now, each time you exhale, let negativity flow out of your body. Let go of fears, worries, emotional pain, hatred—the visualization is easy because as you release, the water is flowing down the drain unless your sink is stopped up, which would definitely be a sign you are, too! Watch the water flow away from you, let your mind push out those nasty thoughts, and experience the liquid movement on your hands for magickal triple-play action.

If you can, see the energy of yourself mixing with the water and clearing as the water runs. At first, you may mentally see dark stuff coming out of yourself and mixing with the rushing water. Keep pushing the energy until you mentally see that it is clearing. You may wish to use a chant or charm of release at this point. Water also takes whisper magick extremely well, so methodically whispering your chant, charm, or prayer, with a louder verbal push at the end (or allowing your voice to drop to being almost inaudible) impacts the working with an extra oomph. This simple technique also works in a variety of healing situations. Don't let the simplicity of the chants fool you; there is incredible power in attunement with the elements.

Release Water Chant

> Water move, water flow; let it out, let it go.
> Water move, water flow; carried off, tidal tow.
> Water move, water flow; release, release, make it so.

Twisted Thoughts

I'd like you to pull a paper towel off a roll and twist it. I'll wait while you go do that, okay? Twist it really, really good! Now examine it. What do you see? What was large (a sheet of paper towel) is now condensed, collapsing in on itself due to your force. Let's make believe that the end that is closest to you is where you are right now, and the end farther away is where you want to get to—the result of all those twisted thoughts in your brain. Even if we unroll the towel without tearing it, the texture will be different. The towel is changed due to your action. Conclusion: every action has a reaction, even if the change only appears minimal, but that's just the beginning of working with the paper towel.

We are going to twist the paper towel up again. Wait! Don't do it yet. Don't wad it. If you mushed it into a ball, I will bet, dimes to dollars, that you are stuck with something in your life that you are not happy about. So! Let's twist that towel again, but this time, before you start, think about how you are feeling now. That mental position represents the end of the towel closest to you. Begin to twist the towel. Reflect on how you wish to be feeling in the future. More confident? Happier? Healthier? Continue to twist the towel until you are "feeling" that desired goal. Hold the good feeling for as long as you can. Now, put the towel down in front of you with that outermost end, the one with the good feels, pointed toward you. Notice that the towel will unfurl a little bit. This tells you that there will always be adjustments you didn't think of in your quest for the better you. That's okay. Life works out that way.

No. We are not done with the paper towel. Wipe your face with the towel. Get your sweat and skin cells on it, and as you are wiping your face, envision that same good feeling that you pushed into the paper towel.

Nice!

Thank Spirit (or whatever you believe in) for the manifestation of your desire as if it has already occurred. Be grateful! Burn the paper towel.

No. We aren't done yet.

Take a new paper towel. Wipe the paper towel on your face. Try not to crumple it up. Next, write or draw on the towel exactly what you want: again, happiness, joy, prosperity, whatever. Breathe on the paper towel; as you exhale, tease the towel with your energy. I am not kidding. Don't push energy into the towel with your breath right away. With the first breath let the energy go a quarter of the way to the towel, and then draw it back when you inhale. Second breath, halfway to three-quarters, draw it back. Third breath, with as much dynamic visualization as you can (flames, sparkles, whatever makes you happy), push the energy into the words or drawing you put on that towel. See your words and design glowing with the energy you pushed into your work. Let the light sink into the design. You may see it actually vibrating, and you will think it is a trick of your eyes, but it isn't a trick at all. Your senses are combining to "view" the impregnated working. Twist up the paper towel nice and tight. Start with where you are, and turn your thoughts (or flip them—depends on your perception) to where you want to be, which should match the words or design you put on the paper towel. Hold this thought for as long as you can, breathing on the paper towel. When the thought leaves, stop breathing on the paper towel. Put it down and draw an equal-armed cross in the air over the towel. Burn the towel outdoors, thanking Spirit (or whatever you believe in) for your success.

Silly? Looks that way on the surface, doesn't it?

Easy? Absolutely.

Does it work? Try it and find out.

The next step in this exercise would be to incorporate a magickal powder or herbal blend along with your favorite fluid condenser (see chapter 4) in the working. But before we get to that, let's talk about the field of potential all around you.

Working the Field: The Sea of Potential (The Astral Plane and Vital Energy Bodies)

The information below represents the general sequence I use for nightly meditations as well as many magickal operations, including the formulation of magickal powders, oils, and herbal blends. It utilizes the sea of potential all around us, activating the network to all things on a spiritual level. Once you have memorized the technique, it can be done quickly and efficiently. Its success rests on the following three points:

- The clear intent you have prepared ahead of time. For example, if you are concentrating on healing your pet or child or if you desire a new car or if you need food in the home, etc., write out specifically what you want *before* you begin so you don't stumble over choices during the process. Be sure to always add "with harm to none," as that is the highest road when working with the sea of potential and yields the better results. If you are in doubt when setting the intent, then a clear manifestation cannot be formed. Let's say you want a red car—no, a blue one—wait…no…a *truck*! A truck would be better…stop! Or perhaps you want your ex-partner to go away…no! You want that person to fall in a toilet and never get out…wait… a big dump truck to smash 'em to smithereens! Yeah! Yes, I know you want revenge, but in the end, do you really want to pay for it? Again, stop. Think of the consequences. If you are filled with lots of anger or emotional pain, do a spiritual cleansing first, then proceed with a more positive outcome.

- Believe that when you activate that sea of potential, what you desire will manifest. Know it!

- Keep your mouth shut. Don't tell the world you are doing magick for whatever reason you are doing it for. Be silent. You can blab about it after you are done.

If you use this as a meditation sequence, you can work on several different subjects at a time, so you may wish to fill out a 3x5 index card so you have it straight in your head what you will be working on. For example, healing for baby Jimmy who has a bad cold, a good job for Aunt Sally, that Harold receives his benefit check without delay, etc. I will tell you when, in the sequence, you can switch from one intent to the next. However, for the first week of using this technique, I would suggest sticking to one intent only until you are comfortable with the sequence.

Release All Worries, Fear, Negative Feelings, and Clutter from Your Mind. You can do this actively or mentally. Earlier in this chapter I gave you a simple mental release technique that you can incorporate here. If at all possible, never skip the release portion of this sequence or rush through it, as this sets the sea of potential for success or failure. You can release by breathing several times deeply and relaxing, welcoming pure white light into your mind by using the mental release technique or words that you truly mean from the heart. Sometimes, when we are very stressed, it is important to verbally acknowledge release: "I release all that does not serve my life path success" or "I release all feelings of fear, hatred, and sadness. I welcome peace in my heart, soul, and mind." If you skip the release sequence, it is like making a cake in a dirty bowl that sat on the kitchen counter in the high heat of the summer for five days. Yeah. Gross. Some people call this act of release "clearing." Whatever word you use to define it doesn't matter; the act of doing it does! I often use chimes or bells as a clearing mechanism. To assist in the clearing process, you may prefer burning white sage, a specific resin like frankincense or copal, nag champa incense or another blend of your choice. Blessed water sprinkled on the back of the neck, where negativity tends to gather, can also be extremely helpful.

Recognize and Activate the Purity of the Sea of Potential by Casting a Magick Circle or Creating a Spirit Bubble. Visualize yourself surrounded by white or golden light. If you begin this sequence as a meditation, get comfortable and close your eyes. Don't open them until the meditation is completed. If you are working magick, then you will most likely be in a ritual area, by your altar, or sitting at a kitchen table, prepared to do mental and physical activities. If casting a spell is the purpose, using candles, herbs, and oils, etc., have them ready on a surface from which you can easily work.

Cast the Circle. (For a meditation, this will be in your mind; for an alert working, you may wish to walk the circle clockwise three times while you intone the circle casting.) "*I conjure thee, O circle of power, so that you will be for me a boundary between the world of men and the mighty ones, a meeting place of perfect love, trust, peace, and joy containing the power I will raise herein. I call upon the guardians of the east, the south, the west, and the north to aid me in this conjuration. In the name of the Lord and the Lady, thus do I conjure thee, O great circle of power! As above, so below; this circle is sealed!*"

Or Do an Alternative Magick Circle. "*Spirit before me, Spirit behind me, Spirit to the right of me, Spirit to the left of me, Spirit above me, and Spirit below me: bless this working and keep me safe. So mote it be.*"

Note: You can replace the word *Spirit* with any word you like: angels, Goddess, the particular name of a deity, etc. You can use one of the clearing, grounding, and centering techniques in my *MindLight* book, or you can recite a favorite prayer, psalm, poem, or verbal charm. Speaking aloud is best when performing spellwork that involves mental, emotional, and physical activity, as the words vibrate along the network of the sea of potential to bring you what you desire. It is not that your thoughts are not powerful enough so that you can work totally in silence—they actually are if you are focused enough—however, our minds are busy, busy, busy, and other thoughts can intrude just at the wrong moment. If you are stating aloud and vibrating the words with emotion, the working will be strong.

Over the years I have heard arguments that casting a circle is not necessary, and in some circumstances I would agree with that opinion; however, I am a "better safe than sorry" type of gal. When I cast that circle, whether by verbal conjuration or mental vision, I know that I have created a safe place to raise power, away from prying psychic eyes and anything else hanging around. I have erected an area free of debris so that I can have a successful working. To me, taking the few minutes to put up that circle is absolutely worth it. Besides, it's good practice; you never know when you are going to have to conjure a circle in seconds. It can happen.

Seal your circle or bubble by saying *"only the good remains"* several times, and then draw an equal-armed cross in the air with your right thumb. You could add the blessing from my HedgeWitch book: "*Peace with the gods, peace with nature, peace within; only the good remains.*"

Personally Connect with the Sea of Potential. Take a deep breath and relax. Thank the universe for the good things in your life and bless those in your home. Then repeat "I *am one with the universe*" several times, allowing yourself to truly be one with the universe. If you don't like this statement, choose another that appeals to you. Some people call this activity "blending," where you let the edges of yourself go and allow your being to flow into the world around you until it touches your idea of the Supreme of the universe. Breathe deeply as you repeat the sentence in your mind several times. Do not stop until you absolutely feel one with the universe. You will feel something give way in yourself; a gentleness of Spirit washes over you. Sometimes you feel a light snap and everything is truly brighter than before. The more you practice, the less time it will take you to reach this quiet, peaceful still point. Some individuals feel a distinct shift in their inner being. You will know the change when it comes, as there is no other feeling like it: totally peaceful, absolutely serene. The last portion of the mental release technique given earlier walks right into your connection with the sea of potential.

Acknowledge Your Connection with the Field. *"The sea of potential is around me. The sea of potential is in me. The sea of potential is around me, and I can do anything!"* Repeat these statements several times until you feel the connection, which may manifest as inner strength, an acknowledgment of your power, a feeling of success, etc. Some people add a visualization of waves of energy lapping around them and through them; others see the sea as golden or white light that smoothly moves throughout and around their body. Others do well with a visualization of blue light electrical pulses. When you repeat the statements for the last time, add *"I activate this sea for..."* and then state your intent. Choose what wording flows from you and works for you.

To Heighten the Working, Gather Power from the World Around You. As you slowly breathe in and out, call the spirits of the elements at least three times for each element, which equates to three breaths per element. I begin by chanting the word *one* and then, when I feel ready, I call *"spirits of earth,"* followed by *"spirits of air,"* *"spirits of fire,"* and *"spirits of water."* I then continue to chant the word *one* until I feel that all are present. An old Basque Witch once said, "Always use the world around you," and I never forgot it.

Next, Connect

For Meditation: State specifically what you wish to be true, with harm to none. Then repeat the statement as you breathe slowly in and slowly out. You are breathing in the energy, lighting it with your thought of what you desire, and then sending it back out into the universe. Think of it like the setup of a volleyball shot: the ball of energy comes toward you, you catch it, you make the ball into what you want it to be, and then you breathe out the visualization into the universe to manifest. Do this as long as you are comfortable. The more you practice, the longer you will be able to hold the thought; however, I have learned that holding the thought for a significant length of time isn't really necessary as long as you do not allow any doubts or other thoughts to interfere with the process. If you do, just repeat this part over again. One person I know likes to activate the outgoing visualization with lightning bolts. Another individual feels their hands start to tingle and get hot. Use what works for you. Don't be afraid to experiment. For example, "*I know that Connie Arber is healed*" or "*I know that I have a fantastic new job that is right for me*" or "*I am joyful that Jacob now owns a new car!*" If you have more than one person on your list that you are working for, now is the time to switch to the next item or person on the list. Close the meditation with your original acknowledgment of your connection to the field: "*The sea of potential is around me. The sea of potential is in me. The sea of potential is around me, and I can do anything! So mote it be!*"

Note: While practicing this meditation you can hold a crystal, a talisman, etc. Complete the meditation by opening your eyes and breathing deeply. If you cast a magick circle, say something like, "*This circle is open but never broken. So mote it be.*"

For Magick: Begin the working, such as grinding and mixing an herb formula, empowering a candle, etc. As you work, state explicitly and succinctly what you wish to accomplish. Feel free to use a favorite chant or rhyme, or listen to a drumming tape—whatever makes you feel empowered. I like the Heathen chant found in my book *To Light a Sacred Flame:* "*May the web of the wyrrd be turned in accordance with my wish and my will.*" Once your materials are ready, it is time to empower them, and we will do it the same way as we do the meditation. The difference here is that you will hold your hands palms toward the physical item, such as the dressed candle, or over the bowl of herbs, or holding a talisman in both hands. You can also hold a wand, your ritual athame, or whatever you use to direct power if you so desire. If I am doing banishing work, I use a pair of black-handled scissors. Yes. It absolutely works.

As with the meditation, it is time to repeat the statement of the desired conclusion you have prepared as you breathe slowly in and slowly out. This statement represents your intent. You are breathing in the energy, lighting it with your thought of what you desire, and then sending it back out into the universe. Tease the object twice before you flood it with energy the third time. See the energy in your mind move toward the object, then recede. Toward the object a little further, then recede. Finally, allow the energy to flow entirely into the object, and keep that flow going for as long as you feel comfortable, strong, and in control of your thoughts. Just as with the meditation, the breathing part is necessary. Nice, long breaths as you pull in the energy of the sea of potential, activate it, and send your intent back out into that same field. When you feel you have finished (which is usually as long as you can hold the thought), begin closure with a statement that indicates the desire belongs to you in the present. Be sure your words are filled with emotional success—that you "feel" positive, joyful, happy. Finish with your original statements: *"The sea of potential is all around me. The sea of potential is in me. The sea of potential is around me and to me, and I can do anything! So mote it be!"* Complete the magickal operation by drawing an equal-armed cross in the air over the items to seal the working. Dispose of or continue to monitor (whatever the working calls for) the items you empowered.

Setting Your Hands

No Matter What I Lay My Hands Upon, It Will Be So

Your hands are always filled with power and the ability to push energy away from you or pull energy toward you. Most people don't think of them as magickal vehicles or tools, yet every time you touch something you take a little of that something into yourself and leave a little of yourself behind. Whenever you lay your hands on any object in magick—be it a string, dried herbs, a sigil, petition, or your tools—that item begins to absorb your energy. What energy it takes into itself is a combination of a variety of factors, including the vibratory pattern of the object itself. Just laying your hands on any item begins the blending process.

If you don't carry the thoughts through coupled with matching action, there is little force behind the touch. For example, you don't really think about your relationship with the thousands of objects you touch each day: a water glass, the steering wheel of your car, the door you open to the grocery store, etc. What separates this type of touch and the handling of objects in spellwork is your focused intention. The thoughts that you impregnate into that magickal object—including visualizations, images, whispered words, etc.—can be combined to direct and create the pattern to manifestation of your desire, which you then activate with the flow of energy. Using the object as part of the process is one type of empowerment.

When you work with your hands in magick based on intent, this is called "setting your hands." Anytime you work with your hands, you want to set those hands on the spell vehicle with extremely clear intent that is not clouded by negative thoughts or muddled emotions. In this book we use the sea of potential to activate a working, while your hands push and distribute intent into the herbs and powders. The energy naturally runs from the sea of potential into yourself, and your hands guide that energy. Many people get lost in thinking that they must have a wand or an athame or a sword to direct the energy, and that is fine; however, next to your mind, your most important magickal tool is your hands!

For a week, practice awakening your ability to direct energy with your hands. Look at them like they are a marvelous magickal tool. Several times a day gaze at your hands; turn them over and pay attention to both sides, remembering the power they promise. Experience the amazing feeling that you have when you whisper several times, "I *awaken the power within myself!*" As you breathe in, imagine that you are taking in the glittering energy of the sea of potential. Let that energy run through your body like a river of enlightenment. As you breathe out, push that power into your hands. They may just tingle or become amazingly warm. Rather than letting the energy go to waste while you practice, hold your hands over your heart and say, "I *heal my body, mind, and soul. So be it.*"

Every human being has the ability to access and use their own incredible power, which can be directed through their hands. You may wish to "set" your hands right before you work. The choice of how you do this is entirely up to you. The following is only an example:

Close your eyes and breathe at least three times deeply. Focus your thoughts that your intent is to gather power and prepare your hands for working magick (or Reiki or even fixing a broken toy). Wash your hands with water or a mixture of water and salt, repeating, "*Only the good remains.*" Dry them off with a clean towel. Again, close your eyes and breathe at least three times deeply, then whisper the following: "*I awaken the power within myself. I awaken my hands as amazing tools for magick!*" Breathe deeply and connect with the sea of potential, running the energy into your hands. Then, when you feel energized, say, "*No matter what I lay my hands upon, my desire will be so!*" Go about your magickal activity (or fixing that broken toy).

Once you practice this exercise for several months, all you will have to say is "*I set my hands*" and it will be so because you have trained yourself to awaken the power within yourself to access and direct what you need at any given time.

I Need a Miracle

Miracles really do happen. We've all been there—a time when we desperately need assistance, and we call out and say something like, "*If I ever needed a miracle, it would be now!*" Perhaps the need is fueled by fear, and you vibrate the air around you with your request for assistance. When you ask the universe for a miracle, you are activating the field and drawing the required energy to you with a super boost of wave-like energy. You are pushing the thought out beyond yourself to touch "whatever" that can help; at the same time, you are expecting a return (belief), actually widening that pipeline so that energy can flow out, which coalesces into a pattern, which is pulled back because you are expecting it.

When you ask for a miracle, you aren't micromanaging energy, you are setting an extremely firm intent, often driven by a heightened state of emotion, that feeling of great need. You don't require sex or drugs to get to that point of possible manifestation. You need help, and you need it *now!* And the universe responds. Relax and think for a moment; recall when you have called out for assistance without trying to micromanage the outcome, and then everything fell into place, not perhaps the way you thought it would, but it works out usually for the best just the same. Many people attribute miracles to a god/goddess form, and I am not debating this; what I *am* saying is that you are quite capable of accessing that assistance anytime for anything.

The Balance of Magick

The sea of potential technique discussed earlier works on the premise of *as above, so below; as within, so without.* When you do magick or visualization techniques, an imbalance is created; the manifestation of what you desire is the balance. Think of it as a seesaw. You put out the energy dictating what you want and one end of the seesaw goes down. As everything works on the premise of balance, to create an even surface once again, the desire manifests on the other end of the seesaw, and the end that went down comes up and levels so that the board is parallel, thus creating a leveled existence. This rule of magick, action equals reaction/polarity, is a Hermetic teaching. Magickal powders, incense, room sprays, perfumes, oil blends, and herbal blends are highly effective in creating an aromatic trigger within yourself that can assist you to create positive thoughts or the thoughts that will lead to the manifestation you desire. These positive thoughts, in turn, help to bring the balance, what you desire. This is one reason why correspondences in magick are so important. By gathering things together that are of the same thought or emotional vibration, we are helping our minds stay focused. By practicing that gathering process in a spiritual way, we widen the road for better success, clearing the pathway to our dreams and goals.

The problem with using the word *imbalance* is that people generally see the word with a negative connotation. "What do you mean I'm creating an imbalance when I think? Isn't that bad?" Think of the sacred double spiral. One spiral represents your thoughts going out into the universe; the other spiral shows those same thoughts coalescing into form in the universe. The spirals are connected, showing a one-dimensional representation of how your thoughts affect the universe and how the universe changes your thoughts. When you see a spiral design, you don't see good or bad; you just see the symbol of what is.

Sacred Double Spiral

As an experiment, try using this symbol on your work surface. As you grind herbs or do a particular spell, the spiral is a reminder that what you put out, you receive. Try inscribing the symbol on a candle the next time you do candle burning magick. How does that work for you?

Mirror Technique

If you are still trying to wrap your brain around the concept of balance/imbalance, think of a mirror. What you do in front of a mirror is always reflected back to you. Shine a light in the mirror, it bounces off the surface and back to you. That is exactly what the universe is like. If things are really crappy for you right now, create a mirror backdrop. No kidding. Pick a mirror in your home and stand it so that it faces a wall. On the wall, put pictures and other items of what you want your life to be like. Each day stand in front of that mirror, with your dream life as the backdrop, and imagine yourself living the life you desire. The key is not to look at yourself and pick out the flaws; the idea is to look at yourself smiling and happy in the new life you wish to create.

You can also create a bulletin board that is filled with things you desire, so that every time you look at it, you are encouraging yourself to think the thoughts that will bring you what you want. The mirror technique is more active, as you can move, smile, even create mythical conversations. If you feel that creating a backdrop is too time-consuming, you can paste photos around the edges of the mirror so that your reflection is ringed by what you desire to unfold in your life.

Remember, the sea of potential is always around you. It never goes away. Sometimes the hardest challenge of all is to keep in mind that it is even there!

Acceptance or Denial

Let's consider the meaning of the words *off* and *on* and visualize a light fixture switch plate. When something is considered "on," it is a *go* thing—power flowing—a *yes, yes, yes* feeling. When we think of "off," such words come to mind as "stop," "I don't want that," or "stillness." Very basic analogies would be:

- off/on
- yes/no
- accept/resist
- want/don't want

When you accept or want something, the feeling is usually positive. When you resist or don't want something, feelings are often negative (at most) or unsettled at least.

All magick is either on or off, yes or no, accept or resist.

Ever watch a kid play with a light switch? On/off, on/off, on/off—drives you nuts, doesn't it? The universe thinks the same way when you broadcast your feelings on a subject where clarity is nowhere to be found. You do? You don't? What the heck is it? Make up your mind! Constantly flipping that switch in your field and in the sea of potential around you leads to defeat or dissatisfaction.

For at least one week, with everything you do, with everything you think, either push the mental button on or off, depending upon your needs. *No extraneous thinking.*

When you push the mental button on, run energy as given under the setting hands topic above.

When you push the mental button off, block the negativity energy.

In life, it really *is* that simple. On or off? Choose.

Link, Sync, and Sink Magickal Technique

Quite some time ago I created the link, sync, and sink technique, a mental method to effect change, to help me when working on healing magicks for people and animals. It works for in-person and long-distance healing applications and is an incredibly simple visualization.

Say the individual's name aloud three times. Breathe deeply several times and close your eyes. In your mind, blend with nature and Spirit. Use the sea of potential technique to set your intent, then repeat the individual's name three times again if they are not present (you can skip this if they are with you).

Link: If the person is with you, lay your hand on the top of their head. If it is an animal, put your hand where you can without the animal minding. If the person is not present, see that individual in your mind. If they are present, the linking process has already begun. If, however, they are not present, link yourself to them using some type of connecting visualization that makes you comfortable: a silver cord, a wave of energy, something that you can "see" well. I find it easier to link at the third eye, but you can choose another part of the body.

Sync: This is where you blend the intention energy (healing, joy, happiness) with their life force, which is often represented by how you feel about that individual coupled with their image in your mind. When you think of any being (person, animal, and even plants) you have a "feeling" about them; this is part of the totality of their signature on this plane and how it vibrates as you observe it. Often, we ignore this feeling because we are so busy processing a billion things at once. When we slow down, relax, and breathe deeply, we can access any individual signature. Granted, some people shield themselves well. However, part of being on this planet is having our own vibratory address (for a time). It is best that you are in agreement with the person on the change required (joy, happiness, healing, love) as this will speed the process. For long distance, visualize that you are breathing together. If they are present, ask the person to breathe in tune with you (or you them, doesn't matter). Whether they are with you or long distance, I now close my eyes and use a spinning light visualization where my light of intention spins together with their light. To me, this light is multicolored and turns to white when the sync has taken hold.

Sink: Visualize the energy slowly sinking into the top of their head and traveling down into all their chakras. Because I practice Braucherei whisper magick, where chants are a part of the process, I begin chanting something that matches the intent. Try to hold the visualization of spinning energy as long as possible. Once you have gone through their chakras, you can concentrate on where the pain or difficulty might be within the body. When you lose the light or the visualization, the work is done. Seal with an equal-armed cross over the individual if they are there or in the air if they are not present. The work is done. Let it go. Wash your hands in running water or rub your hands with salt to break the connection you have made. Some practitioners prefer to use holy water or Florida Water.

To make the linking process easier in long-distance applications, you may wish to hold a photograph, an unwashed article of clothing they have worn, jewelry that belongs to them, a pet collar the animal has used, etc. There are some people who shield all the time, so it can be difficult to affect them even though you have their permission to work the healing; when this occurs, think about any in-person association you have had with them, particularly if you have touched them. Think of *that* moment or a conversation, when you shook hands, when they may have hugged you, etc. Think about what you know of them: favorite colors, flowers, animals, hobbies, etc., to help you make the connection. Make what is familiar to them familiar to you by surrounding yourself with mental pictures that the individual typically holds for themselves (although they may not be yours). For family members and close friends, the key to opening access to their astral body is love. This energy is honest and pure, and it can easily slip through the shield, particularly if the love is shared between yourself and that individual.

The link, sync, and sink technique also works with a variety of magickal techniques, from empowering powders and herbal blends to obtaining a new car. The process isn't just used on living creatures; it also can be employed on inanimate objects for a variety of workings, such as warding a property, drawing money to you, syncing a poppet to your needs, etc. The more you practice the technique, both with people and objects, the easier it will become, and you will find the speed of manifestation a great blessing when you really need it most. When you are using it for attracting an inanimate object, such as a car, visualize the vehicle you want, and rather than breaking the connection at the end of the working, pull the car toward you and imagine your hands touching it. How would the surface of the car feel to you? Link that memory of physical touch to a feeling of joy.

In this book we are blending with the energy of Spirit, the universe as a vehicle, plants, herbs, trees, and the elements to bring joy into our lives and into the lives of others. I realize that we often physically look to the sky when we release energy. That is one of the many meanings of the occult teaching "as above." In working with the earth elements, I stumbled across the following technique, literally, which changed my perceptions on magick and energy flow. Perhaps it will be helpful to you as well.

Blue Lightning Ground Exercise

A quick search on the internet shows a fascinating grouping of articles about plant and tree communication through a variety of chemical processes, their root system, and fungal supporters. While some dismiss this as not being true, other scientists are forging ahead, continuing to gather documentation that networking among plants truly does exist. Most magickal people who wildcraft, garden, and work with herbs, plants, and trees agree that there truly is some type of communication, whether it be spiritual, chemical, or both. Just because we don't understand it and haven't been able to quantify it doesn't mean it isn't there. And once you feel it, you won't need convincing.

In this exercise we consciously join the chain in communication by using the ground. For the first time, place your hands on the ground outside. Rather than thinking of Spirit up above, concentrate on sending your communication into the ground. We are using the ground as our conduit of linking to something somewhere else that is also on the ground—a person, an animal, an object. I like to use this technique for healing, where I follow the method of connecting given below and send healing information to an individual who has requested it. I literally whisper my chants into the ground. You choose who or what you wish to connect to.

Begin by activating the sea of potential as shown earlier in this chapter. Sit quietly on the ground and place your hands out in front of you on the earth. Take several deep breaths and center yourself, then say, "I *awaken Mother Nature*" (or the earth or whatever words that you choose to link yourself with the communication network that roots in the ground). Choose wisely because you want to make the right connection for your perception. This is important.

Then say, "I *gather the healing energy of the universe to travel into the earth and heal her center.*" This lets nature know that you come to her with gifts of love and healing, that you are looking to link into the communication network, and that you are not a threat. Link, sync, and sink with the earth. Close your eyes and fill the ground around you with feelings of love. Keep doing this until you lose the thought.

Next, imagine that the information you wish to send is a net of connected blue lightning that will travel across the ground to the intended individual. It will reach them, travel up through the soles of their feet, and connect with their aura. You can then sync with the person and sink the energy into the physical body (or you can just choose to connect with the astral body of the individual). Whisper your chants, prayers, charms, and words of healing, keeping your hands on the ground and thinking about the person. You can use a magickal powder or herbal blend, grinding the powder into the ground with your hands as you intone your words.

When you are finished, say something like, "I *am grateful for this change and embrace well-being for myself and for (the person's name).*" Break the earth connection. Make an equal-armed cross on the ground with your finger to seal the spell. Thank the earth for her assistance in this matter. Leave an earth-friendly offering of your choice such as birdseed, water, cornmeal, etc. This offering helps to connect the vibration of your intent from the sea of potential to the physical world. You are pulling what is needed from the astral plane to the physical plane. This offering "sets" or "anchors" your desire with love and gratitude—two energies that help to bring the target to form.

I have used this technique for a variety of purposes, particularly long-distance workings where there is no way you could get there in time. Such instances have included protection for children, help to stranded travelers, healing for those in emergency surgery, catching a criminal, and for amber alerts.

If you work magick with friends or family, you may wish to use this exercise to heal the area you live in on a weekly or monthly basis.

I have created a small, private outdoor place with a circle of stones where I can sit and practice this. I cleanse the area after each magickal act with sacred herbal water of rosemary and lavender.

> **Caution:** If you use the process of link, sync, and sink or the blue lightning ground exercise to obtain something from another, such as stealing, the universe will ensure that you pay for the theft. Therefore, never link to a particular item that belongs to another person, like Grandpa's coin collection. The caution of "misuse of power means the loss of it" is not an old adage for nothing. Your actions and your thoughts will always lead to balance.

Summary

In this chapter we discussed several mental and spiritual techniques to enhance your magickal practices. Try none of them, try all of them; the choice is up to you. In the next chapter we will cover the supplies and practicalities for working with magickal powders and herbal blends.

CHAPTER TWO
Tools and Supplies

I conjure thee. These are the words I use to set in motion almost all magickal operations that I perform, including my ritual circle casting. Please note that in my tradition we start with the north; however, in many practices magickal individuals begin in the east. The choice is entirely yours.

> I conjure thee, O circle of power
>
> So that you will be for me
>
> A boundary between the world of men and the mighty ones
>
> A meeting of perfect love, trust, peace, and joy
>
> Contining the power that I will raise herein
>
> I call upon the guardians of the north, the east, the south, and the west
>
> To aid me in this conjuration.
>
> Thus, in the name of the Lord and Lady, do I conjure thee,
>
> > O great circle of power and protection.
>
> As above
>
> So below
>
> This circle is sealed.

"I conjure thee" are the most powerful words I speak every single day. These words have great meaning for me and I use them as a powerful trigger for the manifestation of what I desire.

What do these words mean? Should you use those words?

Let's take a look in the *Oxford English Dictionary* for the meaning and derivation of the word *conjure*. The basic Latin meaning is *con*, translating as "together," and *jure*, "swear." Initially, the word meant the following:

- to swear together
- to bind together
- to band together
- to combine
- to make a compact by oath

To *be conjure* meant "to be blended," "to appeal to something sacred," "to restrain a negative force by calling to something higher than oneself." As early as 1450 practitioners of Christianity were "conjuring the Trinity" (Father, Son, and Holy Ghost) to do their bidding, mimicking the Pagan religions and practices before them. In 1535 there is a reference to "conjuring holy water" by "praying over it that whosoever they sprinkle therewith may receive health as well of body as of soul."[1]

The idea of the word *conjure* representing something bad occurred when the word became linked with political uprising, witch trials, and other events in which individuals conspired against the ruling class. In the 1500s a conjuress was a sorceress. It also meant slight of hand, trickery, and deception (legerdemain). Around the same time people used the word in association with invocations, charms, and spells.[2]

In 1649 there is reference to this classic invocation: "I conjure thee, O creature of Galbanum, by the living God, that thou be for our defense."

At first thought, you might assume that Galbanum[3] is a demon.

Nope.

It is a gum resin used in incense and medieval medicine. In this instance, the practitioner was—through the words spoken—commanding the resin to bind to their intent. In essence, they were, by word, link-

---

1   *The Compact Oxford English Dictionary*, second edition (NY: Oxford University Press, 1999), 316, sections 742 and 743.
2   Ibid.
3   For those interested in the galbanum resin, I found the following link: http://www.scents-of-earth.com/gaabinsp.html. (There are others. Research. Enjoy!)

ing the purpose (protection, healing) to the field of the resin. "By the living God" is invoking "active (living) perfection (God)."

Herbal and Braucherei/Pow-Wow magick rely heavily on "the word." Not the word of a divinity (although those words are used), but upon the words you speak and the way you present them to the universe. You will find a great deal of Braucherei in this book, and in my daily practice I rely heavily on these Pennsylvania German magickal techniques.

The thought creates the word. The word shapes the field. The field acts upon the body, mind, and soul.

That is Braucherei.

That is conjure.

In this book we are working with my technique of utilizing the sea of potential, the word, herbal powders and herbal blends, binding them together to enhance our development of spirituality and bring joy to ourselves, our families, and the world.

Let's conjure!

Getting Started: Supplies, Timing, and Tips

A magickal powder is a formula of dried herbal ingredients ground and blended by the practitioner for a particular purpose, such as love, health, protection, prosperity, etc. An herbal blend is usually a high-quality mix of dried herbs chosen for their color, magickal properties, scent, and texture. Sometimes these blends are lightly ground or not at all. As all things in the universe have a unique vibratory pattern, the ingredients in a magickal powder or blend are constructed to match the energy vibrations of what you desire to manifest, thereby either attracting the object or situation to you or removing unwanted energy patterns from your field of being.

Magickal powders and herbal blends enhance your mental magicks, affirmations, meditations, rituals, spell casting, and daily living by supporting your work through color, texture, shape, and energy pattern. They help you to create a bond in the physical world and assist in building a stronger bridge to what you wish to manifest. Herbs are living tools that, when awakened to your desire, can help you to connect, create, and fulfill any purpose. Just like you, they are one with the pure, positive potential of the universe.

How Magickal Powders and Herbal Blends Can Be Used

Similar in formulation, magickal powders and herbal blends are used in a wide variety of magickal practices and techniques. Examples include as offerings to the gods, gifts to the beloved dead, in gris-gris bags, to stuff poppets and dream pillows, for enchanted potpourri, added to incense, or scattered around empowered candles, to name just a few. Magickal powders and herbal formulas aren't just for spellwork. They can be used in meditation, affirmations, healing salves (depending upon the ingredients), prayer bags sewed into clothing, and other spiritual practices that do not require spellcasting.

In this book most of the formulas given can be used both as herbal powders or magickal blends unless otherwise indicated. The list below is an example of the versatility of both powders and blends. Some of the suggestions work better with powders and others with blends.

- loaded into candles (a small hole is hand drilled into the bottom of the candle)
- sprinkled around the base of a candle
- as a candle coating (wherein a candle is rolled in honey and then coated with the powder)—please note this is a highly flammable option and should be done only under controlled circumstances
- used in conjuring, gris-gris, or prayer bags
- stuffed into dolls, sachets, or pillows
- added to blessed water, which can be sprinkled around a room, meditation area, magick circle, or left as is in the center of a table or altar
- used in the laundry
- added to other spell components

- hidden under carpets
- added to polymer clay projects (jewelry, figures, runes, etc.)
- added to paint (for painting ritual tools, cards, wooden objects, etc.)
- sprinkled over divination tools
- poured into a ritual bowl over a petition
- added to incense
- rolled into petition papers that will be burned
- left at the base of a tree
- used as an offering in a cemetery
- poured over the top of something that has been buried
- placed in rattles or drums
- left as offerings, particularly outdoors or on your altar
- sprinkled into foot tracks
- sprinkled at front and back doors of a business or living area
- added to the ritual bath (body-safe herbs only)
- used in spiritual cleansings
- added to handcrafted soaps (body-safe herbs only)
- added during the brewing process of handcrafted candles
- folded into paper or cloth packets to be put in pocket, purse, wallet, or placed behind pictures
- added to ritual oil that is used for anointing people (body-safe only) or for dressing magickal candles
- used in sachets for clothing drawers, office drawers, in closets, etc.
- added to bottle and jar magicks such a money jar, a room blessing jar, or a jar to repel unwanted influences
- added into the layers of a rolled beeswax candle (only a small amount should be used, and powder should be placed near the bottom edge of the candle)

Research into magickal powders uncovers a compendium of recipes that differ from town to town, state to state, and country to country. Their use can be found in a variety of magickal practices, including Hoodoo (a magickal system), Voudon (religion), Santería (religion), Wicca/Witchcraft (religion), Druidism (religion), Braucherei (Pow-Wow system), and more. Ingredients chosen for any powder or herbal blend are influenced by individual teachers and practitioners as they learn and grow in their chosen craft, religious beliefs, cultural habits, and the availability of ingredients. This array of individuality makes formulas highly valuable.

In most cases, a formula is designed either to attract or repel unwanted energies; in the herbal world many plants have the capability of doing both. For example, chamomile is used for stress relief, banishing worry, or dissipating fear. The flowers are also added in many success and money spells to draw good fortune to you. The fruit of a peach is sweet and vibrates with the energy of success, love, and prosperity; however, the pit of the peach is poisonous and is used to protect the person who carries it and to banish hungry ghosts and astral nasties. The peach pit can also be used to dispel debt.

It is important to remember that every formula—either passed down from generation to generation or found in print—first began as an intuitive process wherein ingredients were mixed and matched to fulfill a mental need. The need may have been focused on healing, heightening one's spiritual desires, or bringing money or food into the home. Many formulas can be used not only for powders and herbal blends but also for magickal oil and blessed water recipes as well.

Types of Herbal Powders

Where herbal blends are relatively straightforward—putting the herbs in a bowl and mixing them, perhaps adding a few drops of essential oil, fluid condenser, or a fixative such as orris root to complete the physical process—magickal powders are a bit more complicated due to the grinding process. There are basically four types of magickal powders:

Mass Market Powders: Those with a fine base talc, sometimes colored, sold in novelty stores, over the internet, or in catalogs for magickal purposes. If not made by yourself, these mass-produced formulas contain little herb and a lot of talc (sometimes arrowroot or rice flour is used). Unless you know the practices of the supplier, you have no clue who made it, what it contains, or how old it is. Talc was originally used as a base to cut costs and save time, and it could be blown quickly into the air if necessary. This type of powder is not to be ingested.

Machine-Ground Herbs from Health Food or Organic Suppliers: While these are not sold as magickal powders, they are used by magickal practitioners in their powder blends. This type of product consists of herbs and roots finely ground by a machine from a supplier whose primary function is to sell dried herbs to the public for consumption or topical use. From my experience, these powders do not retain their scent or texture and are so fine that they can be hazardous to your lungs during the mixing process, although they can be used in a pinch if you are missing an ingredient in your own powders. Another drawback is that you have no idea of the product's age and because they are so finely ground, one herb can look much like another. When purchased in bulk for large batches of powders, this type of product cuts costs, saves time, and can be easily blown into the air. This kind of powder could be ingested depending upon the selection used. Follow supplier warnings and instructions as not all herbs sold this way are edible or safe.

Personalized Powders: The third category of powder is hand ground with a mortar and pestle or a coffee grinder and is coarser in nature. This type of powder is more likely to retain the original scent of the herbal ingredients. Ritual setting, hand movements, and sounds uttered during the grinding process do much to enhance the energy pattern of the powder. If color is desired, diamond glitter (used in soap-making products and gel candles) can add that "flash of Spirit" and merge with your color correspondence. Colored talc can also be utilized for this purpose; however, it is messier and can stain clothing and other materials. The practical rule here is to put color in powders that will only be seen by yourself, not those that you will use around the general public. This third type of powder is usually made by yourself or a trusted friend or practitioner, and typically contains a variety of unnatural or unusual elements chosen for their vibratory associations. Just like a recipe for a good apple pie, each ingredient is chosen for its ability to blend with the others to create the ultimate formula. Minute amounts of essential oils or fragrances can also be added to heighten both the aroma and pattern of the formula. A fluid condenser ramps up the power. Orris root is often added to personalized powders to assist in their preservation, both aroma and storage quality. This type of powder is not ingested; however, you can easily make your own herbal powders or magickal blends that comply with food-safe standards.

Food-Safe Hand-Ground Magickal Powders: Commonly used in cooking magick, these consist of standard food-quality herbs such as pepper, parsley, sage, lemon verbena, etc. As there are a wide variety of edible herbs, basic formulas are easy to grind, combine, and use, particularly if you feel your magickal powder selection is not safe from pets or children. This powder does not contain any additives.

Why Make Your Own Magickal Powders or Herbal Blends?

Making your own powders or herbal blends allows you to tailor the ingredients to a particular, private purpose. From choosing something special for your healing circle or Samhain ritual to helping your daughter dump the crappy, abusive son-in-law to asking for mental clarity in an emotionally charged situation, being able to design your own formula helps you to intimately manage the energies you wish to promote and blend your thoughts and the herbs together during the mixing and grinding process. From stress relief to good fortune, working with your mind, your hands, and the spiritual world of plants can bring great satisfaction in any situation. Making your own powders and herbal blends is an individual statement of power and allows you to intimately experience the bond of all things.

Your own magickal powders and herbal blends are extremely economical. Powders cost less to make, do not waste our natural resources, are easy to store and simple to use, can be mixed with many magickal practices, and lend well to secrecy. "To be silent" is a high priority if you are looking at magick as a science governed by quantum physics, where the fewer observers, the better! As significant quantities of the herb are not needed by the practitioner for either powders or blends, when shopping for ingredients one can choose the higher-priced organics, which usually carry a better aroma and are of better quality. If you wish to gather herbs from the wild, little is needed to dry for your personal magickal cupboard, thus conserving our wildcrafting resources.

If you raise your own herbs, making powders and herbal blends allows your enchanted garden harvest to last through the long, cold months of winter. Since you have grown the herbs yourself, you know their age and, very importantly, you know how they grew, what you put in the soil, what rituals you performed in the garden to help them grow, and what the season was like. Here, as a gardener, you have communed with the living spirit of the plant. You have lived the bond between plant and human through watering, weeding, touching, caring, or perhaps just observing, depending upon the nature of the plant. You know what was in the soil, the angle of the sun across the plants any given day, and perhaps rushed to save them a time or two from frost, hail, or violent storms. You may have already performed lots of magick surrounded by those living plants, perhaps a summer solstice ritual in the garden or a Mabon celebration with friends and family as you harvested some of the plants. You may have learned the best way to dry those plants for the greatest yield, both for food and for magick. Here, the bond of being, the oneness of the all, has already been experienced with those plants, creating a stronger platform for your magickal work.

Making magickal powders and herbal blends can be a fun lesson in teaching students. Not only are the students able to take something home with them, they quickly learn the properties and correspondences of the herbs, grasp the importance of the ceremony chosen, and experience a broad range of magickal techniques in creating one simple formula. From selecting whole dried herbs, they become more intimate with the magickal plant world. They learn consistency, texture, color. Most importantly, students learn that the powder is an alchemical pattern in itself that can be enhanced by the spiritual practices used in its creation and become a powerhouse in their personal magick. All plants have their own individual DNA, just like humans, and their pattern of individuality combines with your work to create a powerful tool in the magickal powder or herbal blend.

Magickal Powder and Herbal Blend Additives

Powder and herbal blend formulas are often unusual due to a variety of additives. These additives are used to strengthen the formula, knitting the desire tighter to the herbal bond and creating a unique bridge to the ultimate manifestation.

Additives can include ground gems, stones, feathers, shells, and bones; ashes of a petition or photo; graveyard dirt (of which there are several varieties); saltpeter (highly flammable), iron dust, rust, and glitter; shredded and pulverized paper money, newsprint, pictures of saints or gods and goddesses, parchment talismans, rune pictures, printed words of power or intent, pictures of a goal, names on a business card or court document (use a copy), a logo from a company or school, a phone number, internet IP address, or tarot cards; dirt from a bank, a jail, a successful corporation, your job, or the property of someone who has been trying to hurt you; scrapings from a car, gravestone, church, or statuary; naturally shed cat whiskers (for balance) and cat claws (for protection); a dog's tooth (naturally lost, not taken) to command people; salt, sugar, colored powder, eggshell; resins such as myrrh, dragon's blood, frankincense, or copal; brick dust or pulverized rune stones; menstrual blood, saliva; essential oils (one or two drops only), liquid fragrance (one or two drops only), and my favorite fluid condensers (which you will learn how to make in this book).

This is just a simple list. Additives, like practitioners, can be unique and endlessly creative. These items were chosen for their ability to make a single bond to the intended goal. The purpose of the additive is to build a unique connection to the goal that your consciousness deems empowering.

Basic Supplies for Creating Your Own Magickal Powders and Herbal Blends

The following supply list represents an example of what I have used over the years to make and store magickal powders and herbal blends. It is a simple guideline that you are free to change.

Glass Bowls: Use for mixing. Some practitioners believe that metal bowls taint the blend; however, others feel that the metal actually helps to enhance the work—only you can choose what is right for you. You will need at least two bowls if you are making a powder, one to blend the raw herb mixture and one to hold the finished powder after grinding (or during the grinding process if you are making a large batch). Clear bowls work well because you can see what you are doing through the entire process, making sure all ingredients are thoroughly blended before storage. Metal containers, on the other hand, are light and less likely to break if you drop them. And, metal bowls will also sing (vibrate) during the stirring process, which does add a special energy to the blend.

Wooden Spoons: Some practitioners use individual spoons hand-carved with magickal sigils, words of power, or other artistic designs. Others use sticks, bamboo skewers, or their fingers during the blending process. A few use a metal fork, particularly if they want the metal bowl to sing.

Mortar and Pestle: Use to break up large herbs or roots for herbal blends and to grind herbs and roots into powder form for magickal powders. The size of the mortar and pestle depends on the number of ingredients, how large a batch of powder you choose to make, and the consistency of the ingredients. For example, a larger, heavier mortar and pestle set is extremely handy for tough roots and barks, such as angelica root, or resins, such as dragon's blood chunks. Every herb breaks down in its own way. For example, lavender fluffs, which makes it a difficult herb to add to a smooth powder. You can either leave it whole or use a heavy mortar and pestle to break down the buds. If you put lavender in a coffee grinder, it tends to get puffy. There are herbs that retain moisture, like pumpkin seeds, which can clump your powder. You may wish to use the heavier mortar and pestle to break down the seeds, and then press your results with folded paper towels before adding them to your powder blend. Resins like frankincense and copal can be ground in a coffee grinder; your results may be somewhat sticky but not unmanageable.

Mallet or Hammer: Use for crushing raw resins such as frankincense, myrrh, and dragon's blood, as well as some of the tougher roots: Solomon's seal, angelica, etc. The hammer also can be used for creating protective brick dust or pulverizing gemstones. Some individuals use a heavy metal meat tenderizer.

Measuring Spoons: These can be useful in ensuring that the more aromatic ingredients do not overpower the lighter elements. They are extremely helpful in designing a formal magickal recipe or when creating a formula that you wish to repeat or share with others.

Kitchen Shears: As I mentioned earlier, although some magickal practitioners frown on using any metal in a magickal process, others don't have a problem with it at all. Kitchen shears can be very helpful in the pre-grinding process. For example, if you have dried long sheaves of lemongrass and you are ready to grind some of it for a cleansing powder or blend, or perhaps you are making your favorite magickal cleansing soap, cutting the leaves into tiny pieces helps to release the natural oils and makes the grinding process easier. Lemongrass is tough, and you could be grinding all day just to get what you need if you don't use the shears.

Safety Mask: This can be obtained at your local hardware store and is used to protect the lungs, mouth, and nose area when grinding herbs, particularly if you are using a coffee grinder or adding sulfur, saltpeter, or any kind of fine dirt, chipped gems, or glitter in your formulas.

Coffee Grinder: This works wonderfully for that final blending process and can create a variety of powder weights from rough and coarse to medium ground to a very fine powder, depending upon the ingredients. A good grinder can also be used for bits of copal, frankincense, myrrh, and for some pre-crushed roots. In our busy society you may not have several hours to sit and grind everything you need by hand. I agree that the more time you spend grinding the herbs while uttering prayers, spells, songs, or incantations can help to strengthen the bond of the powder, but this is often unrealistic when it comes to time management. I can hear you now: "I'm sorry, I can't pick up my granddaughter today from daycare because I will be busy grinding a very special magickal powder." Yeah, right.

Magickal Powder Journal or Notebook: You think you will remember…how could you forget? Especially since the powder worked so fast or so well in your magickal operation! Unfortunately, time passes and a year later, when you have a need for that formula again, you may remember the key ingredients but not every single element. Writing down all your magickal recipes—and including the date, the reason for its creation, and, later, the outcome—is an essential part of the enchantment process and gives you written documentation of your work as reference for future applications. I have three journals spanning approximately five years each that contain a compendium of formulas. It's fun to look back over the events and see how I have changed personally, and how some of my techniques have changed as I continue to learn. These books are so used and worn that the covers are coming off and many of the pages are stained, but to me they are priceless.

Essential Oils or Liquid Perfume Fragrances: Only 2–3 drops are used for small batches of powder or herbal blends (12–14 for larger quantities); be careful of overpowering the natural aroma of the work. The oil can be added to the raw herb mixture or massaged in with the fingers when the grinding process is completed. When using an explicit formula, if an ingredient is not available in the herbal form, many times an essential oil may be added in minute amounts to replace that necessary dried herb. Not only does this round out the magickal pattern of the formula, but the oil also heightens the aromatic properties of the mixture, which can affect the performance of the practitioner in positive ways. As a result, many of your personal blends may contain both herbals and oils to capture the totality of the magickal essence.

Eye Droppers: Use for adding minute amounts of essential oils, fluid condensers, or fragrances to your powder or herbal blend mixture.

Storage: Once your powder or herbal blend is made, you may choose to complete the empowerment process and then store it, or store the powder or blend until you wish to empower it for a particular purpose. Select the storage that best suits your lifestyle. Storage depends on quantity made and the shelf life you desire. For example, the shelf life of an edible magickal powder is approximately four months in plastic, six months in glass, or a year if you use a food sealer. The general rule for nonedible magickal powders is six months in plastic, one year in glass, and two years if you use a food sealer. However, some practitioners feel that nonedible empowered powders or herbal blends stored in glass actually gain potency. There are individuals who will use a powder that is twenty-five years old simply because it was empowered by a deceased individual who carried masterful abilities in life. Powders and blends created during a special event, whether personal or astrological, are also thought to be potent in their own right, due to the energy pattern of the special occasion. For example, powders can be made from herbs and flowers used in a handfasting (wedding), wiccaning, or initiatory celebration. The same applies for astrological events, particularly those that will not occur again in your lifetime; however, other cycles, such as full moon, new moon, and dark moon, are commonly used for specialty powders.

In Process/Collection Bag, Box, or Lidded Jar: These are holding areas for projects in process. They can be as decorative or as plain as you like, from highly decorated boxes and jars to machine-stitched and appliquéd bags to a good old paper sack. These containers hold the herbs or ingredients you have collected until the right timing occurs for you to actually create the powders and blends. They can also be used as an energy-holding vehicle, where you gather all the ingredients together for a particular blend that you want to use for an individual person. For a holding bag you may like to use black (the absence of color) or white (the blend of all colors), depending on your intent or preference. In Braucherei we often bury items in the ground or in jars containing dirt gathered from place relating to the issue so that the object can gather power and be "birthed" at a later date.

The timing for this process is usually from moon to moon, but we use the method with other numbers as well (3, 9, 21). You might choose to have a variety of containers that apply specifically to a favorite signature powder or a theme, such as prosperity, healing, banishing, etc. Holding jars and containers come in very handy the more involved you become with the art of powders and herbal blends, particularly if you have a very busy schedule or if you have a very busy household where folks just can't seem to keep their fingers off of your stuff. It may take you an entire month to gather all you need for a very specialized powder: this might include items collected on a Spirit Walk, things ordered from the internet, herbs picked up on your next grocery store run, dirt from a specific graveyard or business, blood gathered on white cloth from a menstrual cycle, a certain plant that you had to drive for several hours on the weekend to obtain, or a gemstone that a family member sent you from across the country as a result of your request. Perhaps you see a banging planetary configuration coming up and you want to use that to make a sigil for a powder associated with that type of positive energy, which will work well for a powder that you wish to make, but you don't have time to gather all the supplies right now. Design the sigil at the right moment, wrap it in black or white paper or cloth, and add it to your intent bag.

Having a place to put these items until you are ready to use them saves so much time when you are ready to actually grind and empower the powder or mix the herbal blend. There is nothing more irritating than searching through a compendium of drawers, boxes, shelves, and jars, saying to yourself, "I *know* I have that! I even remember when I got it! Where the heck is it now?" If you spiritually cleanse all the items before you put them in the container, they will begin to blend together in your mind as a result of your mental purpose. Yes, you will have to take the process further for the realization of your intent to occur, but this initial step can help to fine-tune the work. If your bag or container is large enough, you can even add the candles, incense, and other components of ritual or spellcasting that you will be using in a working.

For example, I make hand-rolled beeswax candles that contain magickal powders, and I paint the bottom of the candles with a fluid condenser that matches the intent. When moon phase and planetary timing match my intent, I will roll a candle for a named person and add it to the bag. That way, when you are ready to do a healing spell for Susan, you already have everything prepared, saving you precious time. If a powder or herbal blend is for a single individual, put their photograph or full name in the bag first along with an initial prayer for assistance to help you find exactly what you need for this working. As you add items to the bag or jar, say the person's name aloud three times, indicating your intent of healing for that person. By the time you actually put everything together, the focus is already there because you have layered words and energy into a pattern linked to the person. This is truly mystical web weaving; like the spider with her web, you are constructing (weaving) a foundation pattern with your actions to accomplish a specific goal. The things in the bag are energetically sticky because of your intent of attracting something specific. At the proper time of your choice it will be your job to catch the goal, wrap it up, and internalize it, which will lead to its fruition.

For an individual person with a specialized need, you may wish to use a paper bag as your collection point and then burn the bag once your spell has been cast or the ritual performed as part of your ceremony. Non-disposable containers can either be washed out with holy water or cleansed with salt or a mixture of salt, lavender, and rosemary. I keep a jar marked "cleansing wash" with these three ingredients in my workroom. You can use it dry or add a teaspoon to blessed water whenever the need arises. I also have a resin cleanser that is pre-ground and mixed frankincense, myrrh, copal, mistletoe, eggshell, and a pinch of salt, which can be used in a variety of applications, from adding a teaspoon to cleansing conjuring bags with other ingredients to burning the resin mixture on a charcoal tab. Whether the holding container is permanent or temporary, I mark the outside (or put a paper inside) that indicates what the collection is for, along with a listing of the ingredients I have already collected. This way I never use the ingredients for the wrong person or intent. Here is one of the sigils that I designed to hold and protect the energy of my temporary or permanent containers:

Eyes of Spirit Sigil

This sigil is entitled "Eyes of Spirit." Write your intent in the box in the center of the design. You can redraw the sigil or use a photocopy. I often change the planetary symbol at the top of the sigil so that it is in tune with my intent. In this example, Mars is the associated planet. If I wanted to draw something toward me, I would use Venus. If I desired dreams, heightened intuition, or healing work for women and children, I might change the top symbol to the Moon. For success and my will, the Sun. For communication and solutions of all kinds, Mercury. Saturn for protection, foundation, rewards, or karmic work. I also use the modern planets: Neptune (creativity), Uranus (freedom), and Pluto (destruction and significant change). This design can be placed on the bag or container or as a sigil to go with your working.

Witness Stick: This isn't a must-have ingredient, but I began using this technique about five years ago, and it works extremely well. The witness stick (usually no larger than 3–4 inches in length) is a small stick that you have collected from outdoors before a working, often gathered on a Spirit Walk. It is one from the ground; you do not take a living limb off of a tree or bush, although you can remove a broken stick out of a tree or plant that is unattached and has not yet touched the ground. Both have worked for me. You can use a different wooden stick for each working or you can use one stick for a particular theme; for example, one stick that you have gathered for prosperity rituals and a different one for healing. The stick "witnesses" your spell, takes the energy into it, and then you carry the stick with you until you receive what is asked for or you can leave it on your altar until the desire has come to pass. If someone tries to carry your stick off in the meantime, this is your cue that you need to let the stick go because the working is already in place and it is only a matter of time before it will come to pass. In this case, return the stick to the wild. Otherwise, a witness stick for attraction can be kept. A witness stick for banishment should be burned or buried off your property. The witness stick remembers your words, feelings, and the energy you raised.

Beeswax Sheets: Use these to make your own rolled candles using your herbal powders as the main ingredient. Of all the candles on the market, beeswax seems to hold the power better due to its natural structure designed by the hands of Nature herself. Over the years I have made candles from all the waxes: paraffin, palm, soy, etc. All of them have chemical additives. In fact, when researching soy, I found that soy wax can't be "all natural" due to the process of making it. (This statement is always subject to change with advancements in the industry.) I found that beeswax takes your charge better, particularly if you put the candle in the refrigerator for approximately half an hour before the magickal operation. The chilling process not only helps the wax absorb better, but the candle also burns longer. You will find instructions on how to roll your own powerful beeswax candles in chapter 5.

Powderboard: A powderboard is a flat portable surface that is used for meditation, ritual, and spellwork. For working with magickal powders, the surface should be satin smooth. This type of board is used to draw sigils or write someone's name with your powder on the surface during a magickal application. I have found that flat sticks and a metal ¼ teaspoon can be helpful in the designing process. If this is too complicated, spread the powder on a piece of clear glass and draw your design in the powder. If you use a piece of clear glass for your powderboard, you can place printed or drawn information under the glass (such as a spirit circle, a person's name, etc.) or the surface can be opaque. Like any other magickal tool, the powderboard should be cleansed and blessed between every working. I have also used wooden cutting boards, although the powder tends to stick to the wood during cleanup. Powders are spread on the surface in the desired design, then activated either by passing a candle flame over the pattern while chanting or by setting and using your hands, teasing the energy to the artwork and then back again several times before actually filling the design with the energy. The powder is then used in the next step of an application (such as loading into a candle) or dispensed where you wish to place your intent. If the work was all about the sigil, then you may want to take the powderboard outside and blow the formula into the air to release the magick. When the powder will be stored for later, you can draw the sigils in the powder on the powderboard as a part of the construction of your formula. I use this procedure particularly for astrological or runic powders, where I draw the symbols of the planets, signs, or rune glyphs into the powder before storing.

An Herbal Altar: This is a sacred space that you use to honor the spirits of the plants. It can be a table or a cupboard with a flat surface (such as a hutch)—the design of the furniture you use is entirely up to you. If you are fortunate enough to have a shed or greenhouse area, your working herbal altar may be placed there. Practitioners may incorporate the altar and herbal storage together so that items for magick and ritual can be easily accessed. Often the altar is facing the east, but this is not a necessity. Working with herbs can be a messy process. There are those practitioners who opt to make most of their powders and blends in the kitchen using the portable powderboard as an altar for easy cleanup. There is no right way to honor the plants, create an altar, or make a powderboard. The universe loves creativity and beauty; enjoy the freedom!

Charcoal Tabs Designed to Burn Incense/Noncombustible Incense: Your herbal blends and powders can be burned loose on charcoal tabs nested in ash or sand in a firesafe bowl. Always double check all ingredients to ensure that the herbs you are using are nontoxic. For example, I would not add woodruff, mullein, wormwood, nightshade, or other poisonous herbs to an incense blend. You can make incense pellets out of your herbals for burning on charcoal tabs by adding a few drops of honey to the herbs or powder and rolling the mixture into small balls.

Choosing Herbal Ingredients

Although this book provides many formulas from my private collection, mastery comes with the design of your own recipes and the positive results of your work. We are fortunate to live in a time where we can draw from the knowledge of various cultures, societies, groups, and families that have published herbal books and information both in printed form and on the internet. This information includes correspondences (lists of herbs that vibrate well together, that blend well under particular astrological influences, or that have colors that positively affect the blend). As a student, you might wish to use this information or you may choose to rely on how you feel as you work with the herbs yourself. In the end, if your recipe works to assist in creating your intent, then that formula is considered successful. See the appendix for herbal resource information.

Where to Work?

Although you may think that a ritual room or area is the answer, most practitioners I know work on their dining room table or in the kitchen, or, when the weather is beautiful, outdoors on a patio, porch, by a ritual fire pit, or in the garden shed. I've used all those places, including my home office on occasion. Yes, powders can be made in a ceremonial environment on an altar; but, they also lend themselves extremely well to where your heart is, and your heart is usually in the center of your home, which is either the dining room or the kitchen. These are also easy places to clean up any mess as a result of the grinding, blending, and mixing process.

From interviewing several individuals all over the country, I've learned that all of us use some kind of mat, tray, or plate for the final magickal blend and empowerment. For example, I learned a great deal of herbal magick firsthand from author Ray Malbrough. Years ago Ray taught me to use clay plates painted with various designs depending upon the need for activating my powders and herbal blends in our Spiritism work. I have a plate for general work, one for manifestation powders/blends and magicks, one for healing, one for petitioning my patron, etc. A friend of mine in Texas learned herbal magicks in Haiti. He uses a tray. The decoration and design of this surface is highly individual. I've also created a planetary board by burning the sigils of the planets on the surface of an oval piece of unfinished basswood and a runic board by using the same material and technique. I stained both boards with my own plant-based dye recipe, then added a sealer on the boards to withstand moisture. This way, I can use them from preparation through to spellcasting. I took my time with all these projects; the journey was half the fun!

Where to Start?

• • •

There is only energy that is affected by portals, gates, paths, and patterns. It is not human. It does not think. It just is.

Ray Malbrough taught me that the process in enchantment can be just as important as the actual magickal act. In the process of choosing, collecting, honing, deciding, blending, and mixing, intent is added to a working. If you have difficulty visualizing in ritual or meditation, then the props you use as well as the preparation you have done help to give your work the jolt it needs to form the required pattern of manifestation. The process in any magickal working (meaning the beforehand actions) contributes to solidify the goal you have chosen, as long as you haven't cluttered the prep time with negativity, fear, or doubt.

Sometimes the longer you take to collect the necessary ingredients for a powder or herbal blend can actually help to dispel some of those unwanted thoughts. As you gather each item, you may become more excited about your project. This emotional joy and enthusiasm seeps into your work, encouraging it to gain power and momentum toward your desired conclusion. Sometimes I spend lots of time creating the containers that will hold my powders and herbal blends; I paint, Mod Podge, stain, sand, engrave, etc., letting my creativity flow. I add embellishments such as ribbon, natural or humanmade charms, and glitter (oh, how I dearly love glitter)! Tin, wood, or glass (I don't use plastic because I want the greatest shelf life), I will spend hours making sure the container that will hold my finished powders and herbal blends is creatively pleasing. After all, to believe in magick, you must be willing to create!

Where to start when you wish to design a magickal powder or herbal blend? *With your intent.* What precisely do you want to draw toward yourself or push away? What is the issue you desire to work on? Are you looking for a particular object (such as a car, a computer, or a new pet), to fine-tune an ability (such as divination or dream work), or to enhance something about yourself (such as your creative potential)? Perhaps you need to solve a problem or create an energy field around yourself or a loved one (called protection magick or warding).

And herein lies the biggest hurdle in magick: clarity of purpose—knowing what we really want. Most humans, including myself, are pretty darned wishy-washy when it comes to goals: today we want this…no…wait, not that…perhaps the other thing…shoot! I have to do the laundry. I have to pick up my mother. I have to pay that electric bill. And even if you had that goal somewhat settled, well! Life takes over, and your thoughts tumble onward (but not necessarily upward), and we let go of the goal, just like that. *Poof!* Gone!

Sigh.

A magickal powder or herbal blend can be designed for any purpose; you need only to begin with clear intent. This is where your notebook, pad of paper, or 5x7 cards can come into play. When wording your intention, keep it clear and concise and include all the elements of your desire. I keep a pad of graph paper handy when designing my powders and blends. I might spend a few minutes or several days reworking my intent on this pad. I also write down things that come to mind during that time period: good quotes I hear, conversations from friends that I think are pertinent to what I'm working on, or thoughts I have of a spiritual nature that may help me to fine-tune my intent. Then, after I am satisfied with my goal as it is written (although I can still change it), I will work on collecting what herbs, additives, or oils that I feel will best match that intent. Once the working is done, I will write down the final formula, date, moon phase, and what sign the moon was in during the process in my powder/blend notebook. Like everyone else, sometimes I'm in a hurry and just make sure I put the right date so that I can look back later in an ephemeris to check out the moon sign or astrological energies I used.

Oh! And I doodle. Yes, I doodle while I am thinking, and many times I may use that same doodle drawing, pulverized, torn, or burnt, in my powder. Sometimes this doodle contains magickal sigils such as runes, a pentacle, or just spirals of lines and dots. These days, that's my signature ingredient.

The Doctrine of Signatures

In discussing correspondences used in European occultism, the study of herbs can be traced from ancient Sumer (located in present-day Iran) and then to the early Greeks. One of the first writers to address the field of plant medicine and its association of astrology and magick was Dioscorides, a Roman. His book, entitled *De Materia Medica*, was published around AD 77, approximately 2,000 years ago. For quite some time, future writers on the subject studied the author and his work rather than doing field experiments themselves. By the 1500s the European printing press was going full blast. Brave thinkers like Agrippa von Nettesheim (1486–1535), Johannes Trithemius (1462–1516), and Philippus Aureolus Paracelsus (1493–1541) were pushing the envelope of government and church guidelines. Rather than just reading and studying what had already been written, they did experiments on what they wanted to learn. Their work included alchemy, medicine, herbs, astrology, theology, and more. They reexamined the classical works such as Dioscorides and made revisions based on their own experiments. For plant lore, this meant traveling to other areas, talking to healers of different nationalities, and then bringing information back to test for themselves.

These men (Agrippa, Trithemius, and Paracelsus) and many of their contemporaries were confident that a world soul existed—that we are all linked together in some way. It is from this idea that the correspondences involving herbals, astrology, and magick were researched, developed, studied, and, most importantly, written down. It was Paracelsus who said that the body was not a separate thing but a house for the soul, and therefore the physician should treat both body and soul to turn the sick person into a well one. Today Paracelsus is considered the father of pharmaceutical chemistry, modern wound surgery, and homeopathy. He was also a magician who used folk remedies, amulets, talismans, and a variety of studies to heal his patients. He traveled all over Europe, talking to doctors, barbers (who often seconded as physicians), wise women, sorcerers, alchemists, nuns, bath attendants, magicians, knights, princes, kings, gypsies, and monks. From the low ranks to those of nobility, from the intelligent to the simple-minded, he collected as much information as he could for the purposes of healing. Paracelsus's work, the doctrine of signatures, created correspondences that are still used today based on the plant's family, the conditions in which it grew naturally, its shape, leaf type, root system, color, etc., and its effect on the body, both physically and spiritually.[4]

For example, one procedure to heal a skin disease was to mix the particular parts of four herbs together, then squeeze the juice into a bowl and add a small amount of soap. This is the medical part. The prescription goes on to instruct the healer to take a small amount of blood from the patient at sunset and pour it into running water. The healer then spits three times and says, "Take this disease and depart with it!" (Still common today in the realm of Braucherei, Hoodoo, Santería, Voudon, and more). The healer is also instructed to walk back to the house by an open road and to walk each way in silence. The timing and the procedure for transferring illness to running water, spitting, uttering words of banishment, and walking to and from the water in silence is clearly magickal[5]—or is it? There have been recent experiments wherein a drop of blood taken from the body and removed to another room will react to an event that the body is experiencing. How much of magick that seems so silly may be based in quantum science? We just haven't gotten there quite yet!

Let's look at that "walking in silence" part. In the science of the mind, we know that any conversation can change circumstances, muddle thoughts, and interject elements that we do not desire. In silence, an observer cannot change your mental activity. If you are the healer, you need to be focused on the healing—not on fear, not on failure, and not on what someone had for dinner last night who decides she must break

---

4   Paracelsus, *Paracelsus: Selected Writings*, 43.
5   Kieckhefer, *Magic in the Middle Ages*, 64, 65.

the silence and tell you because she can't stand not being the center of attention.

Silence is golden. Really. Golden light, empty of negativity. Let your mind wander on this one. Gold, the Braucherei preferred color. Gold, the rising of the sun (new energy). Gold, the setting of the sun (banishing, putting to rest). Gold, the height of noon-day power. Gold: winning, courage, loyalty. What scientific associations, as well as personal ones, can you find as a result of your own contemplation in that odd, old spell? What comes to mind when you think of the word *gold*? Gold also stands, astrologically, for the solar noon, a time of great power for magickal workings. The solar noon is when the sun is at its highest elevation in the sky. The clock time of the solar noon depends on your longitude and the current date. Some magickal practitioners feel that this time is best for success workings. There are apps you can put on your phone or other device that will tell you when solar noon occurs at your location.

Many practitioners work with the original doctrine of signatures, *Culpepper's Herbal*, *Cunningham's Encyclopedia of Magical Herbs*, Paul Beyerl's *A Compendium of Herbal Magick*, and Catherine Yronwood's *Hoodoo Herbs and Root Magick: A Materia Magica of African-American Culture*. You will also find herbal information from my own research in many of my books, including *A Witch's Notebook*, *Solitary Witch*, *HedgeWitch*, and *HexCraft*. When you begin working with plants by creating your own formulas and blends based on size, color, shape, medicinal properties, growing experience, root examination, and experimentation, you are compiling your own doctrine of signatures. Have confidence!

One of these days, science, medicine, and magick will finally get together and rather than spitting at each other from opposite sides of the triangle, they will find enlightenment in the common ground that already exists but is just being ignored. Today, the doctrine of signatures is going to a whole new level in the interests of health, healing, and spirituality. We see more interest in Amazonian and Native American shamans and, in the process, spirituality and science. An example is the work of Julia Graves in her *The Language of Plants: A Guide to the Doctrine of Signatures*, which you may find extremely useful in your spiritual practices.

Magickal Correspondences

All things everywhere consist of energy. This energy pulsates (fast or slow) in unique mathematical/geometric patterns. A correspondence is a relationship between two patterns either by size, shape, color, element, or historical lore. There are angelic, animal, herbal, gem, astrological, color, symbol, element, and deity patterns in modern magic, to name just a few. Patterns that are much like each other work well together and, when linked, build a network of energy you can use in your magickal operations. This system of light energy is usually referred to as patterns working in sympathy. Correspondences often fall into subcategories that relate to the elements of earth, air, fire, and water. Other categories used are those of gender; some planets, for example, are seen as feminine, and others as masculine. It is the same with herbs, gems, and stones. Gender doesn't mean the item is just for boys or just for girls—here it can mean active energy (male) or passive energy (female).

The creation of the associations between items began in ancient Sumer. In their view, the arts and crafts had been revealed to them by the gods above and were unchanging. Everything must have its name to assure its place in the universe, and when you knew the "true" name of something, then you had power over it. In essence, they believed the name held the item energetically in place.

Among the earliest Sumerian documents are lists of stones, animals, and plants, classified on their outward characteristics. This belief was also paralleled by the ancient Egyptians. The advent of Christianity didn't change the idea of linking names and energy patterns together. As I mentioned earlier, Paracelsus worked out his own doctrine of signatures in the 1500s by studying classical Greek and Roman writings and conducting his own research. In Braucherei healing magicks it is essential that the given name of the sick person be used, as to speak their name identifies the person to the universe and provides a clear pathway for the healing to take place along the name's energy path. The individual's name is to be spoken three times, thereby assuring the universe of the correct address to which the energy is to be sent. The doctrine of signatures took on a whole new face as Europeans and others immigrated to the United

States. They brought plants with them to retain their traditional beliefs; "in some cases, those imports had a significant impact on the country's agricultural development."[6] They learned about plants here that they had never seen before and added Native American knowledge of indigenous plants, enhancing and improving the growing storehouse of information. Individuals of African and island descent brought their beliefs and their inventive style of turning everyday items into great objects of power. This cauldron of information, much of it by word of mouth, bubbled into many of the magickal correspondences we have today.

You will find several correspondence lists in this book, including astrological symbolism, herbal information, colors, and more. Each section has a few tips I've learned along the way that may help you in the construction and use of your own formulas. I have provided these lists so that you can design or enhance your own powders, herbal blends, spells, meditations, rituals, and magickal operations. It is my hope that you will find this information helpful not only for the gathering of your formulas, but for magickal timing as well.

I have learned that plants will literally reach out and touch you if they are trying to tell you something or share energy. They may brush against your leg or your arm. They may be sick (if you are taking care of a garden, for instance) and wish to attract your focus to their needs. Pay attention to your emotions and what rises within yourself as you feel the gentle (or sometimes smack) of the plant. I know you might laugh and call me a copycat, but I do have a whisper technique for healing and taking care of sick plants. I talk to them about what I am doing (watering, fertilizing, etc.) and how beautiful I know they are going to be. I tell them I am so sorry that they met with difficulty, and that now I am directing my energy to help them grow and become amazing. Now, you may say, how silly or how stupid or how strangely saintly of you. How did you start doing this?

Because I was dead broke and wanted a pretty garden.

Yup.

---

6   Davis, *America Bewitched*, 27.

When my kids were small, money was super tight and there just wasn't extra to buy beautiful plants at the greenhouse. So I would wait for late July and buy the plants on sale across the street at the hardware store. These plants were usually half dead and less than fifty cents each, left to languish in the boiling sun, sucking up the parking lot dust. I would take them home and tell them how much I loved them and how beautiful they could be and how I would be so appreciative if they could grow and be happy. I often used Braucherei chants in a sing-song voice. On summer solstice I would take my boombox outside, turn it up to full blast, and play classical music followed by Enya for them.

Yup.

Much to my amazement, year after year, those broken and decrepit plants would bounce back. To this day I will buy plants that look dead at bargain off-season prices just so I can whisper them to health. I have three rose bushes I purchased this year for a few bucks at a season-end sale. They are all doing beautifully. I will be the first to admit that it was touch and go with one of them, but he eventually joined the program and is blooming merrily along.

Go figure.

The Elements

According to the *Oxford English Dictionary*, the word *element* has a mysterious origin and is first found in Greek texts meaning "complex whole" or "a single unit made up of many parts." From the ancient up to medieval times there were only four element associations in Europe—earth, air, fire, and water, and, if you were occult oriented, the fifth element was spirit. Cornelius Agrippa and many others called this spirit the quintessence. Other cultures, however, such as China, carry a different set of elements: earth, fire, water, wood, and metal.

Today, although scientists list more than 100 chemical elements (with some being manmade), magickal people continue to rely on the five basic building blocks of medieval occultism, using some of the additional elements of the modern age to support the original five, depending on the spell or ritual. For example, silver (an element/metal) is used in various spells and is a symbol of the divine goddess, feminine mysteries, moon magick, dreaming, and psychism. Many would see silver as being associated with the earth because it comes from the ground, but others may choose a different correspondence association due to its possible stellar origins. Gold, another precious metal, stands for the god, male mysteries, success, prosperity, general well-being, and all magicks associated with the sun.

The current theory of the origins of gold tracks its creation as a result of the explosion of a massive star, becoming a supernova:

> Ultra high precision analyses of some of the oldest rock samples on Earth provides clear evidence that the planet's accessible reserves of precious metals are the result of a bombardment of meteorites more than 200 million years after Earth was formed.[7]

Gold piggybacked a ride to this planet via asteroids/meteors. If this is true, it is most interesting that gold and silver are heaven sent and therefore not attributable to the overall earth element category, and that the ancients already attributed these metals to gods and goddesses. Something to ponder. I mention the information about silver and gold because many formulas created by serious alchemists and occultists contain a small amount of gold or silver. When you reach the fluid condenser section in this book, you will find the choice of gold as the driving force of the original formulas. When these fluid condensers are added to magickal powders and blends, they increase the vibratory pattern of the overall formula and help to hold the charge longer, allowing you to send the energy as you choose in a more directed fashion.

Earth, Air, Fire, Water

When researching herbs for magickal and medicinal use, you will often find a primordial elemental correlation to earth, air, water, and fire. Over time each of these elements has been assigned spiritual and magickal associations to understand the world around us and our actions in it. Each one of us processes these connections differently, yet we know that these

---

7 See https://www.sciencedaily.com/releases/2011/09/110907132044.htm.

elements have a primordial energy that affects the earth plane. What is universal is the energy; what is *not* universal are the names we attach to it.

> The universe contains the seeds of all things, drawing toward themselves what they need to grow. At the moment of the acknowledgment of activation, air particles gather together, forming the cosmic wind of karma. This movement activates the fire particles, which gather together to create heat. They ride upon the cosmic wind. The fire particles enable the water particles, which condense to form a torrential rain filled with lightning. This rain vibrates with the intent, and the electrical charge energizes the seed. The earth particles gather and combine with the other elements, and thus solidification of anything is born. The fifth element, spirit, pervades everything and assists in assigning the "address" (pattern) within itself, as Spirit was there before the correlation, and it will be thereafter.[8]

Looking at manifestation in this way, we see that it is a process of waves, with one wave calling another in a succession of steps to create a whole.

In Braucherei, homeopathy, holistic medicine, etc., there is the observation on the imbalance of the elements in any particular malady. This imbalance begins with the original thought, the seed; the amount of each element it draws toward itself and how those particles behave are predicated on the continuous thought.

A final reason for using the four elements in magick is the commonality they share with everything on this planet. The elements are a conduit to each living thing wherein energy can travel to reach its target. We all walk on the earth. We all drink water. We all use some type of fire energy for heating or cooking or growing food. We all breathe air.

We are all connected through the elements.

Universal Element Exercise: The Magick Egg

Many times people say to me, "This is such a mess. I know how I got here (or maybe not), and I just don't know what to do to fix it. What do I work for? Do I do lots of spells and rituals? Do I throw magick at it all the time?

---

8 Dalai Lama, *The Universe in a Single Atom*, 89.

I am filled with so much hatred (or fear or worry or pain). Do I just do one thing and then forget it?" These are tough questions that each of us face upon our life path. When I feel this way, I go back to the beginning (or what I believe to be the beginning) and consider what thoughts and behaviors I may have used that created the mess in the first place. And then, as is my nature, it seems, I say to myself, "This is ridiculous! I no longer accept this—not for any reason! I will rise, and I will move forward. Now. This minute. Today! What do I want? Joy! What do I need? Joy! What will I manifest? Joy!" And then I feel this line of determination rising within myself, this spear of power that breaks and shatters the crap. And I do an action that vibrates with the message of change.

When you just don't know which way to turn, grasp the glowing spear of change within yourself and do any physical action that moves your inner compass in the direction of positive change.

The following exercise can help you move in a new direction or assist in solidifying a positive direction that is already in process in your life. I suggest doing a spiritual cleansing (see chapter 5) and then proceed with this exercise to work for joy.

You can't go wrong with joy.

Joy fills you with feelings of happiness, peace, and rightness of action; it expands beyond you and filters into the universe, attracting more joy.

Joy heals.

I have mentioned that all magick begins with a release and ends with a release. Before you do this exercise, I humbly ask that you forget absolutely everything negative in your life. Turn your back on it. Acknowledge and agree within yourself that you will accept the healing power of joy in your life. The exercise, from start to finish, only takes a few moments, and it is best if you are in a place that is peaceful and won't be disturbed—but, conversely, if you have to, it can be done in the bathroom stall at work.

Yup. Done that. Actually, worse: in a porta potty. (Hey! There wasn't any other private place!) And, even among all that shit, *it worked.*

Begin by sitting quietly. Relax. Begin releasing negative thoughts. Now, stand up and turn your back so that you are facing the opposite direction. This is a physical action that affirms you are releasing anything that is holding you in a negative pattern.

Acknowledge the sea of potential as given in chapter 1. Realize that it is in you, around you, and part of you all at the same time. It permeates you. Activate that sea of potential for joy.

Next, let your feet become rooted to the ground as though you were a tree. Raise your arms like the branches of that tree and tilt your palms to welcome sky energy. Visualize yourself as the Pagans of old, one with earth, sea, and sky.

Fall back into a relaxing position, one where you are comfortable holding your hands, palms up, out in front of you. It is in your hands that you are going to manifest joy. Visualize a beautiful seed in your palms: a big one! A brightly colored one! A sparkling one! This is the seed of joy. Cover the seed with long deep breaths. This is the karmic wind that shakes the seed, urging it to awaken and bring joy into your life. This wind, like the sea of potential, permeates the seed and becomes one with the seed.

Slowly switch from the idea of the wind to the concept of fire, the warmth that surrounds the seed and urges it to come alive. Breathe deeply several times, envisioning the fire tickling the seed, then slowly sinking into the seed so that now your seed glows with warmth. It is highly possible that your palms will become warm. The licks of flame (and you can turn the flame from red to blue if it helps) call forth the rain, the water of life, gently misting around the seed, then gather power and coalesce around the seed. Right before you sink the water into the seed of joy, see the bolts of lightning crackling within the water.

Sink the water into the seed of joy along with the flashing light. The seed now glows, sparks, feels warm, and moves as if it is straining to come alive. The flashing light calls forth the earth particles; they dance in your hands around the seed, vibrating, jittering, and shaking as they come in contact with the other three elements. Your hands may begin to shake. See the earth particles sink into the now very active seed of joy. Take a deep breath and bring that vibrating seed in your hands into your heart chakra. Hold your hands over your chest, tilt your head up, raise your elbows…wait for it…wait for it…because this is the moment of birth…

and then fling your arms out with a large exhale of breath, palms facing up to the sky, loudly proclaiming, "I birth joy!"

Your whole body may tingle with delight or you may feel a boost of adrenalin. Know that as you birthed the joy, this energy has permeated your body, mind, emotions, soul, your astral bodies, and the space around you. It clicks into all that is you.

Take a nice deep breath. Express your gratitude to the universe, and touch the One that there is.

Blend with it.

Feel it.

Welcome the peace.

Welcome the joy.

You can use this exercise for any manifestation you desire. A simple way is to begin with the feeling of joy and then focus that feeling on what it is that you desire. For example, do you feel that a new job will bring you great joy? (Notice I didn't say "do you think"—it is the connection of feeling we are after here.) Then link the joy to the working for the new job. The other important lesson of the magick egg exercise is to realize the joy when you receive it. For example, let's say you did the working for joy, and during the day you received an unexpected visit from someone who brings you great pleasure the moment you see their face. That fleeting moment? That was your joy. Recognize it. Be grateful for it.

The magick egg is another technique to put in your magickal toolbox, and you may find it extremely helpful in a variety of circumstances. You can empower any physical item, plant, animal, or human using this method, making adjustments to the situation and the individual. Here it is the base method that is important; you take it where you want it to go.

Primordial Elements

In discussing the primordial elements in relation to plants, we are categorizing energy function and plant design rather than chemistry. Such correspondences indicate the similarities of the plant that best match one of the primitive elements. These similarities, then, are carried forward in our choice to use the plant in magick, where the primordial elements have a spiritual function assigned to them:

Fire: Motivation, passion, creativity and the electricity of form

Air: Thought, memory, communication, logic, the throttle (or not) of energy placement

Water: Intuition, emotion, flow, the pathway between the conscious and subconscious

Earth: Stability, foundation, condensation of power/pattern into a single form

These associations differ depending on the magickal person, their previous training, their mental process, and to which group (or not) they may belong. There is no one "right" association to these primordial energies.

Some people choose to believe that the primordial energies have conduits to manifestation on the earth plane. Consider them pipelines that govern the behavior and flow of the primordial patterns of fire, air, water, and earth. They are known as:

Fire: Salamanders

Air: Sylphs (fairies)

Water: Undines (mermaids)

Earth: Gnomes

These beings are thought to be the connection between the astral plane and the element as it is expressed on our plane of existence. If you have trouble seeing them as "beings," try thinking of them as portals or some other type of connection mechanism. What is most important is that you understand that any name is an effort to quantify and understand a particular energy pattern and its use; these names have changed over time as our cultures have changed. Remember, to give something a name is to give it power and funnel the energy into a single pattern. The more the pattern is acknowledged by other humans, the stronger the pattern becomes.

In magick, the elements are also categorized as methods in which to release collected power (such as a spell), using the material world as a link to the astral, where the desired change will take place. Here, the elements represent devices of release:

- Fire creates a change through combustion

- Air creates a change through dissolution or evaporation

- Water creates a change through blending and dilution

- Earth creates a change through decomposition

Some magickal practitioners link the elemental signature of a plant to the same element's method of release. For example, if you collected some herbs for their relation to fire, then they would be dispatched through the element of fire. Conversely, there are other practitioners who do not match the elemental signature of the plant to the method of release.

These element release factors (fire, air, water, earth) also correlate to human influence and behavior, and it is believed that when the target person encounters the element in their own life, the element attaches your magick to that person. If you have used a matching fluid condenser (for example, an earth condenser to earth magick release), it is thought that the condenser guarantees the attachment of that element to the target and that the working will hold your charge until you dictate the release. The element combined with the liquid fluid condenser dispenses the power like an injection from a syringe, ensuring that there will be no loss of the pattern you have created from the time of the inception of the original working to the time of the delivery. Basically, your work won't get lost in the mailroom of life. Think of the element release methods as railroad lines named for each element (earth, air, fire, water), where each train only carries a single element.

For example, let's say you created a spell for love using water element signature plants (all plants that have been categorized as associated with water in the doctrine of signatures). In this spell you only want the individual to feel that they are loved; you are not trying to make them love you. Perhaps you have a friend who is going through a difficult time or Grandma is in the hospital and you can't get there. I would like to step aside here just for a moment: when working to influence another, such as in a healing or a love spell, the target always has the right to reject that energy, and the inner core of their being will choose whether or not to accept or reject what you have sent. There is always a choice. If you are worried about this murky territory, state in your working that "So-and-so has the right to refuse this work. If the energy is rejected, please send it to someone who has asked for it and needs it." Rather than you be the judge and jury, let Spirit choose.

You might place the herbal mixture in a bowl of water that is chilled to 34 degrees Fahrenheit. As you stir the water, you would sink your feelings of love and compassion into the water, visualizing the person to whom you are sending the love. Add several drops of the liquid fluid condenser and continue stirring. You may feel the energy ramp up a bit after the condenser has been added. Keep stirring until you lose the thought of love to your grandmother. Blow three breaths into the water, then seal the working by drawing an equal-armed cross over the bowl. Strain the herbs out of the water and throw them away; they have no further use. Thank them with gratitude. Place the strained water in a container and then release it in a body of water such as a river, a creek, or the ocean. The release, water to water, is important to keep the chain of the element intact. The theory is that whenever your grandmother comes into contact with the element of water (washing, drinking), your desire is immediately activated, and she will feel your love.

Let's say we wanted to create an incredible masterpiece of art, writing, or music where we feel we need the fire of inspiration and creativity. We could choose herbals with only fire signatures and roll them in a piece of paper that has our magickal doodle (see chapter 5), our name, and our intent written on it. Dress the rolled paper with a bit of fire fluid condenser, then burn the paper tube in a firesafe bowl, chanting "I welcome the fire of creativity into my work" or whatever verbal charm you choose. Blow into the fire three times while it is active, sending your intent into the flames. Continue speaking until only ash remains. Throw the cooled ashes in the trash. Whenever you come in contact with the fire element via a warm room, a heated stone, sitting in the sunshine, working by candlelight, etc., the fire element will activate the spell that you have cast for yourself.

How about money? Once upon a time it was barter, not money. The ancient concept of material wealth doesn't really equate to our modern times where money is considered wealth, but money is nothing more than a concept, a construct of moving energy predicated on what you believe to be of value to you. Just so you know, there is no real gold or silver backing your money; that went away a long time ago. Now it is just paper and ink. Traditionally, the earth element was used for money, bringing things into solid form. Today, you may find your money magick works better if you concentrate on air as your element of choice vehicle instead.

Just as we can make a universal fluid condenser to work with all elements, so, too, we can create a universal herbal mixture or powder to work in the same way. To do this, we have two choices: use two herbs of each element signature to create the compound or use two of each classical planetary signature to create the compound. The element compound will have eight ingredients. The planetary compound will have fourteen ingredients. Use the example below for the element compound or create your own. The planetary universal compound for fluid condensers is given in chapter 3. It, too, can be used as an herbal powder or blend.

Element Universal Compound

• • •

patchouli (earth), oak bark (earth), sage (air), mistletoe (air),
ginger (fire), sassafras (fire), violet (water), chamomile (water)

I have given you the smattering of occult historical information about correspondences and elements in an effort to show you that for thousands of years religion, science, and practitioners of the occult have been trying to understand how the sea of potential works, and in this effort they have assigned various patterns and links, hoping that by doing so they could learn and utilize the secrets of the universe. Early science tells us that matter has four states: solid, fluid, gaseous, and plasma. As we have progressed through the centuries, another state was added, then substates, etc., on into quantum physics. We learned that subatomic particles also have "states," and so on. What we have to look at today in all the vast material the ancients have left us is their logic, their jargon, and their experiments. This is not to say that what we have isn't accurate; it is simply that each individual has to ponder their own translation and throw out the red herrings. I believe the biggest error is the idea that a process must be complicated to work or else it has no power. Too often I have seen a variety of bells and whistles in magick and ritual that don't need to be there and actually clutter up the process rather move it swiftly forward, needlessly costing you time and money.

If a correspondence doesn't appeal to you, there is a reason why. Use your own logic and intuition to consider why you intrinsically feel that the traditional association would negate rather than help your work. Advances in the study of plants today give us a plethora of information on their medicinal value as well as their growth patterns, and that analysis can tell us exactly how that herb will work in association with any given occult-related practice. When in doubt, use the traditional correspondences as your foundation, then fine-tune your enchantment with additional study.

Matching Herbs and Additives to Your Intent

As you learn, you will discover that a high number of herbs are of the banishing variety, yet due to color or aroma also have been employed historically to draw specific energies toward you or are used to heighten your own vibrations through scent alone. Earlier, I gave you the examples of peach, where the plant can be utilized for both drawing and banishing. An aromatic example is lavender, used to eliminate stress, promote restful sleep (by banishing unwanted energies), and raise your personal spiritual awareness all at the same time due to the aroma—stemming from the peace and tranquility you may feel as a result of wafting the scent into your field of working. Lavender is an excellent herb to use at the beginning of any rite, ritual, spell, meditation, or cleansing, as it banishes negativity and heightens spiritual awareness.

During your selection process, are there any herbs that you should not use? I've learned over the years not to use an herb, flower, or root that you inherently dislike; if you are making a powder for someone else, never choose an herb, root, or flower that *they* don't like. For example, let's say you are creating a healing prayer powder or herbal blend to put in a sachet for your favorite Aunt Jean, who is currently ill. She can't stand the scent of lavender, so although it would be a right choice as far as intent, it would be an unfortunate choice for Aunt Jean. When making blends for others, listen to their aroma likes and dislikes. Not only does this show that you care, but it also indicates you have learned that the spiritual vibrations of the plant do not fit with the energy pattern of the individual.

The deity or spirits served during the process of making a magickal powder or herbal blend are also relevant to the overall construction of the formula. For example, I have a dark goddess blend that was created specifically for the energies of Hecate, the Morrighan, Bast, Dame Holda, and other goddesses who deal with justice, magick, and protection. It is an offertory formula that can be used as a powder or herbal blend and includes strong, aromatic herbs such as patchouli, African basil, lavender, and graveyard dirt from the gates of a cemetery (where spirits of protection were petitioned).

In Afro-Caribbean structures (Voodoo and Santería) the ingredients used are considered to be owned by the spirits and have no planetary associations at all (though again, the knowledge of the practitioner can negate this statement). The herbs are categorized as sweet or bitter, which has nothing to do with the taste but rather with the properties and characteristics of the plant. The bitter herbs are used to remove evil, negativity, bad luck, etc., where the sweet herbs bring in the money, prosperity, love, luck, health, etc. In the European mixtures and many American practices (such as Braucherei/Pow-Wow) the planetary associations of the plant replace the cultural spirits and taboos of the Afro-Caribbean counterparts. For example, in Braucherei a highly potent formula for success and prosperity involves herbs gathered and dried under the astrological sign of Leo. This magickal recipe includes all things yellow or gold or associated with those colors such as sunflower petals, marigold seeds, chamomile flowers, and dandelion root or leaves. Even banishing herbs such as rosemary, nightshade, lemongrass, and hyssop are thought to retain greater power when harvested under the sign of Leo at noon.

The spirit of the plants and your acknowledgment of them also plays a significant role in your selection process and ultimately in the power of your powder or herbal blend. If you have grown the herbs yourself, you may already have a connection. If not, then you will need to connect with those spirits as you select, prepare, and blend your formula. Your belief in what runs the universe and how everything fits into the design of that universe affects how you perceive plant spirits. Each and every person will have a different definition from which they work. This definition is based on their experiences, knowledge, beliefs, and intent. Over the years, as I have worked with plants and become an avid gardener, I have learned that (to me) plants are light spirits. They have energy waves that we would attribute in our world to "feelings." They do communicate. They are affected by your actions and your emotions. Scientifically, I learned that each and every plant has its own individual DNA. Every plant, then, combined with its spirit and its structure, is unique. The more you work with herbs, flowers, and resins, the more intuitive you will become in your choices for a particular powder or magickal blend.

As a magickal rule of thumb when choosing ingredients, hold the herb in your hand (if you can) and close your eyes. Relax and let the spirit of the plant speak to you. Tell the herb of your intent and see what flows through your senses. Is the aroma heightened? Do you feel good? Do you see beautiful lights in your mind? These are all affirmative answers to the choice of that herb for your blend. If, on the other hand, you don't feel anything or if you feel uncomfortable or see nothing in your mind, the answer is no, this is *not* the herb to use for your formula. You can also use a binary divination system that employs a white stone and a black stone in a small pouch. Phrase your questions where the answers would be only yes or no. For example, you may receive a yes that the spirit of chamomile is willing to work on your intent, but when you choose to add chamomile and nettle together for your intent, your answer may be no. This is also a good way to determine if the formula you have developed is complete. Your last question can always be "Is there something missing?" If the answer is yes, let your intuition guide you on what additions may be necessary. The binary system, once you learn to trust it, can be a convenient element in other magickal operations as well. By the way, your inane desire to choose only the white stone because you know what it feels like can be negated by using two objects of the same size but different colors such as a black button and a white button.

What if you don't have the physical herb and are purchasing over the internet or perhaps choosing where to go to wildcraft? Use the same type of meditation by calling the name of the herb or flower aloud first several times or turn the herbal name into a three-minute mantra. You can also hold a picture of the plant in your hand as you concentrate on contacting the oversoul spirit of the plant.

How to Spiritually Wildcraft

The word *wildcraft* means to gather plants and fungi from the natural world. Wildcrafting is also a process, a spiritual blending of yourself (mind, body, and spirit) with the natural world around you. Both exciting and peaceful, there is nothing like walking into the woods and fields in search of unique ingredients for your magickal work. A whole new level of being surrounds your soul, filling you with a universal oneness that you simply can't experience by buying herbs from a store. Walking with Mother Nature and learning about her builds a rapport between yourself and the world around you that simply can't be purchased anywhere.

In talking with magickal people who wildcraft, every one of them is in agreement that herbs gathered spiritually—by honoring them, talking to them, blending with them—bring about a whole new level in their spiritual growth. They find that these herbs, when used in enchanting operations, seem to carry more power because the herbs were gathered in a sincere, communicative way. Your work, then, from start to finish, is a dynamic process that vibrates better to your chosen intention. In chapter 1 we talked about the Spirit Walk, which lays the groundwork for spiritual wildcrafting. The more you accept the process of wildcrafting into your life, the more exciting life becomes! When you actually agree to connect with the spirit of Nature, she will step forward and speak to you to help you with your problems; you just have to be observant and welcome the information given to you.

The process of wildcrafting is unique to you: only you know what you think and how you feel. Only you can interpret the messages you receive from the plants. It all begins with your belief, your intent, and your willingness to open the door to communication with nature. Put your logical mind in the wings of your brain and let your intuition have full throttle. Once you actually allow the communication to flow, your personal learning curve will soar.

Safe Wildcrafting Tips

- Dress appropriately for the weather, the terrain, and the dangers of working in the wild. If the area is new to you, do a little online research of what critters you may encounter and what gear you may need to safely navigate. Always carry water. Always have gloves and use them when handling poisonous plants or plants that are unknown to you. Be sure to have an offering for the plant; some individuals use water, some use tobacco, some cornstarch. I don't recommend fertilizer, though, as you could kill the plant.

- Research what plants are endangered in the area, and avoid harvesting those.

- Have a field guide for the safe identification of plants. This could be a trusted friend, a book, or an app on your phone. If you are unsure of what a plant is, it may be poisonous; don't harvest it. Return home and do more research. You can always go out again. There are several apps through which you can ask an expert if you are not sure of your own identification.

- Carry storage bags with you, as well as a pen and small slips of paper or a marker to write on the bag. You may correctly identify a plant while outdoors, but if you have several different herbs by day's end, you may not remember what you collected, particularly if you are new to the process.

- Have appropriate tools for harvesting: bolline, heavy-duty scissors, or a type of pruning tool; you know what works best for you.

The Process of Wildcrafting

Wildcrafting is an intuitive spiritual process. Before you leave on your outdoor venture, you may wish to do a meditation or ritual, particularly if you have an urgent need in your life. You might like to write down your intent on a piece of paper and carry that paper over your heart or place it in a special wildcrafting magickal bag you have made. When you reach the area, take the time to sit down and do your sea of potential exercise. You might like to hold your intention paper in your hand, rubbing it softly with your fingers as you do this. Allow yourself to drink in the elements around you. Whisper to nature your intent of today's outing. Be aware of all you hear and see. The animals, birds, and insects of the area will also speak to you. Make a mental note of both the usual and the unusual; brightly colored birds or raucous, chatty birds have a message for you. A large gathering of a particular type of insect or an unusual one also has something you need to know.

When you reach the plant you wish to harvest, honor it with a prayer. Tell the plant what you are doing and why. Ask for permission to take a portion of the plant. If you feel good, the answer is yes. If you feel frightened, have an upset stomach, or experience fatigue, that plant does not wish to share at this time. It may be ill or it may be the last one in that area. Never take the largest, most beautiful plant or flower. That is the queen of that plant in that area—the energy matrix, the focus of the pattern, the vortex of the energy. If you are interrupted in your harvesting, that is a sign that you should move on. There is work here that you are not aware of, and you may upset the balance by taking too much or the wrong thing.

I always leave an offering of gratitude when I wildcraft plants. This is an appropriate energy exchange that will vibrate on a higher soul level; it is not in vain. Before you leave the area, ask Spirit if there is something you may have missed. Wait a few minutes, relaxing or in meditation, then leave. On your way out you may find something that Spirit wishes to ensure you receive.

Wildcrafting in Your Own Backyard

Pay particular attention to what is growing around the building you live in—no weed is really a weed; it is a plant with a message. If you maintain a garden, you will notice that weeds may not be the same from year to year. Weeds are messengers of Spirit. What are they trying to tell you? Research the weed; how does its purpose and growing pattern relate to your own life? Before you remove the weeds, honor them. As all plants do have a magickal function, consider drying the weeds and using them in your enchantments during the winter months, being careful not to harvest plants that would be harmful to yourself or your family. Spirit will also send you messages with the odd flower, a plant that seems to come out of nowhere, a single bloom where there never was one before, a patch of color that for years has held only ferns or moss or another completely monocolor array. I usually don't harvest the single plants, but I do honor it and give offerings in gratitude for its message. If there are several plants, I often make a fluid condenser from what I have gathered, as the condenser will last for years and if I dried what little is there, it would not last as long.

When an unusual plant enters your life, take the time to sit down, hold the plant in your hands (as long as you know it is safe, meaning nontoxic or not harmful to the touch; for example, you don't want to hold pokeberry in your hands because it can cause contact dermatitis). Relax and quietly ask why it has come into your field. Feel the color, texture, and aroma of the plant within you. Try my link, sync, and sink exercise in chapter 1 with all plants that are new to you or when you need assistance and you believe the plant may be able to assist. Don't forget to write down your impressions so that you can refer to them later.

Do you actually have to physically work with the herb to internalize the message? (Meaning, must you make a powder, sachet, fluid condenser, etc.?) No. Consider the experience like communing with a particular totem animal and work with the plant or herb on a spiritual level. For example, let's say that in a given year your property seems to be overrun by poison ivy or sumac. You wouldn't want to handle these herbs. Take the time to think about your life in correlation with the presence of these plants. What are they trying to tell you? Should you find it necessary to rid your property of that particular plant (as in the previous example), take the time to honor the message and give an offering to Mother Earth in gratitude before removing the plant. You can even tell the plant why it must seek growth elsewhere because it is a danger to your pets or family.

Researching Plants and Herbs for Best Performance

The third season living in our new home presented some interesting plant energy and messages for me. Due to family circumstances, ongoing projects, and the uncompromising spring weather, I did not get outside as much as I wanted to. Something always seemed to come up when I'd planned to wrangle the property into shape. As spring moved into summer, I realized that the wildness of the plant life around me was going full strength and I still seemed to be trapped inside by choice (if that makes any sense). Every time I walked outside I would cringe because my gardens and pots were growing whatever they felt like. And then the heat hit, and I knew I wasn't going to accomplish the regular property maintenance that year. By mid-August I had made a decision. Even though everything looked like heck from the road, I would continue to let everything grow and then actually harvest what nature had decided to bring me in the early fall. I would use those plants during the winter months in my workings. This meant that rather than relying on what I would consciously plant in my gardens (because it was too late), I would rely on Mother Nature to supply what she thought I needed. I don't think my neighbors were too happy with my bohemian decision, but I let it stand. This choice made me go outside my comfort zone and learn about plants and herbs that I had not used before or used minimally.

To figure out Mother Nature's choices, I had to research. I used a MyGardenAnswers App on my phone, the internet, and several books that I had in my library. I also talked to friends who enjoyed wildcrafting. When I identified a plant correctly, I wrote down the harvest date, what I had observed about its growing pattern, its medicinal properties, astrological correspondences, and a plethora of keywords to help me understand and make good use of the plant or herb. I discovered that one of the "weeds" so prevalent that season all around my house was the evening primrose. As I researched the plant, I thought, "Wow! How interesting is that?" The keywords I collected for this plant included protection, remove anger, hunting, fairy potions, love, calming, shapeshifting, luck, goal achievement, antidepressant, attracts bees and butterflies, moon magick, healing of bruises (physical and emotional), and combat procrastination and lethargy. One of its folklore names is "night candle." Up until this point, I had only ever purchased evening primrose in dried form, and of course it doesn't look that great and I never connected well with the storebought offering. However, the message I received from the plant was a bit different than all the keywords I'd found: "You have forgotten to laugh."

And it was true.

My point with this story is that the messages you receive from the plants and herbs won't necessarily fit what others have written about that plant or herb. It is a living being, and it will communicate what it wants regarding what you need. That doesn't mean that you should throw out your research—the new information will allow you to expand your knowledge in a way that is best for you and the work that you plan to do.

I added several plants that season to my magickal cupboard, including the following:

Pennsylvania Smartweed: WATER/VENUS. Stops gossip or makes someone shut their darned mouth; removes toxic substances; inhibits the growth of bacteria; a booster to magickal healing formulas in general. An excellent herb to use in combination with tiger's-eye gemstone when you need the truth of the matter and not a bunch of assumptions or inaccurate perceptions based on faulty data.

Horse Nettle: FIRE/MARS. Diverts negativity so that it feeds on itself; protects; the nightshade family. Horse nettles in a garden actually keep bugs from eating potatoes and tomatoes, as the bugs feast on the horse nettles instead.

Pokeweed: WATER/VENUS. Poisons an unwanted advancement of love or attention; breaks hexes (unfortunately, as mentioned earlier, pokeweed can cause contact dermatitis). The berries were once used to make ink that turns brown with age.

Wild Blackberry: VENUS/WATER. Use for healing, prosperity, and protection, as well as to cause confusion in enemies. The thorns are thought to cut through evil in the aura of a person and shred disease.

Gifted Plants

Spirit will also talk to you through gifted plants—those plants that are given to you as presents for your birthday, anniversary, holidays, illness recovery, housewarming, or just because. Pay particular attention to these plants and their messages. Cut plants can be dried and used in a variety of magickal applications. Living plants carry a deeper message, as the plant or selection of plants have come to you to help you on your spiritual path. I have two African violets that have been with me for several years, one that I purchased when I moved into my new home and one that was given to me as a housewarming present. Both plants are extremely protective in nature and bloom all the time. I talk to them and have even given them names. I dry the flowers and use them in candles, sachets, powders, and conjuring bags. Magickal people often share living and dried plants for magick. If someone offers to give you a plant or you receive a herb you didn't expect, know that Spirit is talking to that person, and this plant or herb is needed in your life at this moment.

Drying Wildcrafted and Fresh Herbs

Many magickal practitioners harvest wildcrafted and garden herbs early in the morning after the dew has dried. If you intend to wash the herbs, you may wish to collect them while the dew is still clinging to the herb, wash them gently, shake them, and then lay them out to dry on soft white towels or white paper towels. There is a folklore theory that herbs placed on white will help them to retain their power. Pick seeds such as dill just before they are about to turn brown. Hang them upside down with an aerated paper bag rubber-banded over the heads to catch the seeds. This also works well for thyme and rosemary.

If I can't get to the herbs when they have dried due to a busy schedule, I place several layers of white paper towels on window screens that I set on shelves so that the air can move above and under the screens. I also tie herbs together with twine when they are fresh and hang them from chicken wire screens or wooden towel racks. Whether I hang them or lay the herbs out to dry, I always label everything immediately. There is nothing more frustrating than looking at a sea of herbs from a successful harvest and not knowing what you have picked, especially if this is a newly wildcrafted herb! Once the herbs have completely dried, remove the leaves—try not to bruise them—and store them in airtight glass (recommended) containers in a dark area. For food, six months seems to be the best rule as the herbs tend to lose their flavor past that time. Magickal herbs, however, are a bit different and can be stored for approximately one year (some even longer). There are magickal practitioners who believe the older the herb, the more power it contains.

A Plant a Day

In 2008 I published HedgeWitch: Spells, Crafts, and Rituals for Natural Magick. That book is a collection of magickal practices that I use in gardening and home crafts such as soaps, herbal salts, and sugars (which can be utilized as magickal powders), tea-leaf reading, grubby candles, etc. The heart of the book was a program of thirteen rites for personal transformation. The word HedgeWitch was my interpretation of finding spiritual avenues for oneself through the blending of one's spirit with the natural world around us and the journey of caring for the physical garden as well as the mental one. To transform, one must be willing to go beyond the self and "ride the hedge" between the physical world and that of the spiritual, which is a pathway that will be unique to each individual. Detractors of the book in the magickal community were upset that I did not follow a more traditional line of thought in the construction of the material, nor did I include medicinal information for reader use, which is often seen as a part of the repoitoire of the HedgeWitch. In public writing I always concentrate on the spiritual aspects of the plants and leave the medicinal information to the experts. I have done the same in this book.

Here, in this book, we take the spiritual idea of HedgeWitchery further by making a concerted effort to welcome the wildcrafting experience into your magickal way of life. To help myself do this, I took a Spirit Walk every day one summer and chose a single plant each day to learn about and study. This opened my eyes not only to the spirituality in the nature of the universe, but also in how I could use these plants in my magickal applications. This type of Spirit Walk may take you beyond your comfort zone, and that is its purpose.

How Many Herbs to Use?

How many herbs used in any given formula depends on the practitioner's choice. There are those individuals who use even numbers for drawing things to you and odd numbers for banishing. Others prefer to use the three, seven, nine, or eleven formula, and then there are those who use the binary divination system mentioned earlier to determine how many ingredients regardless of the numerical outcome. Some individuals go by intuition, passing their hands over the various herbs to choose what is right for their intent. There are folks who choose by color, texture, or aroma alone, given that those choices carry a correspondence that they understand.

I knew one master practitioner who would go on a magick walk. He had years of experience in herbal correspondences from which to draw. He would go out at a particular time (usually astrologically driven) and just walk the city. Yes, the city! As he walked, he would call the herbs to him under his breath, based not on an herbal name but on the intent. His "call" was open-ended. What he stumbled upon or saw on his walk is what he would use given the plant matched the lore he knew so well. If a plant called to him but he was unsure, he would put it in a separate pocket and work with it later to see if it matched his intent. Sometimes this herb was needed for something else, and other times it was for the purpose at hand. Regardless of how you choose your ingredients, again, the intent you have formulated in writing is the basis for any selection.

In interviewing several practitioners who create their own powders and herbal blends, I've found that they all have a variety of formulas based on different criteria. Some of their powders and blends come from the study of other practitioners and books, some blends are driven primarily by astrological correspondence, some by folklore references from family members, and others by color alone. There are recipes based on element, such as all ingredients corresponding to fire or to air. Some of those formulas carry a preponderance of one type of element association, with only a single ingredient corresponding to a different element. For example, my fire spell powder is comprised of herbs corresponding to the element of fire, with one herb (vervain) associated with air. Here, the air element is added to push the fire element. This powder works well when it is constructed when the moon is in a fire sign, and it is best used when the moon is in a fire or air sign. However, it can also be used when you need something to move fast (regardless of the sign the moon is in), and it is particularly useful when the moon is exiting any sign and preparing to enter into the next.

Some of you may be saying, "Oh my stars! This is too complicated!" It only has to be as difficult as you make it. As I said earlier, there are those practitioners who have successfully used herbs based on color and shape alone. For example, my hammer down powder consists of all red ingredients: cinnamon, dragon's blood, dried red hot peppers, red rose petals, and a very odd ingredient: dried red clay that has first been shaped into a petition, written on while still malleable, then dried, anointed (with a magickal oil, pure essential oil, perfume, or liquid fluid condenser), and pulverized to go into the powder. Ah yes, you can be creative and successful at the same time! Hammer down powder has a variety of uses: as an offering to Thor, breaking through blocks, finding success, getting something done or to move fast, or as karmic retribution. One powder. A variety of uses. To ramp it up, add yohimbe powder.

You can also use planetary runes to choose the type and number of ingredients in your powders or herbal blends. You will find this information in chapter 5.

If you wish to use color as your primary focus, here is a list to assist you in making choices not only in herbal work but in associated magickal candle selection as well.

Color Magick Correspondences

You may wish to use the vibratory power of color in your workings, whether you are considering candle colors, altar cloths, sachet bags, conjuring bags, or cloth for magickal packets. You might also like to add color to your powders. Use the information below as a guideline until you choose which colors work best for you based on your intent. You may also wish to use your power color, which is the color that represents the day you were born. You will find those colors listed under the magickal days section in chapter 3.

Black: Return negativity to sender; divination; negative work; protection; karmic retribution

Blue-Black: Heal wounded pride; broken bones; angelic protection

Dark Purple: Call up power of the ancient ones; sigils/runes; government; working with the dead; honoring dark goddesses; spiritual power

Lavender: Favors from others; healing mind; angelic work; Reiki healing; stress relief

Dark Green: Invoking the power of regeneration; growth, nature spirits, and agriculture (such as gardening); financial work (such as long-term savings, investments, or swaying a financial institution; use with brown)

Mint Green: Financial gains (used with gold and silver or honey)

Green: Healing or health; north cardinal point; good fortune and prosperity (with gold or silver)

Avocado Green: Beginnings; healing of toxic relationships

Light Green: Improve the weather; growth; abundance of food (use with gold)

Indigo Blue: Reveal buried secrets; protection on the astral levels; defenses

Dark Blue: Create confusion (must be used with white or you will confuse yourself)

Blue: Protection; stress relief; water magick

Royal Blue: Power and protection

Pale/Light Blue: Protection of home, buildings, young people; pet healing

Ruby Red: Love or anger of a passionate nature; movement; breakthrough

Red: Love, romantic atmosphere; energy; fire magick; south cardinal point

Light Red: Deep affection of a nonsexual nature

Deep Pink: Harmony and friendship in the home

Pink: Harmony and friendship with people; binding magick; creating chaos

Pale Pink: Friendship; young females

Yellow: Healing; east cardinal point

Dark Gold: Prosperity; sun magick

Gold: Attraction; wealth in the home

Pale Gold: Closure with honor; prosperity in health

Burnt Orange: Opportunity; harvest

Orange: Material gain; to seal a spell; attraction of business and monetary opportunity

Dark Brown: Invoking earth for benefits; treasure; dealing with the root of a problem

Brown: Peace in the home; herb magick; friendship; miracles; winning a court case

Pale Brown/Tan: Material benefits in the home

Silver: Quick money; gambling; invocation of the moon; moon magick; prosperity; spirituality

Off-White: Peace of mind

Lily White: Mother candle (burned for thirty minutes at each moon phase)

White: Righteousness; purity; east cardinal point; devotional magick; angelic assistance; cleansing

Gray: Glamour magick of all types

Nature Meditation for Choosing the Right Color and Herbal Ingredients

It is believed that around every person is their own energy field, nested inside the sea of potential. This field is not only a protective layer, but it is also a storehouse of your thoughts that have attached themselves to your body. These patterns cling to the person. You can clear, reinvent, and change the patterns in this spiritual body at will if you realize that the spiritual body exists and that it has interesting stuff in it. This field is often associated with a color and is the basis of many aura-reading techniques, wherein the color signifies whether you are healthy or ill and the general direction of your thoughts on a daily basis. These colors are often associated with the chakras (the seven energy vortexes of the body). The thing is, not everyone can read auras in the traditional sense of simply seeing color or energy. Some people can't see anything at all, and as your mind is filled with a variety of issues on any given day, a single color chosen for a working, technique, powder, blend, etc., may not necessarily suffice.

About four years ago I started reading people—not by aura color but by nature images. At the time I didn't tell anyone about it. I wasn't doing it to share, I was doing it to understand. I would close my eyes and think about that person in their current state, and then reach out into the universe… into nature…blending with it and then asking that I be given images of nature that most closely correspond with the person at this point in time. From there, I would ask for images (or mind pictures) of what was needed to help a person with their problem or to try to understand why they were exhibiting a type of behavior. For this technique, you must learn to trust what you see. However, before you use the process, your own spiritual body should be cleansed in some way—spiritual bath, deep breathing, or mental clearing, etc.—so that you don't confuse your private needs with the needs of the person you are trying to help. As this isn't always possible, having a routine of spiritual cleansing methods on a daily basis keeps your field relatively clear when you need to access the images quickly. I typically sit on my rocking chair outdoors, close my eyes, breathe deeply, say the person's full name three times, connect and blend with the world around me, and then ask the universe to bring me the nature images I need to help that person. In all, the process takes about five minutes, sometimes less, a few times more. When I am finished, I write down what I saw so that I don't forget and can analyze the images for inclusion in the future working.

I do not ask for specific pictures. I just think of my mind as a blank canvas, and a nature scene will develop. For example, with one person I might see a variety of beautiful flowers, with the predominant color as pink or red surrounded by lush green. If I don't know what the flowers are, I don't worry about it. The colors I will then choose for her will be red, pink, and green. I might make the conjuring bag green, the candle color red for her working, and then add pink rose petals in the powder or herbal blend. For another, a woodsy scene may come into focus; I will breathe that pine-scented air or the musk of the leaves on the ground, and I will see beautiful birch trees painted with shimmering sunlight. For this person, I would make sure the herb formula contains the aromas I sensed in my vision, pine and patchouli, even though the correspondences aren't traditional for the type of working they may have requested. I would add a yellow candle (for the sunlight) and a white conjuring bag (the birch). I would also include birch in the herbal blend because that is the tree that I distinctly saw and immediately knew the name. I never assume. For example, in a woods scene, you might reason things are there such as ferns or moss, but if I don't see it in my initial visualization, I don't add it.

The most important part of this technique is not to strain or be judgmental in what you are seeing. Just go with it. Nothing is "supposed" to be there.

While you are doing the meditation/visualization, it is important that you not be disturbed and that you are mindful of what nature is trying to tell you. She may send a slight breeze across your face (the person needs help from the air element to move things along) or several bees might be in your space (this person is dealing with a group of individuals who are trying to change a structure of some kind) or a loud ruckus with the neighbor's cat drifts toward you from the neighbor's yard (someone is on the attack), etc. These are added benefits to the meditation/visualization itself and allow animals and insects to speak to you by their actions.

This type of working is very shamanic and intuitive. Don't worry that you don't have any experience. That isn't important, as nature speaks to all of us all the time. No one person is better than another; all are gifted.

You must only awaken the gift by acknowledging it.

Measuring Herbal Ingredients for Your Magickal Powders or Herbal Blends

There are two ways to measure herbal ingredients for your powder or herbal blend formulas: formally or informally. The number of ingredients (herbal or specialty) in any magickal powder varies; however, in a formal recipe one measures the totality of the whole, always factoring to one. Much like the Eye of Horus, which is an ancient Egyptian mathematical formula for measuring parts of herbs for healing purposes, so too the magickal powder is also a numeric pattern that should always equal one of the measurements (dry or liquid). For example, if you use eight herbs for a particular formula, you may wish to use eight $\frac{1}{8}$ teaspoons of each herb, thus equaling $\frac{8}{8}$ or one whole. If you want to follow the older formulas, using our example of eight ingredients, you will use seven $\frac{1}{8}$ teaspoons of seven herbs with the last $\frac{1}{8}$ dedicated to Spirit, which could be an unusual ingredient such as ashes or powdered stone. To make this clear, let us say we have selected three herbs to use in our magickal powder. We would use $\frac{1}{4}$ teaspoon of each herb; the last $\frac{1}{4}$ teaspoon, a specialty ingredient that is dedicated to Spirit, makes up the whole of one. This is a formal measuring technique.

The informal measuring technique relies more on your own intuition as well as the availability of ingredients. This type of measuring is how my grandmother cooked when I was a child. Over the years, my grandmother learned how much to put in her recipes simply by feel. To her, this type of measuring was a dash, a pinch, a sprinkle, or a cupped hand. She went by her experience and what felt right to produce the most magnificent dishes.

If you want to use a divination mechanism for making a quick choice on a herb, you can use a binary method such as a black stone that stands for no and a white stone that means yes. The stones should be close to the same size and shape. Put the stones in a bag along with eyebright herb and frankincense. When you wish a yes or no answer on a particular ingredient, choose a stone from the bag. This simple divinatory tool can assist in the informal measuring process, especially if you are hesitant about making the right choice.

CHAPTER THREE
Magickal Timing

Of all the techniques I have learned over the years, using magickal timing in my spiritual work has proven the most beneficial. Yes, I had to study. Yes, I had to experiment. Yes, it took a little time to master.

Yes, it was absolutely worth it.

The wonderful thing about learning magickal timing is that you can use a lot or a little; the choice is entirely up to you. There will be situations in your life where you will want to be spot-on with time, and there will be other instances where you intuitively know that a great deal of planning isn't necessary—that the window of opportunity is right to get the magickal show on the road because you feel it is accurate. Neither technique is wrong, and the proof is in your successes.

Timing for Mixing Powders or Making Herbal Blends

Many practitioners gather, grind, and blend their powders or herbal mixes in a ritual environment according to the phases and signs of the moon, planetary hours, or daily correspondences. Generally, in moon lore powders and herbs blended to draw things toward you should be mixed at the new or waxing moons. Powders and herbal mixes for banishment and protection should be ground during the waning moon. Powders for exorcism and strong spiritual cleansings should be prepared on the first day of the dark moon, with the remaining time used for a period of rest (although individual tastes or training can change any of the above definitions).

The first astrological building block for many magickal practitioners involves the phases or quarters of the moon. Throughout the year each full cycle of the moon will carry a specific theme for you. This theme changes depending on your current life path, goals, the time you were born, and what is going on in the heavens at present. When you pay attention to the cycles of the moon, whether you are working with the quarters (the four-division moon cycle template most often used in general almanacs) or the phases (the eight-division template that is a favorite with many magickal practitioners), even the most difficult times can be utilized in an empowering, more spiritual way. The phases of the moon are based on mathematical calculations based on the relation between the moon and the sun. It'd be good if at the exact moment of each of these calculation tipping points some sort of outside event occurs or there is a heavenly bell ringing somewhere in the aether, but that's not the case. Mathematically, the universe is an extremely busy place, and outside events are affected by the demarcations of a bazillion things (okay, so that's an exaggeration, but you get the point). The information that follows is my take on the phases of the moon, how you might be affected by the moon's influence, and how to use what you have at the time to create your magick.

Phases of the Moon

New Moon

The new moon occurs when the moon is 0 to 45 degrees directly ahead of the sun, and its time span for the calculation of activities is from the point of the new moon (0 degrees) to approximately three and a half days after. The new moon is a power point. Here the moon rises at dawn and sets at sunset. Traditionally this time is seen as one of beginnings and starting new projects; however, the actual seed work of any project should have been done two days before the new moon (see balsamic moon information). At the new moon we gather the supplies to creatively push forward on the seeds we planted. This is an excellent time for a Spirit Walk, pathworking meditations, and affirmation building. Usually, the theme of this moon cycle will present itself to you within the first twenty-four hours of the new moon. The meaning of the "theme of the month" is colored by the sign the moon is in as well as her association with any planets in this three-and-a-half-day period.

It is important to listen to your inner dialogue and feelings during this time and to release past failures related to any ongoing project that you wish to add to or move forward on for which you have found new and creative inspiration that will lead you in a needed different direction. In Braucherei many practitioners look forward to the sunrise of the new moon with great anticipation, as this energy can be directed to influence one's life in positive ways. Modern practitioners make nine new moon wishes, writing down what they desire in a journal or conducting some type of spell or rite to complement their nine wishes. It is interesting to look through your past work, usually at year-end, and review what your wishes were each month and if they manifested or not—or whether you have changed in your desire for those things. Observations on what did not come to pass help you to more fully understand your spiritual path and your abilities. This is not a negative analysis. More often than not you may find yourself saying, "Wow! I am so glad *that* did not happen!" And you may see in other months where you changed your wording and direction, which resulted in what you actually received.

At sunset on the first full day of the new moon, you should be able to see the sliver of moon on the horizon; this "time in between," this twilight, is a pipeline of opportunity leading to wherever you wish it to go. This is the time to guide your energies toward what type of possibilities you believe you need to fulfill your desires. Consider conducting a sacred ceremony geared at calling these specific opportunities to you. Sprinkle Honor powder on the ground just as the sun sets and you can see the moon. I particularly like to make my road opener powders and candles approximately two hours before this phase ends and the next begins.

Many times students will say to me, "I know it is the new moon and I should be starting this project, but I really feel like letting go of things, and I know that those activities are usually reserved ritually for other phases of the moon. Yet I feel compelled to do a full spiritual cleansing and other release activity such as cleaning out my garage." My response is always this: have at it! Move with your inner compass. Your navigation system is telling you that your life is too cluttered and that it is necessary to remove negativity and unwanted energies that will hinder your life path. Follow your inner guide. Listen to your feelings. Near the end of this period you will feel opportunity coming. Every month has something special; look for it.

This moon phase begins with a conjunction (power) and ends with a sextile (opportunity).

Crescent Moon

The crescent moon rises at mid-morning and sets after sunset. The moon moves from a sextile to the sun, a glittering point of magickal opportunity, to a square (required adjustment). Use this time to attract open pathways, ideas, and assistance from the universe. In this phase the moon moves from 45 to 90 degrees ahead of the sun. This period of influence lasts approximately three and a half days as well. If you want to get really precise, pull out your almanac and a set of differently colored highlighters and go through the year, highlighting all the sun/moon combinations.

Each moon cycle (from new to new) you will have one conjunction (the new moon), two sextiles, two trines (assistance), one opposition (the full moon), and two squares; this dialogue between the moon and the sun are points of energy that can be used in a variety of ways. As a rule of thumb, the greatest power days are the new moon and the full moon, the opportunity days are those where the moon and the sun are in sextile, the days where things will move forward easily are the trines, and the days where adjustments need to be made in your plans in order for fulfillment to occur are the two squares. In a magickal nutshell this means you have two power days, two opportunity days, two easy days, and two change/adjustment days to work within magickal planning. Again, go with your gut. These guidelines are just that: guidelines.

Students become confused with this type of planning because they think an event will happen right at the precise time of, let's say, the moon sextile the sun (that opportunity period). However, the universe does not run by sun and moon alone; therefore, a corresponding event in the physical world associated with any particular planetary dialogue typically comes at least twelve hours before the exact alignment. Depending upon the universal conversation, this window narrows or expands. However, in magickal timing we take the average, which means that working anywhere in the twelve-hour period before the alignment can render the benefits you need. If you work *after* the alignment, though, you missed the bus. In timing with the moon—meaning we want to catch the full power of, let's say, a full moon—our window to do the magick is usually two hours *before* the event. However, a single dialogue between the moon and another planet lasts only about two hours, so you might want to take that into consideration in your magickal work and, just as with the previous caution, do the work before the exact dialogue, not after.

Back to the crescent moon phase: here you will most likely enjoy some type of external assistance, which could be anything from advice to general information to a gift that will enhance your progress. Your sea of potential exercise done during this phase should result in excellent strides forward; if it does not, there is release work to be done. This moon phase is definitely a time to let go of your fears and bravely move forward. Self-empowerment work does very well during this time. Outside influences will also occur at the end of the crescent moon phase or at the beginning of the first quarter phase (not to be confused with the first quarter moon of the four-cycle system); however, this energy will in some way require that you make an adjustment. For example, you may realize that your research is lacking in some way and you need to look for more detailed information or your child loses or breaks a part of a project you are working on or you might experience a delay because you have to take the cat to the vet. If you look at these adjustments as opportunities for change in and of themselves that are necessary for you to reach your desired goal (and you somehow missed them in the planning portion of your work), they aren't so hard to deal with. Frustration gains nothing. Perception is everything.

Therefore, the first week of the new moon contains two phases, the new moon and the crescent moon. Here is where your creativity really begins to blossom with great ideas, new ways of practice that will enhance your work, gathering and studying new research, etc. This type of activity will flow into your life if you allow it. Again, just as with the new moon, the sign(s) the moon is in during this time period will influence and flavor your experience. Expect opportunities at the beginning and adjustments near the end, and you are ready to go!

Use the energy toward the end of this phase to make aura cleansing powder, good spirits powder, forgiveness powder, debt recovery powder, dreams and visions powder, guardian angel powder, grief relief powder, wishes powder, white owl wisdom powder, and any blessing powders or herbal blends. This timing is merely a recommendation. I prefer to use the phase and the moon in the signs, which may not always correspond to the above guidelines.

If you want to catch the rise of this moon, begin your work at noon. To grab the setting energy, use midnight.

This moon phase begins with a sextile (opportunity) and ends with a square (adjustment).

First Quarter Moon

The first quarter phase (not to be confused with the first quarter of the four-division system) is when the moon moves from 90 degrees to 135 degrees ahead of the sun. It opens with the required adjustment energy and closes with a "full steam ahead" attitude. We are now into our second week of the cycle; this is a time for pushing forward and applying your talents. Problems only arise in this phase if you have been ignoring messages from the universe or if you have somehow jumped the track of your original desires or have been mishandling the energy available to you in some way. Here, you are creating the first layers or levels of a project, and often you will feel like sparks really can fly from your fingertips! This is a go-go-go time unless it is inhibited by your own thoughts and actions. Midway through, the energy just flows—here is the time to do the magick to help push any project forward for success.

Powders and herbal blends made here are usually designed for all manner of attraction from money to motivation, fast healing, abundance, and general success. In this phase you are often committed to getting as much done as you possibly can, and you may find yourself totally immersed in a project. Without realizing it, you will be motoring through past fears and doubts, leaving them in the dust as you forge ahead. Let your creativity flow. During this time you may look through your notes and feel the urge to create a powder or blend you've been thinking about. Many fluid condensers can be brewed at this time as well, depending upon the moon in the signs and other astrological dialogue.

Near the end of the phase you will feel absolutely magnetic with ideas, people, things, animals, and events. You can feel "the draw" within you. When you hit that emotional high, that's the time to do the attraction magick. Check the signs the moon is in for your greatest navigational success.

This phase opens with a square (adjustment) and ends with a trine (ease).

Gibbous Moon

The moon rises in midafternoon, sets around three in the morning, and moves from 135 degrees to 180 degrees ahead of the sun. A time advantageous to detail work and personal growth, this is where you apply the new information you learned in the previous phases and use those ideas to enhance yourself or current projects. Group work is heightened at this time, and the exchange of energy, creativity, and ideas will push any project or organization forward. Now is a good opportunity to work with a magickal partner or family members on agreed-upon goals. This phase opens with a trine (ease), ends with an opposition (needed changes for balance), and performs particularly well when you realize that with the opposition you stand in the middle; all you need to do is balance the energy. The opposition is the full moon, and the twelve-hour period before it (which falls in the gibbous phase) can be an extremely active time. Your hands may literally pulse with power, a signal that you should be directing the energy in positive ways. Clarity of purpose often accompanies this phase. Powders and blends for divination, intuitive thinking, and wisdom can be very useful at this time (either to create or to employ in your magicks). In this time of solidification of power, make powders for healing (skin growth, wound closure, etc.). If this is a lunar eclipse moon, the effects of workings last longer (three to six months).

These first four moon phases—new moon, crescent moon, first quarter, and gibbous—are the waxing phases of the moon. Together they stand for growth and attraction. In my Braucherei practice, items worked on for attraction are buried right before the full moon to gather power and then are "birthed" during the upcoming disseminating moon. This could be a sigil, a doll, a particular magickal tool, or a divination vehicle.

Full Moon

The moon rises at sunset, sets at dawn, and travels from 180 degrees to 225 degrees ahead of the sun. We are halfway through the lunar cycle. It begins with the opposition (changes made for balance) and ends with a trine (ease). The waning portion of the lunar cycle has begun, where energies pull away, sometimes to manifest weeks or months later. You have to be willing to let go! It is a good time to go through your magickal cabinet and supply shelves to clean out old spells, organize the flurry of notes you took in the last two weeks, store new supplies that might have come in, label jars, bottles, and bags, or get rid of dust and grime from your finished projects. This is a traditional time of realization on what must be released for you to proceed. What energies are not serving you well? Room must be made in your life by unclenching your magickal fingers and allowing things to leave that are hindering you.

The first twelve hours after the full moon might best be used as downtime so that you can give yourself a chance to review the last two weeks and the work you have done. The theme of the previous new moon has most likely shown itself, and you may wish to begin the waning cycle with a personal spiritual cleansing and workings that target what needs to be let go. Here is where you would use your aura cleanse herbal powders or blends. It's a good time to meditate, sage the house, and plan projects focused on release. This is the "big picture" time of the month, where you sit back and allow yourself to see things from a full-screen point of view. The end of this three-and-a-half-day period may be filled with renewed energy of a different kind, and you may feel there aren't enough hours in the day to take care of your responsibilities and juggle the things you love, too. This is a sign that the work you did in the first two weeks of the cycle is about to bring the manifestation you desire (depending upon the goal). In fact, the busier you are, the better! This flurry means that all is proceeding on course, even if you don't think so. The best way to handle that last half-day period is to keep calm and carry on.

Disseminating

We are now about three and a half days past the full moon, where the moon moves from 225 degrees to 270 degrees ahead of the sun. The moon rises at mid-evening and sets at mid-morning. This is an excellent time to share your work with others, donate to charity, or give a helping hand to those in need. This segment begins with a trine (ease) and ends with a square (adjustment). The adjustment period that occurs about halfway through (about a day or so into the phase) most often centers on one's individual needs and where you feel lacking. Rather than demanding that others must change their behavior, this is an opportunity to change yours. Unfortunately, too many people want to project their needs and use others' behavior as an excuse to demand that others change so that they will be happier. Instead, take this time to find logical, viable solutions for what you can do within yourself to make the changes you desire to occur. You may feel the need to do another personal spiritual cleansing or clean out a large area in your living environment. In my Braucherei practice the end of this phase is the approximate seven-day mark from the full moon. This is when items that were buried in the ground can be unveiled (although sometimes we prefer to wait nine days). This is the birth time. You can perform your own ceremony or acknowledge the culmination of power and then let the item "go" to do its job.

Last Quarter

(Not to be confused with the fourth quarter moon in the four-segment system, although it does cover some of the same territory.) The moon rises at midnight and sets at noon, moving 270 to 315 degrees ahead of the sun. Many practitioners feel that this is the time for the greatest power in banishing work, with midnight being the preferred hour. It's a heavy-duty period where you do your level best to release and push away negativity, evil, and imbalance. Now's a time to banish disease, irradiate infection, and bring down the hammer on what must be removed. Here is where items are buried for destruction and decay—for example, transferring sickness to an object and burying that object at a crossroads where it is not intended to be unearthed, or going through old pictures of people who have harmed you and burning them. Dump old, tattered clothing, items that cannot be repaired, or tear apart and dispose of objects that are brimming with hate or sadness. Towards the end of the three-and-a-half-day period, the movement and organization of household objects or things from the past, such as photographs that you wish to keep, find a natural pathway to restructure, and by physical movement help to freshen what has become stale or forgotten. Fast magicks (things that you wished to have occur quickly) begun on the new moon often play out here.

This phase starts with a square (adjustment) and ends with a sextile (opportunity). In this segment of the moon cycle, you will begin to coalesce new thoughts on what you have learned over the last three weeks and start looking in new directions to move your work forward. The heaviest banishings to clear the way to a better life might be done just as the moon straddles the last quarter and balsamic phases, as close to 3:00 a.m. as possible.

Balsamic Moon

The end of the lunar cycle, the moon rises at 3:00 a.m. and sets at midafternoon, moving 315 degrees to finish the cycle of 360 and conjunct with the sun to begin the next cycle. Of all the moon phases, I've found this one to be the most different as far as how it is used, which depends on choice and past training. There are some practitioners who don't participate in any magickal work at this time. Instead, they clean, reorganize, or rest. There are others who view this three-and-a-half-day period, particularly its midpoint, as "the" time to kick magickal tuckus. There are others who use that last day of the cycle for personal spiritual cleansings, particularly if there has been suffering, such as a long illness, a divorce, loss of a loved one, etc. Meditating on the still point on this very last day, connecting with the sea of potential, and doing cleansing energy work can be most helpful. This is a good phase in which to look around at all your projects and see what can be completed before the new moon. Small tasks are just as important as the larger ones; any affirmative action that clears your calendar is considered a good one. In my Braucherei work, what you wish to stay dead forever is written on a piece of paper. The paper is torn into tiny shreds and the pieces placed in three envelopes. Once the envelopes are sealed, they are burned separately and the cold ashes are kept separate as well. These ashes are scattered at three physical places off of your property—one batch over running water, if possible, before the new moon.

The Moon in the Signs

The moon phases (eight cycle) and quarters (four cycle) are fairly standard with just about every occult teaching; however, the moon in the signs actually has just as much influence (or more, depending on the beliefs of the practitioner) on the overall formula, coupled with the phases of the moon. The moon represents emotion, and emotion is the gas in the engine of your magick. The moon in the signs tells you the emotional tenor of yourself and those around you; basically, it alludes to the type of fuel you have to work with.

The moon passes quickly through the signs each month, spending about two and a half days in each sign twice a month (give or take). This gives you a great advantage to fine-tune your magickal workings. Finding this information on any given day is easy. Unheard of a few years ago, today there are many apps for your phone, computer, or iPad that quickly give you the phases as well as the moon in the signs information for the current day. There are even apps for planetary hour calculations! I use that one not only for powders and other magickal work, but also for fine-tuning my seminars and performing spiritual cleansings when I am out on the road. For example, in cleansings, the people I will see during a Saturn planetary hour are usually dealing with negative authority figures or have a chronic illness. They may have recently experienced the loss of a family member or friend or have lost a job or a house or are having some sort of difficulty with a senior parent. They are looking to get rid of negative energy that leaves them frightened, adrift, unstable, or bound. On occasion, I will see someone who has just received a great reward, a good karmic experience, or who has become an elder in some way, such as becoming a grandparent.

Those who schedule their appointments during the Jupiter hour are much different, and you can see the change in energy. These folks are in the mindset of expansion and good fortune. They wish to remove negative energy so that they can experience a heightened sense of spirituality, or they are looking to increase or develop their knowledge by carefully watching and enjoying the entire cleansing process. However, I will also see folks who have let things go too far in their lives and are seriously backpedaling or people who naturally tend to exaggerate circumstances. Those who will likely ask the most questions and have difficulties with other individuals in general come during a Mercury hour, and people in Venus hours bring presents!

In working with astrological timing, you can also use an almanac such as *Llewellyn's Daily Planetary Guide* that provides an extensive compendium of astrological information and is very handy to keep with your powder/herbal blend journal. You can also use the standard ephemeris if you so desire.

In this book I have included the traditional glyphs for the twelve signs of the zodiac and the nine planets because they are very useful in sigil magick and can be added in pictorial form to your powders and blends. These sigils can be used in conjunction with the moon in the signs and planetary hour information.

General Guideline for Moon in the Signs

Below I've listed the twelve astrological signs and the flavor the moon assimilates as she travels through each sign. I've also given you the category of the sign (cardinal, fixed, or mutable), the ruling planet, the exalted planet (if there is one), the color most associated with that sign, and the element that rules the sign.

Before we look at this information, I'd like to make two important notes. The first is the definition of an exalted planet and the second is about angelic associations. An exalted planet is considered strong when traveling through a particular sign, even though they do not rule that sign. They are also considered less grumpy than usual (Mars and Saturn in particular). They are comfortable there and generally perform very well unless they are afflicted (arguing with another planet or fixed star). Originally, since there were no duplicate exaltations in the classical system of astrology, there weren't enough planets for the twelve signs; therefore, there are a few signs that do not have a classical exalted planetary association, such as Mercury being chosen to be both the ruler and the exalted planet for Virgo. However, modern astrologers have restructured the exalted planetary relationships; unfortunately, they don't all agree, which is why my book may say one thing about an exalted planet and other books or documentation may carry a different opinion. Not to worry. Go with your gut. Exalted planetary information simply gives you another choice, widening the field a little, when you are formulating your own recipes.

There are several angelic powers that match any one planet or astrological sign. In this book I have used only one or two of the most familiar energies. If you would like more information on angelic work, please see my book *Angels: Companions in Magick.*

You can use the astrological sign information to choose when you would like to mix or empower a powder or herbal blend. I have also included the powder/sachet formulas for each sign. These magickal recipes were constructed using the ruling planet and the ruling planets of the decanates involved in each sign. A decan is a subdivision of an astrological sign. To give a more complex interpretation to each sign, ancient astrologers partitioned the signs, adding information that modifies and enhances the sign's energy pattern. These decantes cover ten-degree periods, with a total of three unique subdivisions in each sign. Each decan is assigned the rulership of a planet, which means you can fine-tune your magickal working on any particular day to capture the type of energy window you desire by combining the day, the moon phase, the planetary hour, and the decante rulership. Many people don't want to be bothered with this type of timing; however, a critical issue may make you think (and choose) otherwise. These formulas can be employed for a variety of purposes, including as a significator for an individual person where the sign matches their birth sign or for timing when the moon or another planet is in that sign or as a boost in a particular month wherein the sun is in that sign. These powders are best made during the new moon that matches the sign she is in.

♈ **Aries:** Beginnings, attack, and new experiences; the true "first." The downside? Aries work is famous for only lasting a few days. Although Aries is known as the ultimate "starter" sign, it isn't considered a strong finisher and works better as a set-up for projects that will be worked on in other signs. For example, if you wanted to make a fire magick powder or blend, you might begin the powder when the moon is in Aries, then wait and add more corresponding ingredients under the signs of Leo and Sagittarius, the other fire signs of the zodiac. This collection of sign energy would also add more fire influence to my triple action formula. The Aries moon is good for an initial push in the right direction and fantastic for experimenting with new information or adding newly discovered techniques to a working. An Aries moon is often used for exorcism and banishing rituals where the blast is intended to finish the problem once and for all. The searing power of Aries (if you've ever irritated one) is impressive to behold. A powder or blend made under that same energy packs a unique and particular wallop. However, use it and be done. When the balloon of power is popped, the warbling stops, which is probably a splendid thing. Aries should be utilized not to start a war but to win the final battle. THE SIGN OF ARIES IS A CARDINAL SIGN, MEANING BEGINNINGS. ELEMENT: FIRE. RULED BY MARS. EXALTED PLANET: SUN. COLOR: RED. ANGELIC POWER: AIEL/MACHIDIEL.

ARIES HERBAL FORMULA: allspice, basil, dragon's blood resin, mustard, galangal, bay, spearmint

♉ **Taurus:** Sensual and constant! A Taurus moon favors investment and long-term effects on things you value. Taurus is considered by many as the most stable sign of the zodiac, and if you've ever known a Taurus personality, we should hang the sign "most stubborn" right underneath the word *Taurus*, which makes it perfect for sticky spells. Work under this moon sign and whatever you do will last a long-squared-infinity time—perfect for enchantments for things like a safe home, food, pleasing and functional home decor, caring for your savings account and retirement, comfort, good fortune, steady growth on your investments, and luxury, etc. Some feel this moon sign isn't good for fast cash workings, but I have not found this to be the case, particularly when I employ the sticky quality of this moon by using honey, molasses, spider webs, or glue. Taurus is also known for its appreciation of beauty, and its energy can bring a deep sense of gratitude to your workings, which puts the mind in the right frame for positive change. Many magickal workers choose to use this moon in combination with the Cancer moon for protection and magickal wards, where Taurus represents hearth and home and Cancer guards the family unit. FIXED: STABLE. ELEMENT: EARTH. RULED BY VENUS. EXALTED PLANET: MOON. COLOR: ORANGE OR GREEN. ANGELIC POWER: TUAL/ASMODEL.

TAURUS HERBAL FORMULA: rose, orris, vervain, violet, almond, willow, skullcap

♊ **Gemini:** Movement, intelligence (but not necessarily wisdom), communication, and creativity. Gemini provides a fast one-two punch to workings and reminds me of a boxer who flits about the ring, slamming well-placed punches into the opponent's head and then quickly darting out of reach before getting creamed. Due to this sign's mental nature, it is excellent for powders and herbal blends that will contain sigils, petitions, pictures, ashes, or words. Gemini turns the moon into a glittering courier capable of delivering any magickal package. Powders for games of chance are blended in this sign, as well as in the signs of Sagittarius and Leo. Pisces,

Aquarius, and Gemini moons are excellent for preparing items to be used in divination, and petitioning the ancestors for help during this time is usually beneficial. Gemini, Virgo, and Aquarius moons are windows for the preparation of spell elements (such as a chant or charm), designing a spell or ritual format, or planning the timing of a working. A few hours flipping through your magickal almanac to plan future magickal activities will not go to waste. Some practitioners choose to charge general candles, herbal blends, and powders when the moon is in Gemini, as it is a good "sending" moon. MUTABLE: EASILY MOVES WITH CHANGE OF CIRCUMSTANCE. ELEMENT: AIR. RULED BY MERCURY. EXALTED PLANET: NONE. COLOR: YELLOW, BLUE, OR SILVER. ANGELIC POWER: GIEL/AMBRIEL.

GEMINI HERBAL FORMULA: bergamot, lavender, lemongrass, marjoram, lemon verbena, mandrake, sage, cinnamon, tangerine

♋ **Cancer:** This is the home sign of the moon, and she is most comfortable here. This is where she lets her hair down and wears no masks—where she feels comfortable and empowered. In this sign she deals with things closest to our inner selves: emotional healing issues, psychism to some degree, the "roots" of a situation, women's mysteries, moon magick, protection of almost anything (particularly children and assets that affect the balance of the home or inner self and things associated with your legacy). Powders and blends for general prayer, spiritual cleansing, healing, the care of children, and magickal cooking are ideally made under this sign. Compelling, controlling, and domination mixtures can be constructed as well, particularly powerful in a Cancer new or full moon. Use the Cancer moon for peace in the home. CARDINAL: BEGINNINGS. ELEMENT: WATER. RULED BY THE MOON. EXALTED PLANETS: JUPITER AND NEPTUNE. COLOR: PINK OR SEA GREEN. ANGELIC POWER: CAEL/ MANUEL/MURIEL.

CANCER HERBAL FORMULA: eucalyptus, myrrh, sandalwood, rose, wintergreen, lemon balm, peppermint, calamus

♌ **Leo:** Loyalty, children, talent, creativity, inspiration, gambling, spotlight ambitions, strength. Leo rules gold; therefore, in some traditions, Leo is seen as the ultimate sign for working money and prosperity magicks. Ideal for your career, big sales of your product, or landing the best job ever! Some Braucherei practitioners find the Leo moon, particularly in the sun sign of Leo, to be most advantageous for gathering herbs that will resonate with strength, and that powders made under this moon will hold their charge longer and carry a better boost of energy. Robust and steady courage and passion are signatures of this moon. FIXED: STABLE. ELEMENT: FIRE. RULED BY THE SUN. EXALTED PLANET: NONE (ALTHOUGH MODERN ASTROLOGERS HAVE ATTRIBUTED PLUTO HERE). COLOR: GOLD OR YELLOW. ANGELIC POWER: VERCHIEL.

> LEO HERBAL FORMULA: sunflower, mistletoe, cedar, rue, marigold, chamomile, rosemary, patchouli, clove, cinnamon

♍ **Virgo:** Analysis, solutions, stealth magick, occult mastery, animal magick, order, detail, getting the job done! If you need evidence or proof, use either Virgo or Scorpio moons. Where Scorpio looks for secrets in general, Virgo ferrets out the motive. Valuable in child custody cases or revealing criminals and unfair practices at work, etc. This is the bloodhound sign of the zodiac. Virgo is also useful in making adjustments to your physical situation, including labor and health and breaking bad habits. If you need to "fix it," this is the sign, as well as bringing money and food into the home and healing for pets and animals. Virgo is also used for compelling, controlling, or seduction powders, the closer to Libra without being void, the better. MUTABLE, BUT THEY ARE COLD AND CALCULATING IN THEIR CHANGING POSITION. ELEMENT: EARTH. RULED BY MERCURY. EXALTED PLANET: NONE. COLOR: BLUE OR YELLOW. ANGELIC POWER: VOIL/HAMALIEL.

> VIRGO HERBAL FORMULA: peppermint, vervain, horehound, dill, elecampane, mistletoe, violet

♎ **Libra:** Artistic, socialization, partnership matters, legal subjects (wherein the outcome must be fair). Innovation is a vital energy with this sign, encouraging inventive and intellectual pursuits. Because Libra is the sign of balance (a great rarity in the world), the energies will shift and move like sand under your feet; however, it can be useful when considering all sides of a situation and contemplating the intent of your working. This is the "home beautiful" sign and is a good time to make magickal powders and herbal blends focused on finding a great shopping deal for big ticket items, beautiful clothing, and home decor. When the moon is waning, spells are often performed to destroy a partnership; when waxing, to solidify one. Always remember that Libra acts first on what is fair to the self (me, me, me), and when that balance has been obtained (or at least the self is satisfied for right or ill) it moves outward into the greater world. CARDINAL: STARTER. ELEMENT: AIR. RULED BY VENUS. EXALTED PLANET: SATURN. COLOR: LAVENDER OR PURPLE. ANGELIC POWER: ZURIEL/JAEL.

> LIBRA HERBAL FORMULA: Balm of Gilead, larkspur, orris, plantain, yarrow, thyme, eucalyptus, ivy, linden

♏ **Scorpio:** The Scorpio moon is the power animal of the zodiac because it intensifies everything—feelings, colors, energy, creativity—heightening your ability to summon or banish. It is the moon to use if you just can't seem to get the enthusiasm you need to complete a project or where you just can't seem to raise the energy because you don't see this issue as all that important. If you have been in a rut, the Scorpio moon can help you figure out why. In an activity I call "translating power," feed the Scorpio moon energy into a movement powder (like triple action), with the magick done at the midpoint of the Scorpio moon. When the moon reaches its midpoint in Sagittarius (the following sign), add that moon energy to it as well, then complete the powder or herbal blend. The Scorpio moon is perfect for investigation, quietly finding the truth of the matter, general occult work, magick, giving seminars, sex, release, and gain through other people's money such as inheritance or sales. Scorpio has the ability to shift mass quantities of energy and large numbers of people. It is definitely a powerhouse in any working. Think of a volcano beneath the sea and the impact it has if it erupts. The moon for ending or transformation—you choose. If you look at the broad canvas of enchantment, all magickal actions are a form of seduction; the Scorpio moon gives you a triple-X ticket. Just a note: never lie to a Scorpio and do your best to deal with all things honestly during a Scorpio moon. FIXED: STABLE. ELEMENT: WATER. RULED BY PLUTO (MODERN), MARS (CLASSICAL). EXALTED PLANET: URANUS. COLOR: BURGUNDY OR DARK RED. ANGELIC POWER: BARCHIEL/SOSOL.

SCORPIO HERBAL FORMULA: chili pepper, ginger, nettle, woodruff, tobacco, eyebright, licorice root

♐ **Sagittarius:** Swift. Swift. S*wift!* Sagittarius moon is like an animal that has consumed too many energy drinks: wired (in more ways than one). If you want something to darned well *move*, use the moon in Sagittarius. Legal issues, foreign affairs, philosophy, higher education, publishing, travel, networking. It is also a nature sign—the great outdoors, the magnificent vistas of life. Use the Sagittarius moon for making powders and herbal blends for higher spirituality, communing with nature and beings of a different order (such as angels), or kicking an old project back into gear. Want to make a blend for joy? Use the Sagittarius moon! Opportunity powders and blends, such as road opener, triple action, and hot honey, are often made under the light of this moon, as well as creativity and self-improvement blends. Need to get into a university or other higher education establishment? Create your mojo/conjuring bag during this moon sign. The Sagittarius moon carries an unusual gift: that of allowing you to link quickly to another person or item. Now's a good time to use my link, sync, and sink technique. MUTABLE: EXPECT IT; SAGITTARIUS IS THE FAST-MOVING, FULL-THROTTLE FREIGHT TRAIN OF THE ZODIAC. ELEMENT: FIRE. RULED BY

JUPITER. EXALTED PLANET: NONE. COLOR: GREEN OR ORANGE.
ANGELIC POWER: ADVACHIEL/AYIL.

SAGITTARIUS HERBAL FORMULA: cinquefoil, clove, sage, hyssop,
sassafras, parsley, lemon balm, buckthorn

♑ **Capricorn:** Business, rules, organization, senior citizens, entrepre-
neurship, investment, authority, the letter of the law. Capricorn is
the great stabilizer. If you feel totally out of control or things seem
too crazy to handle, try working when the moon is in this sign.
Good for presenting guidelines, working on the family business,
and long-term goals for the future. Make powders and blends under
this moon to gain unexpected money or favors, or to draw material
necessities toward you—anything that can stabilize your circumstances. This is another steady sign that smiles kindly on reinforcing
something already built and working on career goals. Powders and
blends to make as well as break bindings, hexes, and spells of influence over another are often constructed during a Capricorn moon;
however, let me be clear: left-hand work will do just fine if the target
is guilty, not a victim but a perpetrator. Sending someone to jail is
doable, as well as asking karma to bear so they will get caught. If you
have targeted the innocent or are miffed over a personal slight (like
they took the last muffin on the tray), you may not be overjoyed at
the results you receive and expect them to fight back in unpleasant ways. Efficiency and awareness (learning to blend with material surroundings) are positive attributes of this moon. In the stillness, force becomes form. CARDINAL: STARTER AND THE KEEPER
OF TIME. ELEMENT: EARTH. RULED BY SATURN. EXALTED PLANET:
MARS. COLOR: BROWN. ANGELIC POWER: HAMAEL/CASUJOIAH.

CAPRICORN HERBAL FORMULA: patchouli, Solomon's seal, lobelia,
skullcap, slippery elm, ivy, yellow dock, ginger, rosemary

♒ **Aquarius:** Creating the unique and strange, changing the path,
freedom, individuality, breaking tradition, assisting others, charity,
the element of surprise. The Aquarius moon supports positive social
movement. It is a good time to work on new powder recipes and for-

mulas, letting your mind jump out of that proverbial box and into the universe, where all things are possible! Now is a perfect time to make a creativity powder or herbal blend. As Aquarius is a fixed sign, be careful of the changes you wish to make, for they will be long-lasting. Almost every Aquarius I know is a super shopper with a refined taste that finds a deal no matter how elusive it may be. If we look at this process another way, we see that the Aquarius moon can help us find innovative ways to work on old problems and resolve them while keeping the greater good in mind. If you are trying to hide something, don't do it under the Aquarius moon, as it carries the power of the public. Trends and fads are ambrosia to this moon sign; however, if the idea is harmful to others in any way, it will fall flat. Aquarius is the intellectual jinn of the zodiac and encourages science coupled with magick. Like Gemini and Virgo, the Aquarius moon lends itself well to writing spells, working out magickal timing, and formulas, mixtures, and blends of energy or material matter. Psychic development is encouraged under this moon, including the creation of magickal powders and herbal blends for improving divination skills, creating servitors or thoughtforms to carry out magickal work, and sigil magick. Just remember that Aquarius is fixed-fixed-fixed: what you create sticks! FIXED. ELEMENT: AIR. RULED BY URANUS (MODERN), SATURN (CLASSICAL). EXALTED: NONE. COLOR: BLUE. ANGELIC POWER: CAMBIEL/AUSIEL.

Aquarius Herbal Formula: Solomon's seal, boneset, skullcap, rose, peppermint, bladderwrack, amaranth, comfrey

♓ **Pisces:** Meditation, restful sleep, prayer, dreaming, artistic pursuits, visionary, glamoury, the big-picture-of-all-things. If you are making a powder to influence someone in a positive way, begin with the Sagittarius moon to make the connection and then translate the powder or herbal blend to this moon, as folks tend to be more optimistic when the moon is in Pisces. It is also the time when people are inclined to be the most spiritual and intuitive. If you are looking to help a friend or family member see a personal truth or help them in a situation where it is necessary for them to step back and look at the whole of the problem, this is the perfect time to use that powder or blend. Many occult practitioners use the Pisces moon for brews to confuse an enemy or throw them offtrack with the Pisces moon void, the ultimate time for the least amount of detection. Dream and divination powders, such as sweet sleep, crystal ball, and visions and dreams, vibrate well to the moon in Pisces. Never make the assumption that the Pisces moon (or personality) is weak; that is merely an illusion! A place between the words, the place between the breath, the Pisces moon avails herself of many realms simultaneously. If you lie to her, she knows! MUTABLE. ELEMENT: WATER. RULED BY NEPTUNE (MODERN), JUPITER (CLASSICAL). EXALTED: VENUS (CLASSICAL), PLUTO (MODERN). COLOR: PURPLE. ANGELIC POWER: BARCHIEL/PASIEL.

PISCES HERBAL FORMULA: linden, white sage, nutmeg, dandelion root, sarsaparilla, star anise, basil, yellow dock, patchouli, witch grass

Don't assume that it is always the cardinal signs (Aries, Cancer, Libra, or Capricorn) that will provide the most action. If you want something to move and shake things up all around, use the moon in Gemini. If you want something to move in one single direction, use the moon in Sagittarius. Just be careful with Sagittarius; its ruling planet is Jupiter, which tends to expand anything and everything, so word your work accurately and watch out for the exaggeration of fear (which will ruin your results). Although Jupiter is known as the Great Benefic, it can backfire on you if you are not positively focused.

Finally, if you are having trouble getting something to move in your life, working while the moon is in the last degrees of the sign she currently visits can bring the push you need for the removal of blocks or the closure required for you to move on, providing the first aspect the moon makes in the next sign is a positive one. I realize that this occurs in a moon void (when the moon isn't talking to any other planet in its journey to the next sign); however, the moon void can accelerate or change circumstances in play, but it will only last until the moon changes signs. The same can be said for a Mercury retrograde; I call this the slingshot effect. The twenty-four hours in which Mercury stations and turns direct holds great power; it is pure potential, the stillpoint that can be used to launch whatever is needed to make an incredible change in your life. (Of note, there are two types of moon void, the classical and the modern.)

At this point you may be saying, "Gee, all this is interesting, but I'm just not into it because learning this stuff is boring. I do just fine with the quarters or phases of the moon. My stuff works with that timing. Adding extra stuff to think about just wastes my time." That's okay. You don't need this section of the book to make your powders or blends. But what if I said to you, "Here's a super key: if you look through the list of energies of each moon in the signs, you will see that every sign is actually a blend of the sign previous and the sign that follows!" This is why most people don't really notice the changes in energy from one sign to the next when focusing on the moon and her monthly dance through the zodiac. She moves quickly, and she is the goddess of blending. She carries (translates) energy from sign to sign, creating a very unique brew each and every day. Her formula of manifestation includes the ingredients of where she has been, who she is talking to in the present moment (the other planets), and where she is going.

In essence, she's just like you! And, like you, she carries a plethora of hidden qualities, gems of power that glitter and gleam, talents and knowledge just waiting to be seen.

Magickal Days

Many magickal practitioners work with the days of the week and their rulerships (the planet that rules the day) in timing for the creation or use of their powders, herbal blends, fluid condensers, oils, incenses, and other magickal operations. The day is the base energy, the platform. The planetary hour is the fine-tuning mechanism. Each day is ruled by a classical planetary energy (see planetary hours section).

To gather the most power of any particular day, you would choose the planet that rules that day. For example, if we wanted to create a magickal powder to send someone prayers of wisdom for a seven-day spell attuned only to them, we would use Wednesday (Mercury day) in a Mercury hour, as messages, sending, and wisdom all relate to Mercury energy to blend and empower our wisdom powder. We might also include either a few drops of universal fluid condenser or an herbal condenser made of spearmint herb (clear thought) and a small paper with their name on it ground into the powder. If we are really pulling out the stops using folk magick, we might add a lock of their hair, fingernail clippings, and a piece of their clothing (preferably a small swatch cut from an unwashed shirt under the armpit) and grind that into the powder as well. Yes, smelly, but you get the epithelials and the residue from their moisture. Then, for seven days, in spell, ritual, or meditation, beginning on a Mercury day (Wednesday) in the hour of Mercury, we might light a silver candle that sits on top of the magickal powder. We could inscribe the name of the person on the candle along with the word *wisdom* and rub the powder into the marks on the candle. Each day we would burn the candle for eight minutes or sixty-four minutes (both numbers are associated with the planet Mercury). No, you do not have to do exactly what I just said; this is just an example. You could make an herbal bag for wisdom on a Wednesday in the hour of Mercury that contains the individual's name and perhaps a favored gemstone. That night you could hold the bag and utter your prayers, spell, or meditation in the way you see fit. Don't have a taglock (item of the person)? Use my link, sync, and sink technique from chapter 1.

Listed below are the magickal days, their planetary rulerships, and their suggested theme colors. You will find more information about the planets in the next section on planetary hours. You do not have to use any of the timing information in this book to work your magick; however, if you are the type of individual that enjoys nuance, magickal days and planetary hours are definitely for you!

Monday: Ruled by Moon energy. Primary colors: white, silver, aqua, turquoise, or blue.

Tuesday: Ruled by Mars energy. Primary colors: red or orange.

Wednesday: Ruled by Mercury energy. Primary colors: blue, electric blue, gray, silver, or white.

Thursday: Ruled by Jupiter energy. Primary colors: orange, purple, or lavender.

Friday: Ruled by Venus energy. Primary colors: green, aqua, or turquoise.

Saturday: Ruled by Saturn energy. Primary colors: brown (for wishes and earth), black (for banishing), midnight blue.

Sunday: Ruled by Sun energy. Success in all ventures. Primary colors: yellow or gold.

Planetary Hours:
The Secret to Great Magick

• • •

There is only energy. There are portals, gates, pathways, and patterns, an ever-changing labyrinth. Energy is all there is.

Many astrologers and magickal people believe that the timing of a procedure based on planetary alignments can significantly influence a spell, ritual, meditation, prayer, or planned event in daily life. Astrological timing can be used for a wedding, the start of a new business, or the healing process involved in illness, divorce, or loss of a loved one where release is necessary. Astrological timing, in its own way, can allow us to look at the past as well as the future. By viewing where the planets were (or will be) on a certain day, we can see what planetary energies were (or will be) active at the time of an event. Where the planets are located and what they are saying to each other can provide a fantastic window of opportunity. They can also give us an idea of how a particular situation may play out.

A little earlier in this chapter, I told you how knowing planetary hour information can really help you in your daily life, particularly when assisting other people. Used in conjunction with the moon in the signs, the phases of the moon, and the magickal day, planetary hours can give you amazing results in your workings in the least amount of time. You can even use this combination for fast predictive work. Let's say you receive a telephone call with a surprise offer. Perhaps it involves some sort of risk, and you aren't sure if you want to go in that direction. By looking at the phase of the moon, what sign the moon is in, the day you received the call, and the planetary hour in which the offer was made, you can see the general flavor of the offer. For example, if the offer came when the moon was void (where the moon has no dialogue with other planets), the situation will usually result in "nothing will come of it" unless the moon is in the sign of Cancer, Pisces, Taurus, or Sagittarius. In those signs the moon does perform, though sometimes not as well. Perhaps your offer came on a Tuesday (Mars day) when the waxing moon was in Aries, in a Mars hour. It could either blow up in your face, go forward full-tilt, or be a flash-in-the-cauldron (as Aries has a tendency to let go of things after the thrill has worn off). Much depends on your state of mind, your previous choices, and your goals. Regardless, with a prediction on the fly, with all that fire I would definitely be a bit wary and do a little research into that offer. Then, if it looks good, do the magick and take the risk, realizing the possibilities.

Because you cannot move the planets into the best possible alignment for any given magickal operation—you could wait years drumming your fingers for this to never happen—you can use magickal days and planetary hours in your workings to make things go a whole lot faster or add an extra boost of power to your enchanted endeavor.

The planetary hour system has its roots in the Ptolemaic system used in Greek astronomy, which placed the planets in list order divided into seven-hour intervals, each segment ruled by a specific planet. Although we think of an hour as equaling sixty minutes, the planetary hours are location and date specific and are based on the rising and setting of the sun on any particular day, which changes their length each day (or night). Each of those segments of the day/night is ruled by a planetary energy, and in that section (called a planetary hour) events and activities often coincide with the energy of that planet. In essence, the segments provide windows of opportunity, each flavored in a particular way that can blend well (or not so well) with your intent. There are seven classical planets (those planets that were visible to the naked eye in ancient times), so there are seven types of energy available for magickal activity: Sun, Moon, Mercury, Venus, Mars, Jupiter, and Saturn. As the technique of assigning planetary hours was conceived thousands of years ago based on the classical planets, there are no correspondences for Uranus, Neptune, or Pluto; those planets were not discovered until modern times. You will find those sigils along with their corresponding recipes in the formula section under planetary formulas.

In the past, to work with the planetary hours, you needed three important pieces of information: the planetary tables, the times of the rising and setting sun on the day chosen for your magickal work, and your mathematical location. From there, you whipped out your trusty calculator (and before that relied on your searing mental math skills) using a series of steps to compute the hours for any given day or night. Mathematics were required because it was the only way to determine the length of the hour segments. For years, planetary hours were faithfully used by the few truly devoted who took the time to calculate those hours. Many saw these extra steps as a bother and not worth the effort. I get that; math is not my favorite either. Today, technology has taken a leap and generously offered us apps for your digital device (search "planetary hours" in your app store) that do all the math and location information for you. You can even set an alarm so that you can be notified when a particular planetary hour has begun. Finding the planetary hour today is a super snap and well worth adding the information to your magickal bag of goodies!

General Guidelines for Planetary Hours

The following information is by no means complete, but it can get you started working with each planet. Not only can you use this information for planning, but you can also use it for divinatory and sigil work. Notice that I have included magickal as well as mundane correspondences so that you can get a quick feel for each hour. As with the astrological signs, there are several angels that correspond to the planets; however, here I have chosen the most common. Feel free to change the association in your work. For more information on angelic magicks, please refer to my book *Angels: Companions in Magick.*

☉ **Sun:** Success in all ventures. Wealth, will, gain, prosperity, draw the favor of the rich or powerful, find love, bring and give kindness and compassion, focus your will, gain great fortune, make your presence psychologically invisible (especially during a moon void), dissolve painful situations reasonably. A good time for initiations, dedications, and spiritual path choices. Good for defending your reputation and asking for favors from males or individuals in authority (father, public officials, influential folks, the boss) and help from people who abhor violence and liars. The Sun planetary hour carries significant power when you choose to do the right thing. PRIMARY COLORS: YELLOW OR GOLD. ANGELIC POWER: MICHAEL.

☽ **Moon:** Situations that involve your mother, grandmother, or children (however, sometimes Jupiter is assigned to grandmothers) and herbalists and those that work with the land. The moon is the storehouse of energy. Protection, particularly for family members. Healing of emotions. Any issue having to do with water, travel over water, swimming, etc. Finding lost objects, sending emotional messages, speaking with the deceased. Visionary work, divination, house blessings, preparing any magickal item that involves water or liquid such as holy water, divinatory fluid condensers, potions for moon magick, or oil blends. The Moon hour is often chosen for nuptials, engagements, or the first date. Ribbon-cutting ceremonies, public announcements, and advertising of products associated with women, children, or spiritual pursuits find favor with the Moon. Also used for reconciling with enemies, spells and rituals for peace in the home or peace in general, all manner of healing magicks, and enchantments for your pets. PRIMARY COLORS: WHITE, SILVER, OR BLUE. ANGELIC POWER: GABRIEL.

☿ **Mercury:** Communication of all kinds with the living or the dead. Find eloquence in speech, writing, or body language. Assistance in study, teaching, science, or divination. Mental activities of all types. Writing of all kinds including fiction, nonfiction (general), résumés, job applications, school or home schedules, etc. Working with computers, the internet, and networking through writing, speech, or film. Encouraging a situation to move quickly. Settling disputes among family members. Handling routine labor, errands, shopping, and general phone calls. Ideal for scheduling appointments (as long as the moon is not void). Contacting writers, philosophers, secretaries, designers, and those involved in mathematics, music, and astrology. Because of its quick nature, the Mercury hour is not normally the time for permanent or long-term situations. PRIMARY COLORS: BLUE, SILVER, OR WHITE. ANGELIC POWER: RAPHAEL.

♀ **Venus:** Venus is the great attractor. She is, above all, a magnet. Matters of education, strategy, love, romance, fast cash, shopping for luxury clothing and beauty items, shopping for items to beautify the home and garden including flowers and eye-catching decor. Excellent for shopping spells to find the best value for your money or some type of price reduction or a deal (as long as there is no current afflicting planetary dialogue such as a square or opposition to Venus or Jupiter). Friendships, kindness, socialization, pleasant trips and parties, rid oneself of poison (physical and spiritual). Self-education and designing something incredibly beautiful. War (it is Mars who fights the wars; it is Venus who plans and orchestrates it). A Venus hour is a good time to ask a woman for a favor, particularly if she is related to you or is in a close energy bond with you (such as a best friend). The Venus hour is excellent for the arts, imaginative writing, painting, crafting, theater, and all that glitters of talent and creativity. If you want to turn something old into something of beauty, use a Saturn day and a Venus hour. For asking favors from your mother, use a Moon day and the Venus hour. To engage help from a much older woman, such as your grandmother, ask on a Saturn day in a Venus hour. Venus repairs what the negativity of a Mars action may have brought. PRIMARY COLORS: GREEN, AQUA, OR TURQUOISE. ANGELIC POWER: ANAEL (OR URIEL).

♂ **Mars:** Mars is used to transform the negativity sent toward you by any negative person or act. It is the spiritual fire that disintegrates evil. Mars is also used for winning, sports of all kinds, to overcome or overthrow enemies, file a complaint, or call battle gods, goddesses, angels, or warrior spirits. Crafting anything of fire or metal. Resolve quarrels, gain courage, and work for success where drastic moves must be made. Find and instill personal strength. Remove submissive behavior from oneself and take right action in any given situation. Mars is the forward motion action planet. Uniquely, Mars is considered a bridge or pipeline to other planets—a connector and energy mover. Fire magick of all kinds. PRIMARY COLORS: RED OR ORANGE. ANGELIC POWER: CAMAEL.

♃ **Jupiter:** Expansion of all kinds and petitions for peace, kind words, good teachings, good philosophies, gratitude, honor, and right judgment. The growth of a project, spirituality, faith, and maintaining good health. Like the moon, this hour is also good for engagements and weddings. Jupiter is considered the Great Beneficent and covers the fulfillment of desires, wishes, and goals. Long-term prosperity. Growth of any type. Honor. Compassion. The abundance of food, general good fortune, and happiness. Asking favors from influential or wealthy people or receiving assistance from grandparents, aunts, uncles, or those involved in professional services (doctors, lawyers, bankers). Magicks for "opening the way," finding favor from the universe, blessing anything, improving your own enthusiasm, or putting life back into an old project. PRIMARY COLORS: ORANGE, PURPLE, OR LAVENDER. ANGELIC POWER: SACHIEL.

♄ **Saturn:** Banish negativity and overcome quarrels, hatred, or discord. Banish illness. Establish new rules, guidelines, and financial goals. Excellent for initiating ventures that you wish to last or for starting over after a bad experience. Protection of property. Sending criminals to jail. Receiving rewards for work well done. Although many folks see Saturn as "loss," it isn't. It is the result of what you think and what you do. Situations involving grandparents, fathers, the dominant parent or guardian, or those in authority. Career planning. House cleansings, ghost busting, and personal spiritual cleansings. Saturn's energy is good for breaking ground for your garden or home, laying the foundations of all types, and making repairs. Saturn can also be used to bring a desire for a material object into form. Use the Saturn hour to write guidelines, rules, and structure for a particular project or bring closure to something unfortunate. Saturn also can be used to bind an issue before banishing it or to bind something to you temporarily. For example, if you are shopping and you aren't sure you want to buy that blue coffee maker, envision the sigil of Saturn on it and continue shopping. The sigil holds the object in place until you return and release it.[9] PRIMARY COLORS: BROWN (FOR WISHES AND EARTH), BLACK (FOR BANISHING), MIDNIGHT BLUE. ANGELIC POWER: CASSIEL.

To learn more about planetary rulerships, there are two books that cover classical information that can be extremely helpful in your work. They are *The Book of Rulerships: Keywords from Classical Astrology* by Dr. J. Lee Lehman, Ph.D., and *The Rulership Book* by Rex E. Bills. You may also enjoy Ivo Dominguez's *Practical Astrology for Witches and Pagans*.

There are a few other magickal timing pieces that you may find helpful, and they are taken from classical astrology as well. There are two dead spots in timing other than a moon void of course: when a planet is in the first few degrees of a sign and when a planet is in the last few degrees of a sign. Not everyone ascribes to this theory. In horary astrology when a planet is in the first few degrees of the sign, it is too soon to tell whether or not an issue will come to pass. It means that there are too many energies swimming around out there and the pattern has not been solidified. It is a time of choice and review of all the options before action. When a planet is in the last few degrees of a sign, the situation is already over, done deal, finished. It is time to move on and stop fiddling with the issue. Retrograde planets can also affect a working, but this depends on the subject, what rules it, and what else is happening with all the other planets. With a retrograde planet, change comes within, and then, when the planet turns direct, that energy is sent outward into the world. A retrograde planet can

---

9   Dominguez, *Practical Astrology for Witches and Pagans*, 81.

be very useful, particularly if you need time to adjust something within yourself such as working for more wisdom, studying a particular subject, eradicating a bad habit, etc. The high point power day of a retrograde planet is the day when that planet turns direct. The planet is waking from its work within; it stations (stops) and slowly gears up to send the energy out into the universe. (I should note that the planet doesn't really do this at all—it is an illusion that it does so.) That hour of "gear up" is your sling-shot period where, with all your effort, you send your intent out into the universe—in essence, your work rides the wave of the planet's propulsion of its own energy.

One way to prove to yourself how valid planetary days and hours are is to be mindful of them for an entire week, writing down in a notebook (or dictating on your phone) anything interesting that occurs on a specific day in a particular planetary hour. You may begin to see a pattern, and this pattern is most important because you will learn how you interpret the energies around you through your observation and behavior on any magickal day in any given planetary hour. Each of us is wired differently, and in the matter of planetary hours, one of those hours (or perhaps two) is your *super* hour—your winning hour—your achievement hour. Which hour is it? Only you will know. What makes that hour super for you? It is a combination of many factors, including your body chemistry, the day and time you were born, your current spiritual path, and how you process information. The hour will be unique to you, and the only way to know it is to pay attention to planetary hour information for at least a week, which will give you a general idea.

Those of you who have a copy of your natal chart, make a note of the planetary hour in which you were born and the planet that ruled the day you were born; these two planets can give you a hint on where to start in determining your power hour. Both planets (or they may be the same) were highly active in the vibratory pattern of your birth. During your life they seem to be the times when things will go very smoothly for you, as a rule. For some people, both hours work very well. Others will find that one hour appears to work better than the other. To heighten your overall skills, track both planetary energies (the planet that represents the hour you were born and the planet that represents the day you were born) on a daily basis for three to six months. Yes, I know it means paying attention to data, but come on, the information is about you. How cool is that! And when you are done, you will have confidence that says, "This hour(s) is my super hour, and I'm going to use it in hundreds of positive ways!" Too, the power hours can lead to your power color, gemstone, etc. It will just take a little research to find them. Can your power hour(s) change? Yes, it can, particularly when you experience spiritual growth; what was useful for you before will fade away, and a new hour will help you along your path. The benefit of tracking the hours, even if only for a few days, helps you to become mindful of them.

In some magickal traditions the planetary ruler of the day you were born carries special significance and can show the rulership of your life path. This hour is used for initiations, spiritual cleansings, and other applications. For example, my planetary ruler for the day I was born is Mars. Interestingly enough, Mars sits at the midheaven of my chart. In my life, I have often "gone where no person has gone before." I will often quietly brood over information until I am ready, and then, when it is time? Meet the human volcano. What actually helps me (though many astrologers wouldn't see it that way) is that my Mars is in Pisces; I can take that energy and apply it to the big picture of an issue or look for a more visionary solution rather than just aiming and blowing everyone to smithereens. Therefore, I've found that using red (the color of Mars) in my workings (even though the correspondences don't call for it) helps to boost my applications. If I want to burn a protection candle for myself, I will use red rather than one of the other colors. On my general altar I will begin most workings with a red candle. Many of my personal herbal formulas contain associations to Mars or are red, as this energy works well for me, but it might not enhance the work of someone else.

Using Planetary Energy and Their Glyphs in Magick

I'd like to cover one more super boost tip before we move on, which is using planetary energies and symbols not just as an association for choosing the time of a working or the herbs in a powder or herbal blend, but as powers in their own right. Over the years I have found that the energies of the planets and their associated glyphs can boost your work in ways you never thought possible, and the techniques are so easy that once you understand the thrust of the planetary energies, they take only a few minutes (or even less) to employ. You will find these techniques in chapter 5.

For more information on astrological timing, including retrograde planets, lunar mansions, and more, you may enjoy my book *Solitary Witch: The Ultimate Book of Shadows*. If you are interested in learning general astrology, try *The New Way to Learn Astrology* by Basil Fearrington, which presents the Noel Tyl method. This is an excellent book for beginning students. You may also enjoy Jason Miller's books or classes; see http://www.inominandum.com.

Planning Your Magickal Powder Formulas or Recipes

Although I've provided many formulas in this book for your use, let's go through a checklist for the actual creation of a powder or herbal blend. Before you purchase any ingredients, you need to ask yourself a few questions, some that we have already covered and a few we have not:

- What will this powder be used for?
- Is this a one-time situation or do you wish to make a larger batch of powder to use for several things (such as a spiritual cleansing practice) or to share with others?
- Do you have the time to order special ingredients or do you need to make the powder right away? If the need is immediate, what ingredients can you substitute for those you do not have? If you have plenty of time, will you be planning to wildcraft (gathering yourself and drying them from nature) or choosing your garden?
- Do you want to add a signature ingredient? Some magickal practitioners add a signature ingredient, something that encompasses their essence and melds the powder to their energy field or vibration. This ingredient can be herbal or non-herbal; the choice is yours.

- Depending on the use of the powder, how much magickal timing do you wish to use? What moon phase, day, hour, or moon sign would be appropriate to make the powder?

- Do you want to add the particular energies of a deity, totem animal, or element to the essence of the powder? If so, what correspondences go well with that deity, totem animal, element, or spirit?

- Do you want to employ the energies of a specialty ingredient, such as dirt from the gates of a cemetery for protection or crushed, dried eggshell to ward off all evil or ashes from a petition, etc.? Use your intuition. If you are unsure, try using the binary divination system I spoke about earlier.

- Do you have a particular plan of operation in mind for the creation, blessing, and feeding of the powder? Do you need to choose particular charms and chants that you wish to use during the construction of the powder?

Right. About now you might be saying, "But what about the spontaneity? About solely using my intuition? About trusting my abilities to just let it flow? Lists? Timing? Oh, please!"

In magick, you will find there is a place for spontaneity as well as circumstances where a trusted format can be very helpful. There are times when you might be overly stressed and nothing comes to mind; a ritual of rote, one memorized and done hundreds of times, can keep the focus and raise your vibrations to the level you desire. Or, what if you have several worries and your mind flits from the various angles of the problem? What if there are so many people involved that you can't keep your mind focused on just the right desire? Maybe you are worried that you are not doing the right thing. What if you feel so defeated that it is difficult to even try to believe that you can make circumstances better? In these instances, if you rely totally on spontaneity, you may mentally switch gears in the middle of a working, thereby muddying your manipulation of the field of potential that surrounds you. That sea of potential is just as important as the herbs you chose, the timing you picked, and the words you wish to use. Mixed signals into that field can derail all of your efforts in seconds. Favored tools such as a particular plate or mat that you always use to empower powders, chants that make you feel calm and comfortable, or hand motions and gestures that you do to welcome, mix, or dismiss energies can all play a part in a successful working.

Summary

Chapters 1, 2, and 3 provided ideas for a spiritual and practical foundation in creating your powders and herbal blends. In the next chapter we will discuss techniques you can utilize when making your magickal powders and herbal blends, along with a large section on how to make fluid condensers that are designed to enhance any working.

CHAPTER FOUR
The Power of Fluid Condensers

A fluid condenser is a blend of natural ingredients prepared in a symbolic way using magickal correspondences, timing, and ritual. Don't let the word *fluid* trip you up. Here, the definition of fluid relates to a blend of occult alchemical practices and philosophy that attempt to explain and utilize for specific purposes the unknowns in the fabric of the cosmos—an effort at delineation, practice, and theory where more standard scientific or religious explanations have failed. In the case of the word *fluid*, the relationship in this discussion is one of energy, the field, the fifth element, and spirit, all synonymous and yet…not. When discussing fluid condensers there are actually three types, two of which have no relation to wet stuff in the least: liquid, solid, and gaseous.

Although Western occultism brought this alchemical (spiritual and material) study to the public, the practices have existed long before Rosicrucian, Thelema, and Hermeticism. However, credit is due to them because, as a friend of mine said, "You can thank Blavatsky and those like her for busting down the door."

There are theories on how a fluid condenser operates. Some feel the purpose of the fluid condenser is to securely hold a specified energy (impregnated thoughts) until the practitioner directs and releases that energy to the defined goal or target. In this line of thinking, the fluid condenser is thought to be able to accumulate substantial charges of energy that, when directed properly, can help a magickal working come to fruition quickly and with speed. Think of it as an energy storage locker.

Others believe that the condenser is more of an attraction mechanism, pulling the right combination of power to amplify and assist in solidifying your thought pattern. Then, there are those who believe the fluid condensers do both: store *and* amplify. Regardless of the theories, most people who use a liquid condenser agree that they work extremely well. We have learned that liquid fluid condensers take the charge of sound extremely well, which works perfectly in Braucherei and whisper magicks.

I *adore* fluid condensers!

Pascal Beverly Randolph, best known for his involvement in Spiritualism and founding the Rosicrucian Order in the United States, is currently the oldest traditional link to the discussion of condensers in print. He made mention of them regarding sex magick and love potions as well as making magick mirrors.[10] He was an alchemist (among other things) and wrote voraciously, traveling the world and collecting information that his charismatic personality put to interesting use.[11] Unfortunately, Randolph's experiments contain several ingredients that are considered toxic today, and his alchemical process was somewhat laborious. His fluid condenser formulas included one for coating objects (with successive layers of the condenser), one for adding to potions to be ingested, and a blend of the first and second formulas cited along with perfume and color for use on poppets (which were called "volts").

Fluid condensers with more information, safer ingredients, and a faster way of production were perfected by the Czech occultist Franz Bardon at

---

10 *Mageia Sexualis*, pages 71–76, first published in French in 1931 by Robert Telin fifty-six years after Randolph's death. It is highly possible, as asserted in my copy of the book, that Randolph did not write the work on fluid condensers or on volts, that this was the co-author's handiwork, who produced the material well after his death. In Randolph's biography, *Paschal Beverly Randolph, A Nineteenth-Century Black American Spiritualist, Rosicrucian, and Sex Magician*, written by John Patrick Deveney, the author writes: "The only significant parts that cannot be traced directly to Randolph's works are the section on animated statues, the astrological references, and the systematization and antiquarian elaboration that were obviously added by de Naglowska" (page 364, appendix C). Long story short: the co-author (de Naglowska) severely tinkered with the original work.

11 John Patrick Deveney, *Paschal Beverly Randolph, A Nineteenth-Century Black American Spiritualist, Rosicrucian, and Sex Magician* (Albany, NY: State University of New York Press, 1997).

least eighty years later, and it is in his work that we find the greatest public reliance on this subject in our community today. Most often cited in this arena is his book originally published in 1956 in German, *Initiation into Hermetics*. Bardon was brilliant and meticulous in his work, an exceptional alchemist interested in physical, mental, and spiritual health. His teachings are still very popular. Although Bardon gave excellent instructions on the liquid and solid condensers, he passed over the gaseous ones (fragrance, perfume, incense), indicating that they were not as important in his studies as the other two. Because of this, almost no information has carried through on the basics of creating a gaseous condenser. As a condenser's purpose is to up the ante (so to speak) in the use of the object, we're going to have to use a little creative thinking on the process a bit later in this section.[12] It was celebrated author and witch Sybil Leek, however, who launched fluid condensers in front of the general public with the mass market release of her book *Cast Your Own Spell* in 1970, written in easy to understand prose, which delighted a hungry audience and miffed serious occultists.[13] Although Sybil stayed close to Bardon's work, her own inimitable yet practical style helps to add clarity to the discussion of fluid condensers and quite frankly says yes, you too can make these potent concoctions and be successful at it without killing yourself or going mad in the process. If you get a chance and feel like delving into history, do take the time to read the biographies of Franz Bardon and Pascal Beverly Randolph; you will find most interesting information there.

Unfortunately, for whatever reason, condensers did not take hold in the general magickal community and are rarely sold in occult stores. Those who have an interest in them construct their own. The process to create a condenser is not complicated; however, liquid fluid condensers contain high-proof alcohol, which is a flammable shipping hazard, and also require either gold (tincture of gold) or the blood, semen, or what I like to call "lady juices" of their creator. Incense, liquid essentials, smelling waters, and reed diffuser blends are part of the gaseous condenser

---

12 Bardon, *Initiation into Hermetics*, 245–250 (first published in German in 1956 under the title of *Der Weg Zum Wahren Adepten* by publisher Verlag Hermann Bauer).

13 Leek, *Cast Your Own Spell*, 139–150.

family, and they too require the same unusual ingredients as stated above. Solid condensers consist of the metals lead, tin, iron, gold, copper, brass, silver, and mercury, and a variety of resins. Getting your hands on liquid mercury these days is incredibly difficult because of the increasing information on its toxicity; studies have shown it can cause kidney, liver, and brain damage, and it may lead to other serious auto-immune deficiencies. Bardon's work, the heaviest and most informative of the three, speaks not only of tangible condensers but of the spiritual fluid transcendence as well, which may not be wholly appreciated as much as it should be, and therefore the work has been too often ignored.

An operative in all three condensers is gold, and just plopping gold in the mixture will not do. There is an alchemical process for preparing the gold to be included or you can purchase gold chloride from a photography supplier and make a tincture that is then used in the condensers. This is the easiest way to incorporate the essence of gold in your work. Because the gold chloride is diluted before use, it will last a long time and you can make a room full of liquid fluid condensers if you so desire! Once you have formulated your tincture of gold, it will last a long time because you only use ten drops per one cup of liquid in your final liquid condenser blend. Why gold? Because it is believed to carry the greatest load in accumulation power. Those who do not wish to add a drop of blood (menstrual fluid), semen, or other use the gold tincture as a substitute. There are also practitioners, however, who feel that both should be utilized. Leek assures the reader that this is unnecessary and that the gold tincture can be employed without difficulty as a substitute. She also states: "Keep in mind that they (fluid condensers) are added power to the core idea of the spell."[14]

Are making fluid condensers worth it or should we just use a present-day magickal oil formula and move on?

It's worth it.

Our practices here have shown that the liquid fluid condensers work very well for anointing objects, dressing poppets, creating talismans

---

14 Ibid., 144.

(which many feel may have been its original purpose), and a compendium of other magickal operations from healing to drawing good fortune to work for rendering justice and sending back negative energy. Most popular among many is the universal fluid condenser, discussed by both Bardon and Leek because it is an all-purpose vehicle. However, as both authors state in their respective works, simple (one herb correspondence) and compound (several herbal correspondences) can be made for any everyday (and not so everyday) purpose. When I finally understood the full concept of fluid condensers and what amazing things they could do (and I won't kid you, it took me a while), I made it my mission to create a wide variety of simple and compound formulas. My crowning glory is my Divination fluid condenser because it works not only to boost psychic abilities, but also to make a liar cough up the truth. The Money Draw formula is the most popular with my friends. All of my formulas were developed with specific astrological correspondences. There has been more than one time in the past few years that my neighbors have curiously peeked through the thicket (yes, that's not a colorful stretch from the truth) to see what the heck I was doing out there in the moonlight at three in the morning.

I like to keep them guessing.

Because I make and share my liquid and gaseous condensers, I do not put anything from my body in them at the time of preparation, as that would give an energy connection directly to me to any work that is done by the individual who received my condenser. For me, adding such items, if I feel it is warranted, is the very last step and an optional one. You can make your condensers in small quantities or you can drag out the canning pot and spend the afternoon boiling up a huge batch with all of your magickal friends helping. Where the former makes your product singularly unique, the latter allows trusted practitioners to share their combined energy in both the practice and magickal ritual of the creation. Both types of liquid condensers made here have proven successful.

Liquid Fluid Condenser Supplies

To prepare a liquid fluid condenser like we do here, you will need:

Glass Measuring Cups

A Pot with a Glass Lid: (so you can see the mixture as it boils). We have three pots here in different sizes from small to large. Tall saucepans or small stockpots work well for smaller batches. Most importantly, this pot should only be used for making fluid condensers, never food. You will understand this when you make your first batch of patchouli fluid condenser: the smell stays in the pot almost *forever*. Too, some of the herbs you may wish to use may be considered toxic in some form or another; always research. You don't want to infuse those herbs into a pot that is used to prepare food for your family. At best, the food will taste super yucky. Finally, the boiling herbs will stain the kettle.

A Heat Source: A stovetop or even an outdoor fire setup where the pot hangs over the fire. Although many practitioners prefer gas, this isn't always possible, and I can tell you from experience that your fluid condenser will be just fine if you use an electric heat source. I have a portable induction hotplate that I use for making most of my fluid condensers. It is safe, and I don't have to be in the kitchen. You can also use a slow cooker and simmer your blend for four hours; however, the end product isn't as clear and doesn't hold the fragrance of herbs as well. We made our first Money Draw fluid condenser this way, and the end product performed well; several practitioners enjoyed increased, temporary wealth as a result of adding the formula to their workings. Using the slow cooker does make the process take longer, so I usually use my dedicated pots and the induction hotplate, which takes much less time, and the formula retains some of the aromas of the herbs.

Metal Fine Mesh Strainer that Covers the Width of the Pot: I actually have two strainers, one finer than the other, as you don't want any solids in the formula in the end.

Cheesecloth, Coffee Filters, or Paper Towels for Straining:
Cheesecloth works best, coffee filters second, towels a messy third.

Two Cups of Spring Water

Two Cups of Herb (Fresh or Dried): Please know your herbs before boiling them. If you are worried that the herb could be toxic when prepared, do your research. Today, you can jump on the net quickly to determine the possible side effects of just about any plant, parts of plants, and even whether or not a plant can be safely boiled. If you can't access the internet and don't have a collection of herbal books, use only food-safe herbs that are known to be suited for cooking. If you choose to use an herb that might be considered toxic because the warnings are not applicable to your current state of health (it depends on medical conditions, pregnancy, etc.), never, ever inhale the steam and do perform the cooking process outdoors. Finally, whether the herbs are food safe or not, don't lift the lid for a little peek while cooking, as you will ruin the formula, and if the herbs are not food safe, then you run the risk of poisoning yourself—not worth it. For example, a patchouli liquid fluid condenser has a compendium of uses and is safe to boil, use on the skin, etc.; however, it is deemed unsafe for handling by pregnant women in their first trimester, and it can cause skin irritations to those who suffer from skin sensitivities.

One Cup of Grain Alcohol: We use Everclear; however, please be aware that different states have rules and regulations on the percentage/proof that is permitted to be sold in those states, so I refrain from giving those numbers. The alcohol acts as a preservative for your condenser. Just remember that it is highly flammable and in this recipe is never heated. It is added cold after the heating and cooling process has taken place. Sybil Leek used both fuel alcohol and spirit of alcohol (which is the Everclear or a clear drinking alcohol such as vodka). Although Everclear and vodka are more expensive, they seem to produce a better overall product; my suggestion is to purchase the strongest proof that is legal in your area.

Bottles for Storage: This choice is entirely up to you. You can choose fancy or plain; glass is best, dark if possible. You can even spray paint the outside of a canning jar with black paint and decorate the jar so that your formula looks delightfully magickal (and therefore cannot be mistaken for a yummy dressing for someone's salad). The lid should be tight, although corked bottles can be used. Just check those corks every now and then. You can put all of the formula in one jar or bottle or, after it is completed, pour it into small bottles to give as gifts to friends. Be sure to label the bottle "poison" and give the date created, if possible, and a list of the ingredients you used. You never know who might pick it off your friend's shelf and decide to take a taste or two. This is the same for any type of herbal formula, including the powders and blends in this book. Well-marked ingredients give peace of mind.

Your Gold Tincture: Gold tincture is easy to prepare. Please read the health warnings on your bottle of gold chloride and take the time to study the hazards of use on the net. You are using such a small amount that there shouldn't be health concerns; however, I feel you should always be informed when working with any type of chemical or herb. To be safe, I never touch the gold chloride and always use an eyedropper or pip for dispensing. The formula is as follows: add one gram of gold chloride to 20 grams of distilled water. To help you understand, one fluid ounce equals 29.5 grams. This means you need only a minuscule amount of gold chloride to make your gold tincture. We use an electronic scale to make our measurements (don't forget to add the weight of your container to your calculations). Your liquid fluid condenser only needs 5–10 drops of your gold tincture for every 100 grams (6.7 ounces) of the liquid fluid condenser. There are 8 ounces in one cup of liquid. The recipe I use here renders about two cups of liquid fluid condenser once the alcohol is added; therefore, you would put approximately 20–30 drops of your gold tincture in your room-temperature liquid fluid condenser. Your own measurements are best, as depending on how long and how hard you boiled your initial two cups of water, more or less liquid will be left, and this amount should be used for your final measurement of your gold tincture that you made; this is just a general guideline. If you are confused, there are several conversion charts online that can assist you in your calculations. This part of the process is the most technical portion of the liquid fluid condenser recipe. After you figure this out, the rest is very easy.

Advantageous Timing: Earlier in this book we discussed timing by the phases of the moon, the moon in the signs, the day of the week, and planetary hours. Fluid condensers are traditionally tied to some type of timing mechanism, usually paying particular attention to the moon in the signs and the planetary hour, matching that information to the correspondences of the herbs you are using for your simple or compound liquid fluid condensers. For example, if you want to make a liquid fluid condenser for motivation, strength, courage, or power, you would choose Mars-oriented herbs and make your fluid condenser when the moon is in Aries in the hour of Mars on a Tuesday (if at all possible). How do you find out the magickal correspondences of a herb? Scott Cunningham's *Encyclopedia of Magical Herbs* is a good start. There are several other books available on magick and herbs; one can never have too many!

How to Make the Liquid Fluid Condenser

Making the liquid fluid condenser can be as magickal as you desire. You can begin with a full ritual, create sacred space, or start with a prayer to clear the area. Incense, bells, rattles, or singing also may be a part of the brewing process; it is entirely up to you. I always make sure that all items to be used have been blessed with burning white sage from my garden and tuned with music or bells, as the fluid condensers take very well to magickal sounds. Many times I offer all my supplies to the east, using a Braucherei prayer to begin:

Eastwards I stand for favors I pray
From goddess divine and lord of the day
Earth lends her power and breath sends the spell
Day's end will reveal that all will be well.

Then I continue to chant "*only the good remains*" until I feel calm and serene.[15]

The process itself is incredibly simple. Just put all the herbs in the pot and cover with water. Be sure that you have enough water to cover the herbs; if you don't, make the adjustment—it won't hurt your recipe. Don't forget to put the lid on the pot. Boil at a very low boil for 40 minutes. Do not at any time lift the lid. By using a transparent cover, you will be able to see if you have the heat too high, as the boil will be too furious. My best suggestion is to bring the liquid to a boil and then drop to a simmer. Allow the mixture to cool to room temperature without lifting the lid.

Stir the cooled liquid several times, impregnating it with a general chant or a focused one. I often use: "*May the Web of the Wyrrd be turned in accordance with my wish and my will!*"[16]

Strain the cooled liquid, trying to remove as much of the material matter as possible. Cover the pot and bring to a boil once again. We've noticed that the consistency of the condenser has a lot to do with the amount of water you initially added, the boil time, and the type of herbs used. In some cases it can be almost gel-like at the conclusion of the second boil; in others, slightly thick; and still others, no coagulation is shown at all. All the condensers I have made have worked very well regardless of the thickness after the second boil. The timing of the second boil depends on how much liquid you have left. You must watch this second boil carefully so as not to heat the pot dry. Usually, it will be 20–30 minutes to give you roughly one cup of liquid, longer for rendering less liquid. Bardon reduced his formula to 50 grams or about 1.7 ounces. I either stick at one or a half cup of remaining fluid because I always share what I have made with my magickal brothers and sisters.

---

15 Adapted from Storms, *Anglo-Saxon Magic.*
16 This is from the *Rune Mysteries* book I wrote with Nigel Jackson.

Allow the remaining liquid to cool to room temperature, then strain as many times as necessary to remove any plant matter. To this add an equal amount of spirit alcohol. Stir well. Then add your calculated drops of the tincture of gold that you made. Stir well. I use a whispered chant as I stir both times if the liquid condenser is for something specific; however, I ask only for the blessings of Spirit on the liquid if it will be used for a variety of magickal applications.

The very last step is to add a drop of menstrual blood, semen, or another ingredient that will taglock the liquid fluid condenser specifically to you. This is an optional step.

Your liquid fluid condenser is now ready to be bottled and stored out of direct sunlight. Your condenser can be used for a variety of purposes, from adding a drop to magickal powders and herbal blends to putting a tiny amount in your favorite magickal oil. You can use a paintbrush to add the liquid fluid condenser to talismans, poppets, ritual tools, mojo/conjuring bags, and the bottoms of candles (because the condenser contains alcohol, I am very careful when using it for candle or fire magicks).

Element Recipes for Fluid Condensers

Earth, air, fire, and water are patterns of energy. Each pattern has a guardian "spirit" that watches over it. In chapter 2 we discussed the correspondences of these four elements. Here I have provided their sigils and a formula for each. Feel free to develop your own recipes. You can use a combination of fresh and dried ingredients, only fresh ingredients, or only dried ingredients. The choice is up to you.

Try to keep your magickal timing in line with the formula. For example, you might want to make an earth recipe when the moon is in the earth signs Virgo, Taurus, or Capricorn. Air would equate to the moon in Libra, Aquarius, or Gemini. For a fire formula, you might choose a time when the moon is in Aries, Leo, or Sagittarius. Water would be made when the moon is in Cancer, Scorpio, or Pisces. The planetary hour would depend on the intent. Attraction, Venus. Banishment, Mars. Limitations, Saturn. Expansion, Jupiter. Connection, Mercury. Energy storage, Moon.

Overall success, Sun. These are only suggestions; you choose what suits the situation.

▽ **Earth:** Potato peels, fern, patchouli, turnip slices, horehound

△ **Air:** Lemongrass, eyebright, mint, mistletoe, maple

△ **Fire:** Cedar, dragon's blood resin, ginger, nutmeg, chili pepper

▽ **Water:** Chamomile, cucumber slices, grapes, eucalyptus, rose petals

Universal Formulas, Fluid Condensers, Powders, and Herbal Blends

A universal formula in magick is a blend of herbs, magickal oils, and pure essentials that form an energy link between the seven classical planets through their correspondences. Mixed in ritual, the end result can be used for any circumstance (thus the title "universal"). Universal formulas are based on two criteria: herbal correspondences culled from historical data and what is available in your area. Although unusual items (such as herbs not native to your area) can enhance the formula, those plants that are native to your area or that you have grown on your property have a strong energy conduit to your natural surroundings, particularly if most of your work will be in that same area. As there are many herbs associated with any particular planetary energy, your choice among them may be predicated on your experience in working with a particular herb, research, or your feelings when working with the individual herb.

A simple universal blend has one herb for each planet represented. A compound universal blend has two or more herbs for each planet represented. In chapter 2 I gave you an element universal compound that lends itself well to powders and herbal blends. Here are two formulas for liquid fluid condensers based off of Sybil Leek's and Bardon's work. These formulas are designed with the planetary signatures of the herbs.

Simple Universal Blend

• • •

sage leaves (Jupiter), chamomile flowers (Sun), peppermint
leaves (Mercury), willow bark (Moon), violet flowers or
leaves (Venus), patchouli (Saturn), ginger (Mars)

Compound Universal Blend

• • •

sage leaves (Jupiter), sassafras leaves or bark (Jupiter), chamomile flowers (Sun), cinnamon bark (Sun), willow bark (Moon), cucumber peels (Moon), violet leaves or flowers (Venus), rose (Venus), ginger (Mars), basil (Mars), patchouli (Saturn), ivy (Saturn), peppermint leaves (Mercury), lavender (Mercury)

Liquid Fluid Condenser Healing Spell

(AIR AND WATER ELEMENTS)

One of my favorite uses for the liquid fluid condensers is when working water and air magicks, particularly for healing. This working uses Sybil Leek's technique given on page 147 of her book *To Cast Your Own Spell*, although I have expanded it to suit my Braucherei work. This working was actually the spell I used to test my universal liquid fluid condenser the first time I made it. I used only blessed spring water that I chill to 34 degrees Fahrenheit (the temperature that water takes the best charge, according to Bardon). The water is placed into a healing cooking pot (a pot used explicitly for heating water magicks on the stove) along with the individual's name to be healed written on a piece of paper. I also add the birthdate if I have it. There should only be enough water in the pot to cover the bottom and wet the paper. Next, I add 5–10 drops of my liquid fluid condenser. I have a particular liquid fluid condenser for healing that is a combination of lavender, rosemary, lemongrass, white sage, African basil, and lemon verbena. You can make each of these as a single liquid condenser and then mix them together or you can make a compound liquid fluid condenser with these ingredients all in the same pot.

In this healing spell you bring the water to a soft boil and then state the individual's full name you are working for and the intent of your magick. Link, sync, and sink your mind into the person (or into their aura), breathing deeply. If this bothers you and you don't want to be too attached, sink only into their outer spirit body. Begin chanting your favorite healing chant, holding that individual's image in your mind for as long as you can, or you could envision a silver tether from your third eye to the individual's third eye or a golden energy from your hands flowing into the individual's heart chakra—all will work. Try to fully embrace their image until the kettle boils dry (but if you can't, that's okay). Regardless of your technique, hold the image in your mind as long as you can. When you have lost the thought, the magick is done. My only cautions are that you should not inhale the steam or touch the hot pot with your hands. If it helps you concentrate, stir the boiling water with a wooden spoon used only for this type of work. I have a fun decorated spoon that I embellished by creating a spirit head fashioned out of Fimo clay on top of the handle. I have a friend who uses a spoon with a carved wooden figure on it that he calls "my Spirit of the Divine Circle" because he stirs in a circular motion.

You can end your working in your own way or you can draw an equal-armed cross over the dry pot and paper, saying, "*May this spell not reverse, nor place upon me any curse. May all astrological correspondences be correct for this working. Peace with the gods. Peace with nature. Peace within. Only the good remains. So mote it be.*" Be sure that as you say these final words, you carry the emotion of gratitude that the healing has taken place, especially if you felt worried or frightened when you began the working. You must feel better! At the end of the enchantment, with the operative word being "feel," do what works to make your mind flip from worry to "all is okay, and I feel good." This twist, from fear to delight, can play a significant role in the working. Allow both pot and paper to cool. Burn the paper. Clean out the kettle with sea salt and a dry paper towel, rubbing the bottom and sides of the pot thoroughly with the salt and towel combination. Not only does this clean the pot in the material world, but it also cleans it in the astral as well. To complete the spell, wash your hands and face with cold water, being sure to pat the back of your neck. This is a Braucherei technique that ensures that any energy work doesn't backfire to the practitioner, and it helps to cleanse the aura after an intense healing experience.

I use this spell often because it requires so few supplies and so little time, yet it yields excellent results. It is good for emergencies or when a friend calls asking for healing help or a text message appears asking for healing work and you have a full schedule and no time for a ritual of any great length.

Liquid Fluid Condenser Water Healing Working

This technique uses a clear bowl of blessed, chilled water placed on top of an individual's photograph. Add five drops of your favorite healing liquid fluid condenser. Rather than stirring the water in the bowl, I let it sit perfectly still.

Connect with the sea of potential (as you learned in chapter 1) and activate that field for the healing of the individual; say the person's name three times aloud. Link, sync, and sink your mind into the aura of the individual while staring at the photograph. Cup your hands so that they are loosely around your mouth, then whisper your healing chant directly onto the water as you focus on the picture (that you can see through the bottom of the bowl). Your fingers should be loose enough so that your breath skips across the top of the water. Keep repeating your healing chant until you lose the thought. Seal the working as in the previous spell. Take the water outside and pour it on the ground.

This is an excellent spell to do when it is raining outside, as the water-to-water link will quickly take place. Wash your hands with salt water after the completion of the working.

Liquid Fluid Condenser Single Formulas

The single formula liquid fluid condensers function in accordance with the nature of the plant and its planetary and element correspondences. To fully understand each liquid fluid condenser that you make, research the plant's growing pattern, medicinal uses, and lore. I make most of my liquid fluid condensers from wildcrafted plants that I find in the woods and fields in South Central Pennsylvania or from herbs I have grown in my garden. Here are a few that I have found most useful.

Mega Protection—Wild Blue Violet: ELEMENT: WATER DUE TO ITS HEART-SHAPED LEAVES AND DELIGHT OF MOIST SOIL. PLANETARY ASSOCIATION: VENUS OR SATURN/PLUTO. There are over 400 species of wild blue violet. If you have a garden or property in the Northeast, you will quickly learn just how invasive wild blue violet can be! The plant self-seeds and spreads across the ground; left unchecked, it will choke out your garden, winding in and around other herbs along the base of the plants. Most wild blue violets are actually edible, both the leaves and the flowers, meaning they are happy to play with humans. Medicinal uses under professional guidance include combating cancer and helping with immune deficiency diseases. The flowers have also been used as an expectorant. All this information tells us that the wild blue violet liquid fluid condenser you make primarily functions as a protective and healing mechanism, particularly if you feel like you are being railroaded, cheated, or taken advantage of in any situation. The logic here is like against like to cancel out the problem. The flowers and leaves are also used to change one's bad luck or a run of unfortunate occurrences in your life. The liquid fluid condenser can also be applied to people who have ganged up on you—for example, a negative family unit or a pocket of unhappy people at work. Not only does the plant protect, it breaks apart what has been bound together by unhappiness, cruelty, or downright evil. The aroma is used as a sleep aid, and the blue color is thought to bring peace into an area.

Super Healing, Super Blocker, Dark Mother—Elderberry: SACRED TO DAME HOLLE/MOTHER HULDA.[17] ELEMENT: WATER. PLANETARY ASSOCIATION: VENUS AND SATURN. Elderberry liquid fluid condenser has a wide variety of uses, including stopping an attack, healing, rewards for hard work, breaking hexes, bringing prosperity, and keeping one's home safe.

Liquid Fluid Condenser and Magick Mirror
FOR DIVINATION, TRUTH, AND WISDOM

I love to experiment and find personal satisfaction in taking unusual ideas and turning them into something magickal. Recently, when one of my students wanted to make a magick mirror, I looked through my notes to see the past projects I'd done. I gave away my last magick mirror, so I decided that to help her, I would do some more research and create a new formula. I was working on this book at the time, and designing a new

---

17 See http://hrafnar.org/articles/dpaxson/asynjur/holda.

type of magic mirror would fit right in with the section I was developing, writing instructions on fluid condensers. I decided to review the work of known experts, so I looked into the material of Pascal Beverly Randolph, Franz Bardon, and Sybil Leek. Now, there is something that I have to tell you, and I know that I digress here, but I feel I have to get this out in the open. Trust me, it does apply.

Here goes. Years ago I had several friends who were avid Sherlock Holmes fans. Once a month they would all get together and discuss the characters and stories of this marvelous fictional masterpiece, and, of course, they would also talk about the author, Arthur Conan Doyle. What I found most interesting were the psychological leaps that these individuals would take when discussing the author and his intentions. I saw that some read too much into the stories, and others too little. I didn't think much of it at the time—my career was young, and I was far too focused on my writing and my family to concentrate on my observation. More than twenty-five years later, as I was sitting on my front porch in my favorite rocking chair, I found myself discussing the internet and how much of the information I was reading had no basis in fact, resting highly on inaccurate statements and opinions. These sentiments, by the way, were about something I had written in one of my books that had been taken out of context—nothing new there. It boggled my mind that the comments being made had absolutely nothing to do with my original intent in the material that I had written. In fact, some of the assertions were so far off that I wondered what world these people were living in; it was definitely not mine.

Shades of my old friends and their dance with Sherlock Holmes paraded before my mental eyes. It suddenly dawned on me that this tearing apart and reconstructing of an author's intent was nothing new; people have been doing it for centuries. The process of overthinking written and spoken material happens every day and is as common as drinking tap water. It also dawned on me that, *duh*, many people do not research or read like I do. When I read anything, absolutely anything, I bond with the author as a human being—not an authority, not as a guru, not as a saint. A person. A human who loved to write and loved to share with words.

Their work is a compilation of their purpose in the universe and the flow of where they are going, what they have experienced, and how they have processed that information. I have also learned that the prevailing opinion on any subject may not be accurate; that is what you hear right now because the mavens are busy at work, but what is the rest of the story? There is always more. Is it fact or fiction?

History is rarely correct; we learn new things about the past every day. Researching family genealogy taught me that! I know that there is material that writers don't add into a particular body of work for a variety of reasons, ranging from PR to "I could get sued if I say that" to the word count is too long and there has to be an ending sooner than later. Sometimes you have so much difficulty trying to put an explanation into words so that the thought can be understood by many (it will never be all) that you just pull a section and move on. This process of writing is no different now than it was in the time of Pascal Beverly Randolph (1875) or Franz Bardon (1958). In the times of those writers you could be jailed—and they both were—simply over what you wrote and the experiments you conducted.

So…all this interesting trivia rumbles about in the back of my mind when I am researching any topic. My point to my rambling is that I have learned to look closely at the bones of any magickal work or occult theory. "See the structure," I say to myself. "Go to the base. Go to the foundation. Get to the skeleton philosophy or beliefs on which this information is based." Follow the threads of the flow, backward and sideways, just like researching one's family history. For example, I am always fascinated by commonalities in mystical teachings that logically shouldn't be there, but they are. Today, we have the internet and all the wonderful goodies of information gathering. Not so as we glide back through history, yet we see culture after culture working with the same bones of mysticism with similar methods, whether they were in the Amazon or China or Australia or Alaska. In times when dreams and visions were commonplace, the shamanic heritage we all hold (but don't often acknowledge) unfolded with the desire of personal attunement to help make the world a better place.

In his book *Clairvoyance for Psychic Empowerment*, Carl Llewellyn Weschcke wrote the following before his death:

> Shamans see themselves as intermediaries between the human (physical) and spirit worlds. They enter nonphysical dimensions of consciousness to discover solutions to the problems afflicting their physical (human, animal, and plant) community. Other than induced trances and out-of-body experiences, shamans gain information through dreams and visions. Shamans are almost always in contact with spirit guides who enable their entry into the spirit world and guide them in their journeys, during which they may receive accurate information and instruction as to what is needed to heal a diseased person. It should be noted that such healing is not always accomplished using medicines but often by the performance of acts of penance to balance previous harmful actions. Other times the shaman enters the body (the subtle body by means of his own subtle body) to confront the spiritual infirmity or energy imbalance and banish it from the body.[18]

When I open my copy of Carl's book, the inscription reads: "To Silver RavenWolf, a good friend and fellow traveler in this new age of personal growth and transformation, with appreciation and best wishes. Carl, 7-1-2013." These words always make me smile. That's what we all are: fellow travelers. Folks who are trying to tune in to that shamanic essence on a daily basis to make life better for ourselves and our families, friends, and humanity. Trying to motor past our own self-deceptions, hoping to bring clarity and correct vision into form. Dedicating ourselves to learn and grow in an uplifting and spiritual way.

The unmitigated success of that magick mirror I told you about in the first paragraph taught me a critical lesson. You see, it took me two months to put that mirror together. I made mistakes. I chose products that didn't perform the way I thought they would. I continued to go back and forth with that mirror, having to wait patiently to fix this or get just the right timing for that or fighting the humidity in the drying process...at one point I almost abandoned the project. I worried that because I couldn't

---

18 Weschcke, *Clairvoyance for Psychic Empowerment*, 227.

make the mirror exactly the way those before me had done (the ingredients were toxic so I didn't want to use them) and because I had gone out on a very teetering limb of my own thought process that even though I might have an excellent occult toy, it wouldn't work, and wouldn't that just be a darned irritating thing! Yes, I realize there are lots of ways to make magick mirrors; however, I desperately wanted this to work so that I could share the process with my student (it never occurred to me that this story would end up in this book). Yet I stuck to it, and in its construction I empowered that mirror and the sigil inside it to bring truth, vision, and clarity, and to protect the owner at all times. In fact, the mirror turned from being "just a mirror to see" into a vehicle where energy could be sent or obtained in a variety of practical spellwork applications. I also charged the mirror to have its own radar to let me know if someone was sending nasty stuff my way or if I was doing something stupid that would draw ugly energy forms of my own making—all this from two humble pie plates, a collection of herbs, magickal powders, resins, gems, fluid condensers, wax, stubborn glue, and misbehaving black paint.

Midmorning on July 21 I sealed two pie plates together and finished the empowerment process. I hadn't done any of the pretties I'd planned for it. The idea was to finally get that mirror together and see if it would work. Not five minutes later I received a text message that there was a person in our community who had purposefully cursed me and a friend earlier in the year and that this individual appeared to have met with a recent unfortunate circumstance. I didn't realize it at the time, but this was the forty-second anniversary of my mother's death. I don't know if that has anything to do with it, but I thought I'd mention it as it was actually two mediums who texted me in that time window with the same information—one of those odd notes that you pay attention to now and then. Ya know? There is no such thing as a secret. Ever.

So my response was *What?*—as in why the heck did that individual feel they had to target me, let alone my friend—and *What?* as in an exclamation of the universe giving that person a metaphorically bloody nose. (My actual reply is not fit for print.)

THE POWER OF FLUID CONDENSERS

However, the mirror, made with the formula I am about to give you, absolutely did its job with bringing the information to me, and it wasn't done! Whenever I needed to know anything important, I would be drawn to the mirror. It got to the point where I only had to talk to it and, sure enough, within a few hours or days I would have my answer. Eventually, I named it "the bat mirror."

As Carl said, we are all travelers on the path of spirituality. It doesn't matter what religion you are or what occult order you are in or what title you hang your tools on. I don't care. The universe doesn't care. What counts is what you do, who you help, and what you create. That's our task, to raise the vibration of love.

It is my hope that you take the information in this book and run with it as fast and as hard as you can. Allow the shamanic transcendence to be a part of your being, use the work as a platform to create your own unique, loving vibration. Trust your instincts. Be creative! We all will be better for it.

My magick mirror isn't fancy at all! It is made out of two glass pie plates that I spray-painted black on the backs nine times. Between each coat of paint I brushed on my divination liquid fluid condenser formula. Once it was completely dry, I placed a sigil I'd created on a large bay leaf painted with the fluid condenser in the center of one of the plates. Then I glued a piece of copper on top of that. Next, I added crushed crystals and a powdered form of the same herbs listed below along with wormwood, poppy, and morning glory seeds and a pounded-flat silver necklace. Finally, I placed the other pie plate on top of that one and glued them securely together in a nested fashion, gluing only around the rim. Okay, so that didn't work extremely well because of the glue I chose, so I had to glue it again. Once the glue dried, I affixed black felt to the back of the bottom of the double plate so that the paint wouldn't scuff off during repeated use.

My magick mirror would win no prizes in a beauty contest, but it works amazingly well! The magick mirror fluid condenser formula I used was created with the following ingredients:

. . .

dandelion, tobacco, bay, bladderwrack, eyebright, marigold, saffron, thyme, borage, lemongrass, orange, damiana, orris

The timing for creating the liquid fluid divination condenser was the key to the mirror's success. I chose the summer solstice, as close to the Sun entering the sign of Cancer as possible and still catching the full moon energy of Sagittarius and Gemini in the planetary hour of Venus (an energy traditionally used for creating magick mirrors). I empowered the formula in the woods under the beams of the moonlight, using a circle of tiger's-eye gemstones, quartz crystals, my divination formula, tealight candles, and a ritual bell. It was awesome!

Cornucopia Liquid Fluid Condenser
ATTRACTION MAGNIFIER

This condenser uses only fresh fruits either picked by yourself or purchased at your local fruit stand. I live in the Northeast United States, so the ingredients listed here are those fruits that are easy to obtain in my area. If you reside in another part of the world, feel free to choose fruits that are popular in your own locale. The cornucopia liquid fluid condenser lends itself well to attraction, good fortune, and happiness enchantments, and it is one of my favorites because it vibrates so sweetly. The resulting color is a lovely burgundy. Slice all ingredients and cover with water, then follow the liquid fluid condenser instructions given earlier in this chapter.

Apples: Venus—healing, love, long life, plant communication, stress relief

Apricots: Venus—love, sweet character, grace, inner strength, balance

Blackberries: Venus—protection, prosperity, healing, cleansing, peace in the self, enhance memory

Blueberries: Venus—cleansing, protection, boost intellect, peace in the home, happiness, strength

Cherries: Venus—love, intuition, healing, pain relief, sleep aid

Grapes: Moon—mental ability, fertility, prosperity, healing, cleansing

Peaches: Venus—long life, fertility, prosperity, wishes, love

Plums: Venus—protection, love, balance

This formula contains eight ingredients; seven correspond to Venus, one to the Moon. Where Venus attracts the energy of the formula, the Moon ingredient stores it. This formula is best made during a first quarter moon in the hour of Venus. Venus energy is most happy in the signs of Taurus and Libra. Try to find a day when Venus is happy in her dialogue of the other planets, particularly with Mercury, the Moon, or Jupiter.

CHAPTER FIVE
Silver's Magickal Secrets

This section of the book contains several formulas and magickal techniques to enhance the process and use of your magickal powders and blends. I have included personal thoughts, ideas, and a little history that may be helpful to you.

Beeswax

The use of honey and beeswax in human society can be traced back as far as 3,000 BC in ancient Egypt, where it was employed in a variety of religious and medicinal practices. Honey was offered to the gods and applied to wounds, and the wax was used in embalming and candle making. From ancient Roman market stalls selling wax tablet talismans to modern times, beeswax has provided light, aromatic delight, and pharmacological assistance for man and beast. In candle making beeswax burns slowly and is delightfully sweet. With its organic properties (and the right wick), beeswax candles provide a 98 percent smokeless burn. Approximately eight pounds of honey is consumed by the bees to create one pound of wax; one pound of wax yields about six votive-sized candles. Therefore, it takes about 1½ pounds (roughly) of honey to create a single votive.

To make spell disks, talismans, amulets, Yule ornaments, etc., any type of magickal powder (unless the powder contains a combustible material such as saltpeter) can be added to melted beeswax, and then the wax poured into square, circular, or rectangular soap molds to approximately ¼-inch thick. During the warming process (follow package instructions), stir the warm wax and chant your desire. Remember to sink the matching glyphs of planetary power into the wax. After cooling, the wax disc is removed. If you are having a problem getting the wax to release from the mold, simply pop the mold into the freezer for a few minutes. You can inscribe your charms, spells, and sigils with a heated stylus on the wax disk or carefully use a wood-burning tool. To enhance the indentations you have made, distress the surface using burnt sienna and umber acrylic paints, wiping the wet paint off quickly with a soft towel so the paint primarily adheres to the patterns in the wax. Allow to dry overnight. Small medallions of beeswax can be created in the same manner and used in conjuring bags, sachets, and herb pillows.

Due to its natural color and strength, beeswax is associated with the sun. As beeswax is made by bees from the nectar of flowers, additional correspondences include Venus (society and partnership) and Saturn (organization and structure). In my opinion, a beeswax candle in magick enhances the overall power of the working, ramping it up because of its all-natural makeup. Beeswax candles can be used for magnetizing a desire or banishing negative energy as they are both drawing and repelling in nature. Medicinally, beeswax is used for lowering cholesterol, relieving pain, and reducing inflammation—therefore, if a situation is "out of control" in your life, you might burn a beeswax candle in a ceremony to assist in relieving emotional pain and stop the problem's advancement. You might want to fine-tune your working by choosing a Saturn hour (to limit the problem). Conversely, if you wanted to gain (or make sticky) your ability to attract money or good fortune, you would burn a beeswax candle in the hour of the Sun on a Sunday for success or in the hour of Jupiter (expansion) on a Thursday. For love, burn a beeswax candle in the hour of Venus (or the Moon) on a Monday or a Friday.

Beeswax can be colored black by adding soot or activated charcoal after it is melted and before it is poured. These candles are used to banish negativity or send evil to the grave.

Wax Balls or Jack Balls

You can use your herbal blends and powders by rolling them in balls of warm beeswax or you can melt the beeswax first to liquid, then stir in the herbal blend or powder, adding other ingredients such as bits of torn paper as you roll the cooling wax in your hands. Once the balls are at room temperature, empower them and add them to sachets, conjuring bags, or throw them in a ritual fire. I don't recommend burying them or putting them in water as they could kill wildlife.

Beeswax Sheets for Rolling Your Own Candles

Natural or colored beeswax sheets can be purchased at a local hobby store or you can buy them in bulk online. Your candles will perform better if you keep the following tips in line:

- Cut the sheets lengthwise in half so that your candle stands about 4 inches tall. This size seems to burn better and longer. You can use the entire 4 x 17-inch length to roll your candle or you can cut the 4 x 17-inch piece into smaller pieces for chime candles: 4 x 2½ inches makes a beautiful chime candle with the same burn time as purchased paraffin chime candles.

- Make sure you have the correct size wick for the diameter of the candle you wish to roll.

- Place your powders (only a little is needed) along the bottom edge of the beeswax before you roll it and after you have softened the wax with a heat gun or hair dryer. This way the load is at the bottom of the candle and is less of a fire hazard.

- Roll tightly for a longer burn.

- Be sure to smooth the outer seam on the candle so that it blends into the layer below. If you don't do this, your candle will burn too fast.

By rolling your own candles, you have complete control over the magickal pattern process and, even better, it only takes about three minutes or less to roll your own candle for a specific intent on the fly. Let's say a friend calls you and asks for healing energy after surgery. It will take you only a few minutes to sprinkle bonesetter healing powder across the bottom of the beeswax sheet, add a dash of magickal oil or a drop of the liquid fluid condenser, and roll it up, chanting as you go. You can do a full process of releasing, setting your hands, setting the field, rolling, and then sealing all in that individual's name in a matter of minutes.

The process makes you feel truly magickal because you have created the candle for your intent yourself without hours of pouring wax or having to go to the store to pick up the right color or the right type. By putting your special touch to the candle with herbal powders, the fluid condenser, and so on, you have a fully charged vehicle that matches your energy pattern and the pattern of your intent. I have even taken very tiny strips of paper and written the person's name on it, then rolled the paper slip in the candle, making sure the paper is at the very bottom. I have never had a problem with this; however, fire safety precautions should be taken just in case. I blow repeatedly on the candle as I'm swiftly rubbing it with my palms, running energy into my hands and then into the candle. I may do this for several minutes until I lose the thought. Then I light the candle and watch it burn to see how the situation might proceed with the work I have done.

You can also make beeswax petition sandwiches to be burned in out-door ritual fires. Cut two pieces of colored beeswax so that the sizes are identical; they don't have to be large. Write your petition (desire) on brown paper and dress with your favorite magickal oil, fluid condenser, perfume, etc. Place the paper on one section of beeswax. Top with herbs of choice and finish with the second piece of beeswax. Squeeze the "sandwich" together as part of your empowerment process. Throw these magickal wax packets into your bonfire at the appropriate ritual moment of your choice. This is a creative way to use leftover pieces of beeswax rather than throwing them in the trash.

Using Planetary Glyphs as Runes and Conduits to Manifestation

According to Rolla Nordic, a student of Madeline Montalban (sometimes spelled Madelyn Montalbin, a pseudonym for Sylvia Royals), "In ancient times each rune (planetary glyph) was a talisman made on a special day and blessed with a particular spell. Early man used the stones for guidance, inspiration, and warning."[19]

Using the planetary glyphs as rune vehicles is an easy, delightful way to learn the planetary energies and how they apply to a variety of circumstances. They can be employed for predictive purposes or for focusing on a particular energy in a spell, ritual, or meditation. If you need to know what energy to apply to a specific day or event, select a planetary rune! The following information is a brief compilation of my research and experience using the planets for divination and magick.

Paint the glyphs of the planets on stones or small pieces of wood. You can even use slips of paper to start, and if you really like using the glyphs in your work, you can create a set out of clay, wood, beeswax, or stone later on.

Cleanse, bless, and empower your planetary runes on a Sunday or a Wednesday, or you can make the glyph on its corresponding day in the planetary hour that best matches each rune—meaning you will be drawing, cleansing, blessing, and empowering one or two runes per day according to the information given in chapter 2.

When empowering your runes, using them for magick, or calling upon the planetary energies for assistance, you may find the following invocation useful in your work:

The Invocation of the Planets

Seven planets light the heavens
Seven metals rule the stars.
Seven angels stir the magick
Seven spirits bring the charge.
Seven beasts and seven birds
Seven drums beat out the word.
Seven chakras, seven days
Seven pillars, seven rays

---

19 This quote about using planetary glyphs as a divinatory tool is from a November 1972 magazine article in Sybil Leek's *Astrology Magazine* (page 16).

Seven powers, force and form
Come to me, the change is born
Blend together into one
Bless this place; my will be done!

Intone the names of the seven archangels slowly or intone the seven classical planetary energies slowly (Sun, Moon, Mars, Mercury, Venus, Jupiter, Saturn) in the order that you desire. I have given a selection of angelic names below:

> *Michael*
>
> *Anael*
>
> *Raphael*
>
> *Gabriel*
>
> *Cassiel*
>
> *Sachiel*
>
> *Samael*
>
> *So be it!*

Note: This angelic lineup was taken from the *Conciliator* of Pietro d'Abano, written in 1303 but first published at Venice in 1471. The system is from the scholar Averroes (1126–1198).[20]

There are several ways to read planetary glyphs—you can choose one at a time from a bag or toss them in the left hand (to learn what is coming toward you) and drop them on a soft cloth (I wrap my glyphs in a soft cloth to protect them and then use the cloth as a divinatory reading surface). If, however, you wish to learn what action you should take on a particular matter, then tossing them with your dominant hand is in order. Only those faceup are often read; however, a full reading can include those facedown as hidden energies that are not in play with the particular question but are active just the same. If you would like to read for an individual other than yourself, you can place their photo or an item that belongs to them on the cloth. If the person is present, they can shake the glyphs and scatter them or you can ask them to place a piece of jewelry or a coin on the cloth so that the glyphs can attune to their energy. As with

---

20 Agrippa, *Three Books of Occult Philosophy*, 535.

any divination tool, the glyphs will show the most likely path; you can change what falls if you don't like it simply by applying the runic energies to spellwork, ritual, or meditation to divert the energy in a different direction. Cleanse the glyphs with salt water, holy water, a crystal gemstone, moonlight, or sunlight after each reading to remove connections.

Generally, runes that fall on top of each other or right next to each other indicate a particular theme or event. Runes to the right of the center object speak of the past; to the left, the future; above, conscious mind; and below, subconscious mind. The farther away the rune is to the center indicates the level of power it has at this moment.

Commanding Planetary Energies

Your planetary runes can also be commanded to work for you in ritual, spellwork, and daily life. The process is very easy and improves the more you use it. Simply visualize the glyph of the planet in your mind and connect with the planetary energy, then apply that energy through spoken command and visualization to do what you wish. I first learned to do this with the planet Mercury. I live in a rural area, and I was constantly having problems with the internet and my computer. One day, deep in winter, I couldn't get either the internet or the computer to work properly. I was extremely frustrated as at the time, I had an Etsy business and was trying to take care of my orders. I walked outside, held my right hand up to the sky, and called out Mercury's name three times. I envisioned the sigil of Mercury glowing in the air before me. Then I said, "*I conjure thee, Mercury! By thy power, I command thee to swiftly fix my internet and computer problems without costing me any more money or time! I know you will do this for me!*" I said both statements three times in a loud and booming voice (because I was angry) and then went back in the house, had a cup of coffee, and returned to my office. I sat down at the computer and figured, "Well, I will try this one more time!" And it worked.

About a week later it happened again, and I did the same thing. Once more I grumbled back into the office and the problem was fixed. I actually went through this process several weeks in a row; each time I was able to get the equipment to work. Then I thought, if I can do this with

Mercury, what can I do with the other planetary energies? I began experimenting with each one with great success.

In the meantime, after analyzing what my internet problems might be, I called the company handling my service and told them that the dish was misaligned. Sure enough, it was, and it was fixed for free. As to the computer problem, my husband went to work and asked the IT fellow in the office what the error message I kept getting meant. It was a simple fix. No money involved.

In my planetary experiments I would always sync myself with the planetary energy first. For example, I would think of the sigil of the planet and what its powers were that I knew of. Then I would visualize the glyph shining out in front of me as I commanded it. If I were working with a magickal powder or candle, I would sink the glyph image held in my mind into the powder or candle, allowing it to glow as long as I could embrace the visualization. Right before I knew I was about to lose the image, I would imagine it melting into the object.

Sometimes I would say, "Universe! I *command the power of Mercury to* [add intention here]. *I know you will do this for me!*" That works too.

General Planetary Rune Meanings for Divination, Spellwork, and Daily Life

In chapter 3 we covered the basic energy patterns of each planet (under the planetary hours section), giving correspondences and associations. The information presented below is a keyword version that you may find useful in your work. The first word in all caps is a keyword for easier learning.

Sun: SUCCESS—aggression, authority, confidence, courage, determination, dignity, faith, individualism, leadership, loyalty, optimism, poise, power, reliance, vitality, will

Moon: FEELINGS—birth, creativity, domestic, flexible, food, growth, imagination, intuition, kindness, magnetism, maternal, matter, mother, peace, protection, psychism, receptivity, sympathy, women, visions

Venus: MAGNETISM—adult women, affection, art, beauty, blending, consideration, cooperation, courtesy, devotion, evasion, education, feminine, friends, gentle, group work, harmony, love, originality, refinement, social activities, vacillation

Mars: ACTION—adult males, assertion, beginnings, combat, construction, courage, defiance, destruction, energy, force, independence, leadership, movement, passion, self-reliance, sex, speed, spontaneity, violence, winning

Mercury: COMMUNICATION—adaptability, agility, analysis, awareness, brilliant, changeable, children, critical, discriminatory, efficient, intelligent, messages, paperwork, reason, siblings, versatile, written communication, young males

Jupiter: EXPANSION—benevolence, charity, confidence, dignity, expansion, extravagant, faithful, generous, government, growth, humor, kindness, mercy, optimism, philanthropic, poise, religious, travel

Saturn: LIMITS AND REWARDS—antiques, authority, crossroads, defense, diplomacy, justice, patience, responsibility, restraint, reward from hard work, rules, senior citizens, serious, sincere, structure, thrifty, time

Neptune: ILLUSION—addiction or mental illness, angel work, channeling, dreams, fantasy, imagination, instinct, meditation, mystical work, listening, lying, psychism, purification, spirituality, spiritual healing, wisdom

Uranus: INNOVATION—astrology and planetary work, charm, clarity, divination, eccentric, equality, freedom, good outcome, group work, humankind, internet, inventive, imagination, networking, new trends, objectivity, originality, technology

Pluto: CHANGE—banish, blackmail, compulsions, crisis skills, debts, destruction, dissolution, empowerment, exorcism, inheritance, intensity, investigative, lies, magick, power, secrets, self-mastery, transformation, wills

Astrological Significator Candles and Powders

Astrological significator candles (sometimes called astral candles) represent the individual that is the focus of a magickal working. This candle is the center point to which various activities can be directed (healing, protection, success, etc.). Ideally, the candle should correspond to the individual's astrological sign according to their birthdate through both color and ingredients either already in the candle or placed upon the candle (fragrance, magickal oil, herb or gem inclusions). When you ritually bond an individual to a significator candle, it is believed that a pathway is formed that connects the energy you are manipulating in the working to that individual in a clear, unblocked way. Unlike other magickal candles, a significator candle can be used repeatedly as long as it is employed for the same person. This means you can use a container candle or large pillar in repeated workings for the same individual.

Originally, correspondences for astral significator candles were established by blending the energy patterns of colors, herbs, and fragrances with the mathematical positions of the stars in the heavens, specifically the twelve astrological signs and their planetary rulers. It was felt that by combining these items, a synergy was created that would heighten the focus and power of the working and create a stronger connection to the individual in need of assistance. Historically, the sign placement of an individual was based on his or her rising sign (not the sun sign). Eventually, the focus shifted to the sun sign as the individual's significator. For a complete ritual, three signs can be used—the sun sign, the moon sign, and the rising sign. Most practitioners only use the sun sign when choosing the significator candle, saving the other two signs for use if the situation is severe.

Currently, when you search astral candles on the net, you will find a list of colors and instructions for pouring one color over another to create an astral candle. This practice dates back to a chapbook entitled A *Candle to Light Your Way*, published in 1941 by Mikhail Strabo, a pseudonym of

Sydney J. R. Steiner, the Jewish American proprietor of Guidance House Publishing based out of New York. Steiner wrote several books on Hoodoo and Spiritualism. The author does not give a reference to the origin of these correspondences or color practices in the book. Keep in mind also that the range of colors for candles in 1941 was significantly less than it is today.

Because astral significator candles are formulated on correspondences based on the astrological signs, they also can be used when doing a working when the moon or the sun is in that sign. For example, if you wanted to work for financial stability, you would burn a Taurus astrological significator candle dressed with a money oil when the moon is in Taurus. To fine-tune the ritual, you would burn that candle in the hour of Venus (the ruler of Taurus). If you wanted to learn a secret, you would burn a Scorpio astrological significator candle when the moon is in Scorpio and in a Mercury (information) hour. If you needed to do a working for healing a female friend but have no idea when she was born, you would burn a Cancer astrological significator candle on a Monday in the hour of the moon. Beside the significator candle you would burn a candle that contains healing herbals or fragrances, or is dressed with a healing correspondence magickal oil. Alternatively, you could burn the candle when the moon is in the sign of Cancer.

Astrological Signs

Aries: 21 March to 20 April

Taurus: 21 April to 21 May

Gemini: 22 May to 21 June

Cancer: 22 June to 22 July

Leo: 23 July to 22 August

Virgo: 23 August to 23 September

Libra: 24 September to 23 October

Scorpio: 24 October to 22 November

Sagittarius: 23 November to 21 December

Capricorn: 22 December to 20 January

Aquarius: 21 January to 19 February

Pisces: 20 February to 20 March

Colors Associated with Astrological Candles

Aries: red

Taurus: green

Gemini: light yellow, light blue, or silver

Cancer: pink or aqua

Leo: gold or harvest gold

Virgo: blue or bright yellow

Libra: lavender or purple

Scorpio: dark red, burgundy, or very dark blue

Sagittarius: orange

Capricorn: brown

Aquarius: electric blue or pink

Pisces: aqua or purple

Simple Astral Candle Protection Spell

Choose the astral candle appropriate for the individual for whom you are working. With a stylus or nail, write the person's name on the astral candle if you can. Wrap their picture in tinfoil. If you don't have a photo, use their name written on a piece of paper to encase in the foil. Choose a second candle associated with protective correspondences and set that candle beside the astral candle. Cast a protective circle or intone a prayer of cleansing and protection. Hold the astral candle in your hands and concentrate on the individual it represents. See a silver line of energy extending from the candle in your hands to the third eye of the person. Hold this visualization for as long as you can. Repeat the person's name nine times, making it rhythmic and singsong. Place the astral candle on top of the tinfoil packet and beside the protection candle. Encircle both candles with an unbroken line of salt. Hold your hands over both candles and specifically instruct them to work for you:

Scent and color, wax and wick
Blend together, make it stick
Fill thee now with harmony
As I will, so shall it be.

Light both candles. Take several deep breaths, allowing yourself to relax. As you breathe in, fill yourself with energy from the field around you. Connect with Spirit to heighten the experience. Move from that connection while breathing to connecting to the person you are working for, visualizing that you are breathing protective energy into them and around them. See this energy as white or golden light. Hold the visualization as long as you can. Add a protection chant of your choice or repeat "*Protection for (person's name).*" When you lose focus, the work is done. Seal the working by drawing an equal-armed cross in the air over the candles. Finish with "*I know you will do this for me!*" Allow the candles to burn at least ten minutes. Light the candles every day until you feel the working is no longer necessary. Refresh the packet and candles whenever you feel necessary or at least every thirty days.

Tips on Gathering Grave Dirt for Powders, Magick, and Ritual

They say that when no one else will help you, the dead (your ancestors) will come through. I believe this and have seen it occur many times. One way to make the connection to deceased loved ones is the ritual gathering of grave dirt that will be used later in a variety of magickal workings. Here are some cemetery dirt collecting tips my husband and I have used with great success.

First, follow the rules of the cemetery—you don't have to creep around after dark with pail and spade to collect the dirt you will need. Dirt gathered in daylight works just as well as those furtive scoops purloined in the dead of night. If you need a lookout, take someone with you who is in agreement with what you are doing.

Be prepared. A spoon to collect dirt is *not* helpful. Take a good spade. Will you need one container or many? For example, if you will be visiting several specific graves, you may want to keep the dirt separated and label a resealable plastic bag with which dirt belongs to whom. For general work, we carry cut flowers in a large coffee can; that way we don't look crazy lugging a bucket and a shovel. The large coffee container with flowers hides the spade. Some of the flowers will be left at the gate of the graveyard as an offering to the guardians of the cemetery. We also pour white rum on the ground, say a prayer of protection, and use a lit cigar as incense at the gate. A burning white dressed coach candle declares you come in peace. Dirt from the entrance area is useful for "opening the way" in magickal endeavors. The honoring at the gate is thought to keep anything negative from attaching itself to you, allowing you to leave freely and protected, as well as acknowledging the Spirit of the Crossroads and the power that he holds. To ensure nothing decides to come home with you, soak a piece of cloth in vinegar; after it dries, put it in your pocket to carry with you during your stay in the cemetery.

Once inside, know where you are going. Taking dirt from a random grave can work; however, just whose dirt will you be using? Rather than risk negativity, research is the key, particularly if you plan to take the dirt from a stranger's grave, such as a military or religious personage. Better to use the dirt of a trusted relative or friend if you are in any way unsure. Be careful, by the way, with military graves—it can be illegal to gather the dirt; however, if you are in battle and need the help, and there is no legal issue with the cemetery, a formidable soldier will absolutely do the job. The most powerful dirt we have ever used was from Molly Pitcher's grave. To seal the bond between yourself and the soldier's grave, leave a quarter on the headstone as a sign of honor. Before taking the dirt, utter a prayer of protection for yourself and one of blessing for the deceased. Knock three times on the headstone to awaken the power. Clearly state your purpose aloud. You can also make a petition, such as "Grandma, Susie is in real trouble." Talk to them just like you would talk to anyone. They will hear you. Make the sign of the pentacle on the ground before you dig, then proceed to fill your coffee can. When you are finished, remember to say thank you. Always leave an offering at the gravesite where you took the dirt. Research is extremely helpful here regarding favorite flowers, food, beverages, pictures, toys, etc. Some cemeteries won't let you leave anything but flowers, and then only if you place them in a specific way. If this is the case, pour a libation on the ground and take the container with you. We have also buried items—mainly pennies—where they cannot be seen.

Back home, label your container(s) with the specific date and place where the dirt was taken. If you took two containers with you—one for the dirt from the gate and one for the dirt from the grave—be sure to mark the difference between the receptacles. This is particularly helpful if you are making seven cemetery dirt, where you must visit seven different cemeteries (it's a very potent mix, but it does take time). Dry your dirt in the sunlight; you can put it in your oven at 200 degrees, but this stinks up the house. Sift the dried dirt through an old house screen or mesh colander to remove rocks, pebbles, grass, weeds, and other odd things. Grind the sifted dirt in a ritual circle with mortar and pestle until it becomes a fine powder. A few drops of magickal oil can be used to enhance your formula if you have a particular purpose in mind. If not, store the dirt in a marked canning jar or another airtight container where it can be accessed for a variety of purposes, from banishing nasty people to enhancing a working with help from the dead.

The dead often answer prayers by giving you time, tools, or opportunities in which to take wise action. If you do not seize the opportunity, the assistance is lost. Always pay attention to what is going on around you when you ask for help from the dead, particularly your dreams and the synchronicity of events. Sometimes the most commonplace occurrences are the answer.

Nine Ways to Use Nails, Needles, and Pins with Herbal Magicks

Just how many ways are there to use nails in herbal magick? Many old spells call for the use of coffin nails or nails in general. These days it is tough to acquire legitimate ones, and I have found that wood finishing nails perform very well in place of the traditional coffin nails. Needles and pins can also be extremely useful, particularly when working with fruits and vegetables.

To Keep Out Ghosts: Soak two nails in vinegar or, even better, four thieves vinegar. Pound two nails into a door or window frame—one on the right and one on the left. Perfect if one is suffering from nightmares, night terrors, or children who claim to see ghosties! Empower a combination of thyme, hops, frankincense, and larkspur in a conjuring bag for double ghostbusting power.

To Bring Good Fortune: Paint three nails with gold paint and cover with gold glitter. Use in workings to draw good fortune to you. Wrap nails in paper money, secure with gold thread, and dot with honey or money drawing oil. Add goldenseal herbs to increase the profits of business. Golden needles can be used to replace the nails.

To Banish Evil People: Write the name of the bad person (murderer, thief, abuser, etc.) on a piece of brown paper. Dot paper with vinegar or coat the paper with "send it to the grave" magickal powder. Fold the paper away from you. Nail paper to a dead tree or to the ground in a graveyard.

To Banish Sickness or Disease: Place nine nails, nine pins, nine needles, and broken glass in a jar laced with vinegar. Breathe into the jar nine times, then repeat this Braucherei charm nine times: "*Tetter, tetter, thou has nine sisters; Goddess, bless my flesh and preserve my bones. Perish thou tetter, and be thou gone!*" (*Tetter* means "monster" or "evil being.") Cap. Seal the jar with an equal-armed cross. Place the jar in an eastern window. Repeat the charm once a day for nine days. On the ninth day dispose of the bottle out of the living environment. Add motherwort to the jar if family protection is your goal.

To Banish Chronic Illness: Rub a potato over the sick person. Paint three nails or pins with earth fluid condenser. Pound the three nails into the potato. Place the potato outside under a rain spout. Command the potato: "*As thou rot, so the disease will be taken away from (person's name). I will it so!*" Repeat the command nine times.

To Keep Evil from Entering the Home: Soak a handful of pins in a solution of white sage, rosemary, lemon verbena, Beth root, and vinegar for three days over the dark of the moon. On the last day bless the pins and command them to keep evil and negativity from entering the home. Insert the pins in a fresh lemon—the more pins you have, the better. Hang the lemon inside the threshold or entryway to your home. Replace every three months.

Protection of a Person: Draw an upright triangle on a piece of paper. Put the individual's name to be protected in the center. Add a photo if you can. Put a Himmelsbrief (German letter of protection) on top of the picture. Sprinkle with a protection herbal powder. Dress three nails with a fluid condenser designed for security work. Lay each nail at a point of the triangle, sharp point facing out. Place a protection candle inside the triangle and on top of the Himmelsbrief. Place a banishing candle outside of the triangle. Light both candles, petitioning deity for assistance. Ring the triangle with nine bay leaves for extra protection.

Good Fortune Knots and Nails: Tie seven nails about one inch apart on a long piece of twine (green is best). Make sure they are secure! Fill a conjuring bag with money drawing herbs, a magnet, and your name on a piece of paper. Dress the bag and each nail on the twine with money drawing or attraction oil. Run your hands over the knots and nails (toward you), starting with the nail and knot closest to the bag down to the nail at the other end, saying first: "*I make the bond and establish a secure connection between easy money and me. Money comes to me easily.*" Breathe on the conjuring bag seven times, then chant the following three times as you touch each nail: "*Seven days and seven nights, seven waves and seven lights, seven mountains, seven stars, work my will by my desire. Money, money on the way, the bond is made this very day!*"

Destroy a Glamoury: There are some folks who just always seem to get away with theft, cruelty, gossip, lies, and, worse, murder. It is as if there is some shield surrounding them where they simply escape responsibility on a repeated basis. These con artists aren't just in the criminal world—we see them time and again operating in everyday society, manipulating circumstances so that others are innocently harmed. For this working, you will need one tomato (the more acidic, the better), the individual's name written on a slip of paper dressed with universal fluid condenser, and three pins. As you pierce the paper with the pins, command the powers of Mars to burn away all glamouries so that the individual will be seen and captured for the evil they have done. Cut a slit in the tomato and place the pinned paper inside. Add Mars herbal powder in the slit. Squeeze the tomato closed slowly, envisioning that the juices are the individual's true nature being forced to the surface of their aura so that everyone can see the evil they have done and continue to do. When you lose the thought, immediately throw the tomato in the garbage to rot.

Aura and Spiritual Cleansing

In Braucherei there is an adage that says, "You didn't get sick in a day; you don't get well in a day." Whether you are focusing on health, finances, or relationships, life is a series of energy events and choices that lead us to any one moment. By practicing cyclical spiritual cleansing techniques, we release negativity that can inhibit our work, which gives us a clear field in which to operate. Sometimes, particularly in our darkest hour, we allow a problem or issue to overtake our minds, forgetting that moving forward into a better existence requires a series of steps, not a cataclysmic event. A spiritual/aura cleansing is an excellent first step. You don't need to be capable of taking a giant leap—one action at a time will do. Any type of spiritual cleansing should incorporate a three-pronged approach: cleansing of the body (which includes the energy bodies), cleansing of the mind, and cleansing of the environment where the body spends most of its time or where it receives the most amount of stress. Once you have performed your cleansing activities, I believe you should add a positive endeavor to fill the void made by the banished negative energy. Some practitioners burn a sweet floral candle or scatter glitter to welcome in directed attraction energy.

Many years ago author Ray Malbrough taught me the importance of spiritual cleansing in preparation for my coronation in spiritism. His work has significantly affected my life and my magickal practices. The following spiritual cleansing technique can be used by yourself or done in a group format (which can be incredibly powerful when the group focuses on each person in attendance). The ritual is herbal and word driven, meaning the words and the herbs chosen carry marked power in the proceedings.

As you read through the ritual, please understand that you can change whatever you like; what is important is the sincere action of accepting the cleansing process and the results. This is only one way that I do spiritual cleansings; I have several. I usually adjust the cleansings to the needs of the individual and the circumstances presented at the moment. I will always look at the sign the moon is in, the phase of the moon, and the planetary hour before a cleansing so that I fully understand what energies I have available that can enhance the working.

Many people think that a spiritual cleansing is a once-and-done affair; no. As a rule, I do a complete spiritual cleansing once a month—more if I have experienced a heightened level of stress. A spiritual cleansing can help to banish negativity that others send toward you; by keeping your field balanced and filled with light and good thoughts, you can deflect this negativity. Whenever I am ill, I will drag my carcass into the bathroom and perform a complete spiritual cleansing that includes a shower. I know I feel awful, but I also know that this is my best effort for a speedy healing. I have never been disappointed in the results.

How do you know that the cleansing has worked? If you feel at peace at the conclusion of the cleansing, it has definitely worked. The effects won't last long if you continue to flood your mind with negative thoughts. It is necessary to keep that effort going and to try to rise above the hatred, sickness, fear, or worry that is emanating from your mind.

Who is the winner?

You are!

Spiritual Cleansing Ritual

Supplies

Two white candles, a bowl of blessed water, bells or rattles, an herbal cleansing blend of your choice, and a rolled sage bundle or sweetgrass bundle (the collection of herbs in this example includes white sage, lemongrass, lemon verbena, slices of lemon, hyssop, olive leaf, African basil, lavender, and rosemary), sea salt. Dried or fresh herbs can be used. White carnations (or any cut fresh white flowers). If you are using dried herbals, place them in a white conjuring bag. This bag will be put in the bowl of blessed water with the lemon slices.

Preparation

Have your supplies ready with easy access. I've done this cleansing in good health and in illness, and I've found that having the supplies close to me and ready to go is an added benefit. I keep tools and herbs dedicated to spiritual cleansings in a particular box so that I can use the collection at a moment's notice for myself and others. This box contains a small ceramic plate, a natural rattle, a bell, a natural bath sponge, and cleansing herbs in packets that I've made up during specific moon phases. It also has a lighter, a large quartz crystal, a large smoky quartz crystal, white aura cleansing tea candles and white coach candles, candle holders, aura cleansing spring water spray, white conjuring bags, and a rolled sage bundle. Sometimes I use all the tools; sometimes I do not.

The Ritual

You can cast a magick circle or you can create sacred space by cleansing the area with burning white sage or burning sweetgrass; if you are allergic to smoke, sprinkle the area with a cleansing mist of your choice or a combination of blessed water and sea salt.

Light two white candles and hold them on either side of the individual to be cleansed. If this is you, sit in between the two lit white candles. Connect with your idea of divinity, taking several calming breaths.

Take the sea salt in your hands, rubbing it between your palms. As you do this, intone the following as many times as necessary. Blow into your palms three times after reciting the words—this is to push negativity off of your body.

> *May sickness be no more*
> *May unhappiness be no more*
> *May worry be no more*
> *May hatred be no more*
> *May fear be no more*
> *I cleanse myself of all negativity!*

These words can be changed to suit the circumstances. Let's say you are having a problem with jealousy (yours or someone else's), greed, pain, etc. Craft the words to suit your circumstances.

If you are working with other people, they can be using rattles, bells, and drums during this process.

Take the white flowers and run them all over your body, intoning the same words as before:

> *May sickness be no more*
> *May unhappiness be no more*
> *May worry be no more*
> *May hatred be no more*
> *May fear be no more*
> *I cleanse myself of all negativity!*

When you are finished, break the flowers, drop them to the ground, and step on them.

If you are working with other people, have them surround the person and walk around that individual while making sounds with the bells and rattles. Their focus is cleansing the person and the space around the individual. If you are alone, take the time to find a rhythm with bells or rattles and allow your mind and emotions to let go of all negativity. Allow yourself to transcend.

When you begin to feel a change come over yourself, connect with the sea of potential as indicated in chapter 1 of this book. I am putting the words here so you don't have to flip back to that section:

The sea of potential is all around me.
The sea of potential is in me.
The sea of potential is around me and in me…
And I activate this sea for spiritual cleansing
of all levels of my mind, body, and soul.

Say those words three times, and as you do, feel yourself floating in that sea that permeates your entire being.

Take a deep breath, then place the bowl of blessed water in front of you, between the two white candles. Put the white conjuring bag that contains the dried herbs in the bowl. Add to this a dash of sea salt and the fresh lemon slices. I have found that doing this practice slowly and with peaceful intent can be helpful. Stir the water with your hand several times. Watch the light play across the water. Let yourself merge with the blessed water.

The next step is a rather long prayer. As you say the prayer, dip your hands in the water, then rub your wet hands together. Do this several times during the recitation of the prayer.

Spirit of the Divine, the place of the center, I call thee and ask for
your help and assistance in this work. Empower my actions with
your aid. Please send the positive vibrations of my request to that
which orchestrates the universe and vibrates to the correct pattern
of energy assistance for (state person's name), and do not stop
until the working has manifested on the earth plane in the body,
mind, and soul of (state person's name). To you, I confide my
need: (repeat request). Graciously take this cause in hand and let
this prayer not end without having experienced in some way the
effects of your intercession. I know you will do this for me!

Sprinkle some of the water from the bowl on your body (or the person you are working for).

Hold your hands out in front of you, palms up. Intone the names of each of the five elements, beginning with air. As you intone the words, close your eyes and visualize the power of that element in your hands. Make a note of which element or elements seem stronger to you as you go through the sequence. The sequence is air, fire, water, earth, spirit. When you have finished, take several deep breaths. Again, you will transcend this time, higher than before.

Cross your hands over your heart, as if to pull the energy of the five elements into your body. Intone the following prayer (make any adjustments you prefer, try to keep from being too wordy).

> *Spirit of the Divine, bring me into harmony with the perfection*
> *of the universe. May my higher consciousness hear my voice and*
> *vibrate to create my own healing on all levels of my being. If I*
> *have done anything that facilitates the past negativity I have*
> *experienced in my life, may it be cleared from me immediately.*
> *May I experience a blending of health, healing, harmony, and*
> *gratitude, and may this perfection rebound in my soul and fill*
> *me with the grace of joy and positive energy. With every breath*
> *I take, happiness I make. With every breath I take, joy I make.*
> *With every breath I take, peace I make. With every breath I take,*
> *love I make. So be it!*

Draw an equal-armed cross in the air to seal the working. Dispose of the candles, herbs, broken flowers, and water. Thank the spirits of the plants for assisting you, and leave an offering outside in gratitude for your spiritual cleansing.

You can adjust this technique to cleanse an animal or any object you desire.

Fast Cleansing Techniques

There are many times when a full cleansing cannot be performed. Try these fast methods in a pinch.

Breathe Deeply Several Times: When problems hit, we often forget to *breathe!* Nice, long, deep breaths help to connect you to spiritual energy as well as cleanse the body.

Take a Bath or a Shower: Water is the great spiritual cleanser. A scented bath or shower along with chants of well-being can do wonders in any situation. If time or place is a problem, hold your hands under cool running water. Remember to say to yourself, "I know everything will work out just fine" or "I know everything will be okay." These statements energize the field around you, tapping into the positive potential available and fueled with the vibratory essence of the running water. The statement directs the mind to focus on the solution, not tangle the pathway by worry.

Use an Herbal Blend or Mix (Fresh or Dried): Connect to the herbal world through scent and touch to eliminate stress and rejuvenate the mind. Grind dried herbs into a powder and use in your workings. By surrounding a candle with an herb mix or powder, you are connecting the internal world of your thoughts to the external world, where your desire will manifest. The herbals provide a link —a bridge from the unseen to the seen. Be sure to cleanse and bless your herbs before use. Be clear on your direction and intent. The aroma of the herbs alone can help to erase worry and stress, allowing the mind to focus on the needed solution.

Use Bells or Rattles: These quickly break apart negativity in your environment. While you are at it, pick up all the clutter. Dirt and clogged space hold negative energy fast. Clean and move to get things going again.

Use a Braucherei Technique: Place an egg (raw and still in the shell) in a bowl where it won't be broken. Chant a protective or cleansing charm over the egg, then command the egg to take on any negativity in the room. Remove in twenty-four hours and place under a rain spout. In Braucherei it is believed that the running water from the spout will destroy the negativity collected by the egg.

Using Magickal Doodles
as Sigils for Enchantments

Doodling on paper isn't silly—it is actually a way to channel thoughts into a single focus. Experts tell us that doodling on a scrap of paper is a window to your inner world. In fact, there is a vast pool of study on why people doodle and what those doodles actually mean (in a general sense)—just like interpreting handwriting!

Ladders, squares, and triangles indicate your willingness to work toward your goals. They are symbols of a go-getter—an achiever. Stars show optimism and hope. Flowers and hearts mean a sensitive soul and love. Shapes in 3-D can say that you are willing to see the big picture. A spiderweb can mean one of two things—you feel trapped or you want to trap someone. Dots indicate the situation is unstable or the doodler believes the issue is shaky. Cubes mixed with spirals and circles might mean a solution is possible, but the doodler is unsure of exactly where to find the answer. It can also mean that the doodler really would rather be doing something better with their time! If you don't believe me, do a Google search using the keywords *psychological meaning of doodles*. The top ten will give you a broad range of explanations. Next time someone bugs you for a reading, tell them to doodle instead! (Just kidding.)

Doodles can also indicate what you really think about a person you are talking to or the situation they are describing. Have you ever had a long conversation on the phone and found yourself doodling around the information you took down as a result of the call? When you are finished, take a closer look at your doodle. Not only will your mind have transferred the main points of the conversation to paper, but it will also tell you exactly what you think or feel about that conversation. Even better, your doodle is an effort to map out a solution (should the call have been an issue where an answer is needed) and how you really feel about acting on the advice you may have given or a promise you said you would keep.

The doodle shown on page 179 is the result of someone talking (at length) about the problems they were having at work. They felt trapped, ineffectual, and at a loss for an immediate positive solution. A hard worker, the frustration is mounting, as several individuals at the place of employment are actually working on the baser side of life—lying, cheating, and incredibly narcissistic, creating unfeasible requirements that eat into the individual's private time. Their actions (there are three of them) are severely affecting the rest of the office. Unfortunately, the person in charge is never there and is either jetting around the world or, when in the area, having drunk-fest parties at his private cabin, not giving the least amount of attention to his responsibilities.

What do you see in the example doodle on the following page?

Doodles can also provide a magickal vehicle that allows you to freely focus your thoughts on sigil creation for any given goal, issue, or desire. Magickal doodles are my signature ingredient in many of my powders, herbal blends, and poppets. Once the doodle is completed, I may add other design elements such as a planetary symbol, a circle around the doodle, or runes in a particular area of the design.

Magickal doodles are best done with your eyes closed; that way you can chant and focus entirely on an inner visual image while letting your hand holding the pen glide freely on the paper. You can take as long as you wish to create your doodle, with a general rule that when you have lost the thought, the image is completed.

You can use this doodle in a variety of magickal applications. For example, if you wish to banish a problem, roll the paper away from you and tie the paper with red thread. Pass the rolled paper over your body to draw the negativity out of yourself completely and attach it to the paper. Dot the paper with universal fluid condenser or banishing magickal oil, then burn the paper, confident that the answer you need will be given to you quickly. If you are ill, spit on the paper, add a few drops of universal liquid fluid condenser, and boil the paper in a small amount of water. When the water boils dry, tear the paper up and throw it in the trash. For goal programming and success, burn the paper to ash and add the ashes to another working or scatter the ashes outside. To birth a new venture that includes a desire for stability, wrap the doodle around a rock and sprinkle with earth element magickal powder and an earth element fluid condenser. Bury the rock in the ground on your property or in a flower pot in your home or apartment.

A Magickal Doodle

Creating a Single Number
to Represent Your Intent

There can be a variety of reasons to factor a written intent statement into a single number: the need for secrecy, wanting to know the best number of herbs or other objects to use in a working that exactly matches your desire, or perhaps the number of days that an enchantment will be repeated. You can use the number as a guide for choosing how many candles or gemstones to use, or even for the number of times to ring a ritual bell. The number itself has its own significance, giving you an idea of the strength of your intent in its correlation to what you wish to achieve. The time taken to write out the statement—making sure it is what you desire and then turning that statement into a mathematical vibration—gives the process more power due to the energy you have extended in your crafting. This journey creates confidence because you *know* you took the time to get it right.

One = Beginnings

Two = Partnership

Three = Expansion

Four = Structure

Five = Change

Six = Blending

Seven = Movement

Eight = Self-mastery

Nine = Accomplishment

Ten = Reward or harvest (should you choose to use this number)

The list above represents the meanings I have attributed to the numbers in my work. Numbers carry a plethora of meaning; choose what works for you, what vibrates the best. If you don't like the resulting number of your statement—perhaps it just doesn't feel right—rework your statement and then do the math again.

Using the guidelines given, an example statement of "May my life be filled with joy, happiness, and prosperity in a happy, positive way" factors into the number eight. That's a solid number for this intent, indicating the result is self-mastery, which is exactly what I want. With this number, I will move forward to create a magickal powder using eight ingredients. Are the planets associated with numbers? Yes, they are often found in medieval planetary sigil work (magick squares). Here, I have a more modern list that follows the planetary lineup in our solar system, allowing us to equate a single number to each planet (heavenly body). This list is not to be confused with planetary magick squares or anything else you've seen in other books.

One = Sun (success)

Two = Mercury (communication)

Three = Venus (attraction)

Four = Moon (storehouse)

Five = Mars (action)

Six = Jupiter (expansion)

Seven = Saturn (efficiency/reward)

Eight = Uranus (intensification/individualism/freedom)

Nine = Neptune (creativity/spirituality/camouflage)

Ten = Pluto (empowerment/renewal)

Sticking with my example, the modern planet Uranus, the higher octave of Mercury, is the matching planet. At first, you might say, "That doesn't exactly match happiness," but for me it does. Freedom! I see freedom as a catapult for happiness and joy. Freedom from worry, unhappiness, fear…freedom to see clearly…freedom to work on my passions. So, for me the number is perfect for this statement.

When choosing herbs that have classical associations (seven planets only), you can translate as follows:

- Uranus is the higher octave of Mercury; choose Mercury-ruled herbs

- Neptune is the higher octave of Venus; choose Venus-ruled herbs

- Pluto is the higher octave of Mars; choose Mars-ruled herbs

You don't like my list? No worries. Make your own that vibrates with your needs. Your list is to be a guideline for you that you trust and will use frequently. Your design is best for you. You will also find powder formulas for Uranus, Neptune, and Pluto in chapter 6.

Carrying my example further, to work for a life filled with joy and happiness to match my intent, I would choose eight herbs or ingredients to make my herbal blend or magickal powder, and I will repeat my conjuration (which includes my intent/focus statement) for eight days. One of the ingredients in my powder will be the number eight drawn on my purpose paper, which I will burn and mix the ashes in with the powder.

Those ashes are my eighth ingredient. I could also grind my witness stick (used during the creation of the powder) as one of my ingredients; this would mean I would have six herbal ingredients, one paper ingredient (the ashes of the number) and the powder from the witness stick, which equals eight ingredients. I could draw the number 8 with the powder on a tile and surround that tile with eight candles.

There is no end to your creativity; nothing is wrong. I could also do cord and knot magick, using a length of string that is a multiple of eight and then making eight knots in the string; as I tie each knot, I can repeat my statement of intent. I can carry the cord with me or burn it, making it one of the eight ingredients in the powder. I might even wait for the eighth lunar day or the eighth solar day of the month. Let your intuition be your guide!

How to Turn a Statement into a Magickal Number

Step One: Write out your complete statement, such as "May my life be filled with joy, happiness, and prosperity in a happy, positive way."

Step Two: Remove all duplicate letters: "May ~~my~~ life be ~~filled~~ with joy, ~~happiness, and~~ prosperity ~~in~~ a ~~happy, positive way~~."

M A Y L I F E B D W T H J O P N S R V

Step Three: Using the alphabet sigil key, match the numbers to the letters.

Alphabet Sigil Key

A	1	H	8	O	15	V	22
B	2	I	9	P	16	W	23
C	3	J	10	Q	17	X	24
D	4	K	11	R	18	Y	25
E	5	L	12	S	19	Z	26
F	6	M	13	T	20		
G	7	N	14	U	21		

M	A	Y	L	I	F	E	B	D	W
13+	1+	25+	12+	9+	6+	5+	2+	4+	23+

T	H	J	O	P	N	S	R	V
20+	8+	10+	15+	16+	14+	19+	18+	22

Step Four: Add up all the numbers. Example total is 242.

Step Five: Add the numbers in the sum together: 242 = 2 + 4 + 2 = 8. If the sum is ten or over, continue to add until you have a single digit answer. The single digit is your magickal number for the spell statement "May my life be filled with joy, happiness, and prosperity in a happy, productive way."

Herbal Vinegars for Magick

A book on magickal powders and herbal blends would not be complete without mention of magickal vinegar. The use of vinegar in magick, cooking, healing, and housework dates back over 10,000 years. Its name today, "vinegar," is a French derivative of "sour wine." Vinegar is made from converting any natural sugar (from corn, fruits such as apples and grapes, coconuts, grains like barley and rice, and even potatoes) that is turned into alcohol and then fermented again by adding yeast, where the alcohol is converted to acetic acid. The acidic content of any vinegar varies by type and brand. Most of us buy vinegar rather than making it ourselves, adding additional ingredients for food or magick. When purchasing vinegar to use in magickal applications for banishing (like four thieves vinegar), read the label to choose the brand with the highest acidic content. In your herbal work you may learn about the "mother of vinegar." This is a type of apple cider vinegar that has a significant number of health benefits, including the prevention of cancer, reduction of heartburn, lowering blood pressure and blood glucose levels, weight loss, and even stopping the pain and spread of shingles. Mother of vinegar is identified by the thick strands of sediment lying on the bottom of the bottle. This kind of organic, raw, unpasteurized vinegar is the healer's choice. Vinegar can also remove some pesticides and bacterial growth from fresh produce and be used as a cleaning agent for countertops and windows and even as a hair cleanser and conditioner.

Raw herbs work best in making your own herbal vinegar; however, you can also add magickal powders as well. Wash and dry your chosen herbs and place them in a glass quart canning jar or another glass jar of your choice. Empower the vinegar and warm it. Pour the warm vinegar into the jar filled with your herbs. If you are using a canning jar, place a piece of plastic wrap over the mouth, as the metal lid will react with the vinegar. Label the vinegar with all of the ingredients you used, along with the date you prepared the formula. Be sure to clearly mark if the vinegar is poisonous—you would not want to serve vinegar with horseradish, hot peppers, and grave dirt to dinner guests. Store the vinegar in a dark place for the amount of time you choose (usually two to four weeks). Strain the herbs out of the vinegar and recap the jar for use whenever you need it. I make my magickal vinegar in bulk, so I buy the vinegar in plastic gallon jugs. I warm the container in the sun, then add my herbs and other ingredients. I use an indelible marker and write directly on the plastic all the ingredients, the date, and the unique astrological associations I used such as a dark moon or Mars trine Mercury (to stop gossip).

In magick, vinegar is a balancer and a banisher, removing negativity and assisting in restoring equilibrium in any situation. The herbs or powders you use in your vinegar heighten the focus of the blend. Four thieves vinegar (also called Marseilles vinegar) is a medieval mixture concocted for healing purposes and is one of the most common magickal vinegars used in enchantments. The Marseilles vinegar was supposedly employed by a family of thieves, four brothers, created by their mother so that they could go into plague-infested houses to steal property and remove valuables from the dead bodies. The historical era is debatable, with some indicating the timeframe was the thirteenth century, others the fifteenth century, and even reports from the eighteenth century. As the plague in Europe lasted over six hundred years in one form or another, it is hard to pinpoint when the legend first filtered into public knowledge. The story indicates that due to the vinegar, the thieves did not sicken and die.[21] The ingredients included clove, rosemary, sage, garlic, rue, lavender, and camphor steeped in vinegar.[22] Other formulas included lemon and cinnamon. The thieves soaked a cloth in the mixture and wore the cloth over their noses and mouths. When they were caught by French police, they were offered a reduced sentence if they divulged the secret ingredients of the Marseilles recipe. Since that time the magickal community has developed a host of four thieves vinegar formulas that are offered in printed form or sold in bottles in New Age, Hoodoo, and general magickal shops, and it is considered the go-to blend to rid oneself of negative circumstances and people. The most powerful four thieves vinegar I ever made was on August 25, 2005, during Hurricane Katrina. My formula consisted of rosemary, sage, garlic, lavender, clove, wild rue, hot peppers, lemon slices, and grave dirt.

The shelf life of vinegar is almost indefinite, depending largely upon the preparation and ingredients used. Magickal vinegar is an excellent defensive tool and can be sprinkled or used in bottle magick. Here are a few examples:

- Pour one tablespoon of magickal vinegar into bathwater for protection.

- Sprinkle on the foot tracks of an individual to encourage them to leave you alone. Do this on any day in the planetary hour of Mars.

- Pour on the ground in front of a depraved neighbor's home. You can also pour on a corner of their legal property if you can't get close to the door. A banishment charm should be intoned. This is best done on the dark of the moon.

- In the planetary hour of Mars, add the person's name, written three times, to a small bottle of magickal vinegar. Cap tightly. Bury off your property in the hour of Saturn. Place a stone on top of the place where you buried the bottle. This is a symbol

---

21 Four Thieves Vinegar, Evolution of a Medieval Medicine, July 28, 2016. http://secretofthieves.com/?p-412

22 From *Scientific American Cyclopedia of Formulas* (1910), page 878.

of constraint so that they cannot rise from the spell or escape from the banishing energy. Best done on the dark of the moon.

- Soak small squares of cloth in the herbal vinegar and allow them to dry. Use the material for banishing packets or sachets to ward off sickness and promote healing.
- Food vinegars, those that you have made that are safe to ingest, are used to ward off psychic vampirism; dilute one teaspoon vinegar in a glass of water and drink. It is currently advised by the medical community that you do not drink straight vinegar as it can erode tooth enamel and damage the esophagus over time.
- Pure, unprocessed apple cider vinegar can be used in a spiritual bath (2–4 cups) to destroy negativity or break a curse. It opens the pores and is thought to help in general systemic detoxification.

Salts for Magick and Enchantment

I use salt as a primary carrier for many cleansing and banishing magickal powders. Not only can it be employed to convey the powder, but it can also be boosted with essential oils for bath salts and tub teas. In Braucherei/Pow-Wow, it is generally known that to stop the energy of something, you write the name of the person or event on a piece of paper and put it in the freezer; this stalls the action. To encourage people to be more friendly, you put their name in a sugar bowl. To banish an illness, problem, or individual, you use salt.

Over the years I have created several salt powder compounds for a variety of issues. These compounds can be sprinkled on the ground or rubbed in the hands, placed in poppets (or place poppets directly in the mixture), sprinkled around candles, etc.

Here is a list of salts, along with how I have used them:

Dead Sea Salt: This is my go-to general salt for all banishings and healings. When you need fast enchantment, rub the salt in your hands or on your body, particularly at the base of the back of the neck to break all negativity coming toward you. You can mix the salt with herbal blends to clean out cauldrons or scrub stone altar tops. A salt herb bag can be carried in the purse or pocket and massaged unobtrusively when in the company of negative people. Place the mixture with banishing herbs in a tub tea packet or white cotton conjuring bag and drop in holy water to be used for a spiritual cleansing. Add orange peel powder, chamomile, and peppermint to break bad debt. Adding baking soda and sea salt to the bath is thought to cleanse the auric field.

Gray Sea Salt: Use to break glamouries, remove lies, and change inaccurate perceptions.

Pink Sea Salt: Also known as Himalayan pink sea salt, this is employed to dissolve hatred and unhappiness, remove the pain of a cheating lover, or clear the way to new love. Add spearmint, rosemary, and rose petals to promote wisdom in love choices.

Black Sea Salt: (not the kind mixed with soot, the naturally black salt) Use for all manner of psychic cleansings, for removing ghosts and personal fears, and for breaking addiction work. To remove ghosts from an area, place vinegar in an open glass surrounded with larkspur, white sage, and black sea salt.

Traditional Soot Black Salt: In the 1980s I learned to make what they called witches' black salt, which was used to banish (and sometimes curse) negative energies or people who have harmed you. The blend is messy to make and use due to the activated charcoal base to which salt and other ingredients are added. If it goes gray, you have too much salt in the mixture. Additives include seven cemetery grave dirt (dirt collected from seven different cemeteries), nettles, and sometimes thorns from rose bushes. The blend was prepared on a dark moon on a Saturday, between 12 midnight and 3:00 a.m. or in the hour of Mars or Saturn. Best if done when the moon is in Scorpio. All ingredients are finely ground, then mixed with the activated charcoal. This traditional blend should not be used in soaps or bath salts.

Empowered herbal salts make excellent gifts for magickal friends, especially if you use appealing containers with attractive labels. A general tub tea recipe uses 16 ounces of sea salt and 20–30 drops of a body-safe essential oil. The tub teas can also include magickal powders and herbal blends as long as you have researched the safety of the herbs in regard to medical issues. Essential oils can cause problems with sensitive skin. Be sure to research the essential oil before using it in a tub tea recipe. You should also consult your physician on any essential oils that you use because they can affect individuals with high blood pressure or who are pregnant.

Sacred Spirit Mound

The last exercise/project in this chapter concentrates on blending with the natural spirits in your area. First, take a Spirit Walk and collect as many plants as possible, telling them that you wish to perform a sacred ritual to honor the area, protect what is there, and blend with the spirits of the place. Take as long as you like with your Spirit Walk. You may also find unique stones, unusual leaves, feathers, etc. You will also want to collect nine stones; large or small, this is up to you. You will use them as your sacred circle. Save everything until dawn the following day.

As the sun rises, cast a magick circle and bless the area with an honoring herbal mixture and herbal water (as salt water kills plants). The herbal water can contain cleansing herbs such as lavender and rosemary. The choice is entirely up to you. Do the sea of potential exercise, then stand facing east, holding your right hand so that your palm faces the rising sun. Give the morning greeting adapted from the research of G. Storms in his book *Anglo-Saxon Magic*:

> *Eastwards I stand*
> *For favors I pray*
> *From Goddess Divine*
> *And Lord of the Day.*

Earth lends her power
And breath sends the spell
Day's end will reveal
That all will be well.

State your intent: that you wish to create a sacred mound to honor the area, protect the native plants and animals to your best ability, and blend with the nature spirits of the place.

Dig a hole and place all the items you have collected. You can add any other charms, sigils, trinkets, or objects that you desire. When you are finished, cover the hole and create a small mound. Encircle the mound with nine stones from the area. Seal the working by drawing an equal-armed cross on top of the mound. You can flatten the top of the mound a little if you like so that you can place a candle or lantern there in the days to come. Sit back, relax, and do the sea of potential exercise again, asking that you become one with the spirit of the place. Pay particular attention to any animals or insects that are present during the entire process, as they have messages for you. When you close your eyes, you may see animal eyes in your mind. These are the sacred eyes of Spirit. You may feel incredibly uplifted, at peace, or filled with gentle love; that is nature accepting your request of bonding.

When you are finished with your meditation, thank the place and the spirits and intone a verbal blessing for them.

Be sure to visit your sacred mound often; the spirits will be waiting for you. Bring gifts of flowers, water in a drought, and prayers of love and compassion. The more you work with the spirit mound, the greater the spiritual gifts.

Should you have to move from the area, it is imperative that you visit your sacred spirit mound and indicate why you must go. Leave the mound with a blessing and a gift. When you get to your new home or area, create another sacred spirit mound. You can actually link this mound with the one you left at the old property using the link, sync, and sink technique.

The Chi of Conversation

Every conversation has its own energy, its own pattern, its own chi. In my book *MindLight* I explored the power of your mind in magick and everyday activities. Over time I have learned to listen to the conversations of people and the communication patterns of nature. When we speak to each other, you and I, we usually don't think about the pattern of the conversation. We acknowledge the topic or theme, syncing with each other to make the process enjoyable (hopefully) and desiring (in many cases) to be "in tune" with each other. This feeling of attunement becomes chemical as our emotional responses activate a subconscious energy exchange. Most people don't consider the vast array of energies at play when we speak to each other. We concentrate only on the feelings and then the words. Yes, people talk with feelings first (in most cases), and the formulation of chosen words erupts or floats serenely to the surface, depending on those emotions. This entire combination forms a pattern of energy— what I call the chi of conversation.

I'd like you to think for a moment about a recent positive conversation. Think about how you felt. Reflect on the "pattern" of that conversation. If you could equate the exchange in another form, what would you choose? A color? An aroma? A sound? A thing of nature? Free associate on the mental images that arise from thinking about the discussion, and write down your mental pictures. After a few moments reflect on what you put on the paper.

Now, let's do the same thing with a recent argument or disagreement (or, if you are lucky enough not to have had one, an unpleasant exchange that you remember). It, too, had a pattern, and because you remember it, the pattern is still living! It may be slowly disintegrating, but because you can recall it, the conversation still has its own chi. Write down, as you did before, mental images that you associate with that unfortunate communication. All these mental pictures combined with your feelings are keeping the chi of that conversation alive, and they are (like glue or a nasty, smelly cord) continuing to keep you connected to that person.

In martial arts there is a hand motion that disrupts an individual's chi—a quick fluttering of the hands over the solar plexus area of the opponent that momentarily disrupts a person's energy bodies. This disorientation actually weakens the physical body for a slight window of time. You can cause this same disruption (by various means) in the chi of a conversation. Fluttering your hand over your face as if you are hot, rubbing the palms in a circular motion, concentrating on sinking the water element sigil into their third eye, or moving your hand back and forth in front of you if you are seated at a table are quick methods of chi disruption. All these actions should be subtle. (And you thought those ladies with ornate fans were just having hot flashes.)

Because we have several physical ordinary choices we can make to disrupt or end a conversation, we don't usually think about the energy of the conversation lingering other than in our minds. We can change the subject, we can walk away, or we can punch the person in the nose (not advised). Regardless of the closure we choose in an antagonistic arena, we forget that the chi of that conversation still lives. The pattern is alive, continuing to undulate and move between any two people (or more). It never occurs to most of us to consciously consider the dismantling of that energy other than therapy (where you are carrying all that negative crap on your back like a sack of rotten potatoes years after the initial event took place) or possibly saying "I'm sorry." However, an insincere apology does not carry enough power to displace the original chi of the event.

Let me put it another way: sometimes we are so focused on our hurt feelings that we don't realize the continuing pain is reactivated in our memories because the pattern of the initial event lives on in us and around us. It has attached itself to our energy bodies and, like a leech, it just keeps sucking us dry. This is complicated by our own minds and emotions that have created a perception cocoon around the chi of the conversation. This filtered housing coats the initial negative experience to distance ourselves from the pain; unfortunately, this rationalization makes the stupid thing stronger. Every excuse we make strengthens the original pattern.

The word coupled with the emotion carried upon the breath of life is the pattern of making.

When humans speak aloud, they activate the five elements in and around themselves. Always. Every time. For good or for ill. The power of the word cannot be ignored. Every time you open your mouth and speak, you birth.

The moment you acknowledge the existence of the pattern and your role in the creation of it (no matter how minimal), you have power over it and can quickly and efficiently destroy it and simultaneously dissolve the tentacles of attachment to you.

For one week, I would like you to try the following in every conversation:

- Listen more than you speak.
- Observe while listening or speaking.
- Whenever a conversation turns negative, change the subject.
- Analyze the pattern of the conversation.
- End every conversation on a positive note.

Write down your observations about each day. If any conversation feels negative, at the end of the day dispose of the verbal interchange by agreeing within yourself that you will dismantle it. Visualize the conversation as a net of collected lights, and dissolve the net. As the net dissolves, the lights flicker, dwindle, and go out. When your mind is clear, you have removed the chi of the conversation. To help in this process, you can rub Dead Sea salt (or any of the salt formulas listed in the previous discussion) in your hands as you let go of the negative energy in your mind. Thank the salt, indicating that you are grateful that the conversation no longer affects you, and put the salt in the garbage. If you wish to use a bit more powerful working, mix rose thorns with Dead Sea salt and pour this mixture onto a piece of paper. Envision your feelings and the memory of the conversation sinking into the paper. Call on the animal spirits of the Raven and the Wolf. Roll up the paper and burn it, saying as many times at it takes to mentally let go:

> Raven talons shred you
> Wolf claws shred you
> I shred you.

Throw the cold ashes in the garbage. You can also run the whole mess through a paper shredder; that works, too. This spell also can be used to shred the plans that people are trying to (or have) put in place against you.

The power to converse is incredibly potent when you realize you are always in control, but you don't have to exert control—meaning you are in control of yourself, and therefore it is unnecessary to inhibit another person, particularly if they are just blathering and acting like an idiot.

I have this discussion in this book for two reasons. First, many chants, charms, and spells are spoken. Understanding the power of your words is essential when using them. Secondly, you can change the pattern of any conversation with another person by your own behavior. You can boost your abilities in verbal discussion mode with magickal powders designed to enhance your words and protect you from the words of others. You can learn to immediately dismantle a negative energy pattern before it gets rolling. Later, in private, if the event was disturbing, you can do a complete spiritual cleansing, which will aid in dissolving the conversation's chi and leave you free to move forward. Realizing the chi of conversation, you can now go back and systematically put a personal cleansing technique in action to eradicate each and every one of those nasty memories. Destroy the pattern.

How do you do that? With the realization that you are dismantling something that is actually "there" (even though you can't see it, sort of like the air you breathe), you take back your personal power. You can write the event on a piece of paper and burn it. You can pour your thoughts of unhappiness in salt and then disburse the salt back to the earth, where the energy will be transformed from the negative to the positive. You can choose any type of release you like because now that you know the enemy, you can quickly dispatch it.

If you must go into an environment in which you realize that confrontation is necessary (such as a court case), carry a small natural sponge with you that you have previously enchanted to absorb all negative energy. When you get home, dump the sponge in salt water and do a complete spiritual cleansing on yourself. You can also carry a mix of salt and Mars magickal powder that has been commanded to destroy all incoming evil against you. When you are alone, dump the powder in the trash off your property and away from yourself. If you use either of these ideas, the sponge or the powder, be sure to end the process with a feeling of gratitude that "all will be well."

Voices in the Water

When I was young I learned to whisper magick into running water. You simply stand as close as possible to the running water—a stream is best although a fountain can work in a pinch—and speak your intent. I would cup my hands around my mouth and then whisper my resolve into the water, leaning as close to the liquid as possible so that the moisture of my breath could mix with the movement of the water.

The trick (if you would call it that) is to merge your voice, intent, and breath with the energy of the water and let go of your inhibitions at the same time. This is why the discussion of release was so important in the beginning of this book. To let go of the ego, to merge with the element, brings not only success but a personal fulfillment of oneness with the universe. With voices in the water, the impregnated liquid then disperses your desire into the universe when the circumstances are right for the fruition of your desire, sort of like a time release capsule. You can also work with flame in the same way, though you must be careful not to be too close to the fire as to damage your lungs. Whether using water or fire, I employ powders and herbal blends as an offering to the universe and a seal to the whisper working.

Summary

I hope you enjoyed this chapter as much as I loved writing it. It contains many of my personal ideas on energy, magick, and the use of mental and physical enchantments. Remember, there is more than one level in any magickal explanation. Always! Contemplation and experimentation are necessary to achieve your greatest success. Don't forget to use the DNA of your physicality (a taglock such as a piece of your hair) as well as the DNA of your soul (your lineage) for more power in your workings, particularly for those that involve your own self-improvement mentally, physically, and emotionally. And those repetitive thoughts you have over a problem are a clue to the solution you need. Look for what "feels" right, and that is your answer. Finally, you can't escape your own hatred; you must defeat it.

CHAPTER SIX
Magickal Powders and Herbal Blends

This chapter contains formulas that I have written, used, and sold in candle, sachet, or powder form for the last fifteen years. I have provided only the best of my many formulas—those that myself and my customers, friends, and coven members have relied upon with great success. These herbal blends and whisper charms are most effective if used in conjunction with the information you learned in the first three chapters of this book; however, you are free to use whatever structure you desire and what works best for you. Most of my formulas can be used for a variety of intentions; for example, my angel formula was designed for all workings in which you request the assistance of angelic energies.

Over time you will create your own recipes and whisper chants that will serve you well; those provided here are simply examples for you to try if you like. The formulas can be used in a variety of applications as you see fit. The spells that accompany the magickal recipes are merely guidelines. Feel free to add additional ingredients or matching fluid condensers. Remember, you need only 1–3 drops of the fluid condenser in your powders (depending upon how much powder you have made). If you wish to color the powder, you can use colored sugars, crushed colored chalk, or the color powders sold online for color runs.

There are a few herbs that I have purposefully not included in these formulas for different reasons, but you are free to use them in your own work. These include mullein (which is super fluffy); wolfsbane (highly poisonous and not recommended); mugwort (doesn't grind well and is poisonous); nightshade (poisonous); rosehips (when you grind these, they become a high skin irritant, although they can be added to sachet bags without problem as long as they are whole). This is not to say I don't use poisonous herbs, but I am extremely careful, and I keep all toxic herbs secured. Several herbs are considered harmful to some and not to others; these would include pennyroyal, angelica, calamus, and benzoin.

Please research all ingredients of any formula listed in this book in relation to your medical condition before use. A quick search on the internet of any herb will give you plenty of information on warnings and hazards of the plant. If you have children, grandchildren, or pets or are pregnant, my suggestion is to stick to the food-grade non-poisonous herbs, as the array of substitutions are amazing and just as good. Even then, there are those individuals who have allergies to food-grade plants (such as peanuts and almonds).

I will never forget when my father, who suffered from dementia, rose early one morning and tried to break into my locked magickal cabinet because he was convinced I had his favorite tea in there and believed I was keeping it from him. Of course this was absurd, but such confusion is a commonality of the dysfunction. My point is, you never know what dumb thing someone is going to do. Mark it and lock it. Always.

Please note:

- Your local poison center can be reached directly by calling 1-800-222-1222 from anywhere in the United States.
- When grinding any magickal powder, always wear a safety mask.
- None of the formulas given in this section are to be ingested. They are for magickal purposes only.

Keep in mind that some herbs are a bit fussy to handle. Lavender tends to fluff; I use a heavy mortar and pestle and only grind until they are broken. For herbs from the garden such as marigold, calendula, and saffron petals, I use very sharp scissors to cut these petals into bits as they don't grind well. Another tricky herb is boneset, which has a tough texture; you will probably have to use a screen to separate the powder from the stalks (depending on where you bought the herb or how it was harvested). Dried lemongrass can also be difficult to break down depending upon your equipment. Sometimes I use a large strainer positioned over a bowl, working the herb around in the strainer with the pestle. What can be powdered drops into the bowl, and the remainder is given back to nature with a silent prayer of honor.

Binders/Fixatives

Adding a fixative mixed with essential oils can boost the aromatic properties of an herbal blend and help bind the various energy patterns together to assist in the flow of the intent. These fixatives can be used alone, together, or in raw or powdered form, depending upon your choice of the finished product. For example, orris works well in powders, where oakmoss is better suited for herbal blends.

Angelica Root: Sun; element of fire. Poisonous when fresh, but the drying process is said to eliminate this poison. However, it too carries precautions for pregnant and nursing women as well as those suffering from diabetes.

Benzoin Gum Powder: Mercury; element of air. Has a vanilla-like aroma and reduces the evaporation of fragrance. The additive is used in a variety of soaps and cosmetics; however, there are cautions about skin contact for pregnant and breastfeeding women.

Calamus root: Moon; element of water. Also should not be handled by pregnant or nursing mothers.

Frankincense: Sun; element of fire. Because it is a resin, frankincense is "gummy" in that it will clump after you have powdered it. Frankincense is considered a higher vibration tool; it binds to provide protection, which pushes out negativity, and it is a cleansing and clearing vehicle suitable for all manner of banishings.

Myrrh Gum: Moon; element of water.

Oakmoss: Saturn; element of earth. Oakmoss binds and sets—an excellent one for the stability of a spell or to "set" a weight upon something that should not rise. Saturn helps something to "hold its form."

Orris Root: Venus; element of water. With its violet-like aroma, it is an attraction vehicle and works well to draw things, people, and energies toward you. I wouldn't choose it for a banishing powder due to its planetary properties.

As a magickal powder can be mistakenly ingested if it is scattered on the floor or tossed in the air. You may choose to use these fixatives in raw form rather than powdered, particularly in potpourri, dream pillows, or sachets. Many fixatives have health warning indicators for different medical conditions. Even though this book does not contain any ingestible recipes, when in doubt on the safe handling and toxicity of any plant or root in relation to your medical safety, research is the key. Never rely on a magickal book for health information. Seek a qualified professional or medical material from an accredited source. I realize I have mentioned this more than once in this book; however, I want to make it sincerely clear that you should always be careful when handling herbs, roots, and plants.

These powders or herbs/roots can be used in combination; for example, you may wish to choose one from each element and bind them together dressed with gold flakes or a few drops of universal liquid fluid condenser for a super binding ingredient to be used in several spells or rituals. To bind an enemy, use all the above listed ingredients along with non-poisonous sumac. Stuff the ingredients into a poppet. Wrap the poppet in red thread. Place the poppet in a brown bag of the same ingredients dressed with a raw egg. Bury off your property.

Fillers

I don't recommend using fillers in your raw herbal magickal powders unless they somehow correspond to your intent. Typically, fillers are only added so that the powder can be bulk sold; however, if you are going to draw a magickal sigil with the powder on the ground or on a powder plate, you may find adding a filler helps in the physical construction of the design. Typical fillers are arrowroot, buckwheat hulls, cornmeal, and rice powder.

Arrowroot: Jupiter; element of fire. Luck, purification, healing. Sometimes used as a substitution for graveyard dirt. Antidote for poisonous words or actions. The powder can mold if subjected to moisture. The powder can also gel, which makes it useful if you are trying to manifest something that just refuses to come into form; arrowroot can help the process or speed a spell. (Note that vervain can also add momentum to spellwork.)

Buckwheat Hulls: Venus; element of earth. Lightly crushed buckwheat hulls are used in sachets and poppets to help cut down on the expense of the herbs, particularly in larger sachet pillows and poppets. Ground to make a flour, it can be used in powders for both money and protection.

Cornmeal: Venus; element of earth. A sacred mother herb thought to vibrate well with the intent of protection, honoring deity, safe birthing, and good luck in general. Cornmeal is also used for healing of mental disorders (particularly Alzheimer's) and for wisdom spells and protecting the heart when one has been wounded by the unkind thoughts and words of others.

Rice Powder: Sun; element of air. Rice is thought to guard against all misfortunes, which makes it an excellent additive for protective magickal work. Added to bladderwrack, you can magnetize a metal container during a storm, welcoming the energy of the storm into the bowl. The power from the storm is then used in a protective, defensive magickal application. Rice also vibrates well to the intent of fertility and money magick. Green rice (a formula that includes dried rice, green powder, and other additives depending on the practitioner) is used for drawing money. Poppets stuffed with dried rice are used in fertility spells.

Rough Ground vs. Smooth Ground Powders

Some practitioners prefer finely ground powders whereas others, like myself, like the rougher ground. Although smooth powders are less detectable in magickal practice, rough grounds are easier to clean up in enchantments done at home, are less likely to cause respiratory difficulties, and if you are using the powder as an additive in a conjuring bag or sachet packet, the consistency doesn't really matter. For a pillow, I would use the raw/rough blend or a very rough ground mixture, as you don't want the powder to sift through the material. The consistency doesn't affect the magickal application other than you may have spent more time and energy to obtain a smoother powder, which can enhance the formula through the effort you expended.

Whole Leaves as Carriers

I have a selection of large dried leaves for winter use. In the fall and summer months I have a list of places where I can obtain fresh leaves that I use instead of white or red conjuring bags. Sometimes I write directly on the leaves with an indelible marker and use the leaves alone as an additive. With large leaves you can place the powder, a photograph, charm, or herb blend inside, and gently fold or roll the leaf (depending upon its fragility). You can use colored embroidery thread or even a bit of glue to hold the packet together. You can also use large-leaved vegetables from the grocery store such as lettuce, cabbage, leeks, etc.

The only rule that I've been taught is to never use a rotted plant, as disease or dysfunction has already become part of the plant. I realize that once any pattern is formed it begins to break down; however, if the rot is there, the chaos within the plant won't serve you well and may rebound the work or send the enchantment in a direction where you honestly did not want it to go. When using fresh plants, 4–12 hours is the key; after that, remove the item, whether it be fruit, vegetable, herbal, or other, unless you are working with a particular drying process. It is thought that dying plants (mainly flowers) that have not been told that they will be used for magick or ritual will deaden the chi of an area in dried form.

Use large plantain leaves for healing packets (Venus as in its function in Taurus/Earth). Large dandelion leaves (sacred to Hecate) are useful for strength, divination, and messages, and are also excellent for court cases due to their association with Jupiter. Lettuce leaves are great for protection and love drawing (moon/water). Large maple or sassafras leaves make great packets for money magicks (Jupiter/air). Corn leaves off of an ear of corn can be used for money, abundance, and prosperity packets (Venus/earth). Hollowed-out oranges and lemons are ideal for spiritual cleansings, where you take out as much of the fruit as possible and set aside. Fill the shell with spiritual cleansing herbs. This fragrant vehicle can be used as offerings, as an altar focus, or placed directly in a bowl of water that also contains the squeezed juices along with floating white candles to spiritually cleanse an area through the combination of water, earth, and fire.

Power Herbs

Power herbs are those plants that are thought to add speed or power to any particular spell. They aren't used all the time, usually only when you feel the greatest need. Favorites are:

Celery Seed: Another Mercury/air association, celery seed is thought to bring calm, focused thinking, thereby strengthening the intent of the working.

Cinnamon/Ginger Combo: Cinnamon is ruled by the sun/fire. Ginger is ruled by Mars/fire. The two herbs together combine to speed any spell or working. This combination is often loaded into red candles for swift action.

Mace: An aromatic, golden-colored spice that is believed to enhance mental abilities when casting a spell. It is the outer covering of nutmeg and is related to the planet Mercury and the air element.

Mistletoe: The Grand Dame of the herbal tool box. If you need to ramp up any spell and work for the most power and highest good, mistletoe might be your choice. However, mistletoe is considered poisonous, which is why it is sometimes difficult to find in local shops; however, it can be ordered fresh online. You can even buy a grow-your-own-mistletoe kit online if you are the adventurous type! If you are concerned about the poisonous aspects of mistletoe, note that "in studies of hundreds of cases of accidental ingestion over the years, there were no fatalities and only a handful of severe reactions. One study published in 1996 looked at 92 cases of mistletoe ingestion and found that only a small fraction of patients showed any symptoms…and no fatalities."[23] Magickal correspondences for mistletoe vary; some believe it is ruled by the sun and the element of air. Others believe that Jupiter is the ruler and fire the element. In magick, mistletoe is thought to be an antidote to all poisons and to encourage fertility and bestow good luck. With such a wide range of use, it is perfect for inclusion in almost any working.

Vervain: A vervain liquid fluid condenser is excellent for ramping up the power of a protection spell, bringing peace to the home, and guarding against illness. Here, its Venus correspondence functions as in Taurus, drawing stability, protection, and kindness into the home. The vervain herb in powders is thought to power up its attraction energies.

Yohimbe: Queen of Lust. If you want to make a love powder, yohimbe is the go-to herb; unfortunately, it, too, is considered poisonous (to some extent) as it causes high blood pressure and rapid heart rate. Ruled by Mars and the fire element, yohimbe has the legendary ability to take your love sachets and blends where no love spell has gone before.

> Cast the circle; set the field
> Say the words; breathe your will.
> Seal it up and let it go; your faith in Spirit makes it so!

Always remember to command the powder with a specific set of actions or intent right before using the blend in any magickal application. Tell *it* what to do!

---

23 Anahad O'Conner, "The Claim: Don't Eat the Mistletoe—It Can be Deadly," http://www.nytimes.com/2007/12/11/health/11real.html?_r=0 (11 December 2007).

The Formulas

Abundance

. . .

chamomile, sunflower, orange peel, lime,
vanilla bean, dried melon seeds

My life is filled with positive abundance
And all my needs are met and more
Days are light and nights are bright
Continued joy comes through my door.

This is one of my favorite formulas that works very well as potpourri. To ramp up a summer blend, add dried cherries. For more drawing power in the fall, include shavings of dried apples; for winter, use nuts and cranberries.

This is a joy and happiness blend that concentrates on bringing good fortune, happiness, and joy into your life. I keep a tall glass jar of this formula on my prosperity altar. The jar also includes one small piece of copper, a loadstone dressed with gold magnetic sand, and a High John root. I change the contents of the jar on the spring equinox, summer solstice, fall equinox, and winter solstice, incorporating the preparation and empowerment in my holiday sabbat. The blend can be boosted for aromatic enjoyment by adding your favorite magickal or essential oil along with a bit of oakmoss (to hold the scent).

Add new herbs and re-empower the bag every new moon. Build the power of the bag by adding new items as you feel necessary. For example, you may find an unusual stone or a feather or a little ceramic animal that you know in your heart needs to go in your bag.

Recommended candle color: gold, red, green

Ancestral Honor

. . .

lavender, myrrh, rosemary, frankincense,
hyssop, lemon verbena, eggshell

There is peace in the moment
There is peace in my person
There is peace in my heart

There is peace in my mind
There is peace in my spirit.
I send light and blessings to those beyond the veil.
All hail that which is sacred and filled with joy.

White and purple are my candle color choices for this formula, which fits well in a variety of magickal systems that work with the honored dead. This blend is designed for your ancestors, as opposed to the gede formula, which is for the dead in general. Here, the lavender and myrrh call the dead and the other herbs ensure the visit is sacred, removing any negativity. An excellent blend for Samhain, it also can be used for petitions to specific loved ones, to honor them, or to simply remember them in ritual. Use the herbal blend on your ancestral altar in a bowl; the powder can be sprinkled on the grave or at the gates of a graveyard before entrance. For a named person, add their favorite flowers or scent to the blend.

I've found this formula to be very useful when doing genealogy research, particularly if I am having trouble finding information or making a link. For an ancestry search, write the name three times on a piece of paper, draw the sigils for Mercury and Venus over the name, sprinkle the powder on top, twist the paper, and carry it in your pocket when visiting the graveyard, archives, or libraries. At home encircle a purple candle with the powder or herbal mixture. Burn the candles while you are doing your research. If you have a picture of the person, place the candle on top of the photo.

Recommended candle color: white

Angel

• • •

frankincense, myrrh, lavender,
nag champa, copal

To me, angelic magick is the highest vibratory work you can do in association with calling the Spirit of the Divine. This primarily resin formula can serve a variety of purposes as it seeks the best possible outcome while banishing all negativity. If someone has a drinking problem in the home, nest a citrine gemstone in the formula. This won't solve the problem, but I have found it leads to solutions on how to appropriately handle the issue. When making and using this blend, call out the angelic names you choose, allowing the vibration of your voice to sing out into the universe. You can call a single angel, a specified number (such as the archangels), or a whole host of them.

Recommended candle color: white

Anubis, Egyptian God of the Crossroads
FOR SERIOUS ISSUES OF HEALTH AND PROTECTION
• • •

frankincense, myrrh, cedar, cypress, rum,
ankh symbol on a piece of paper

Hear me, O great guardian of the crossroads
Anubis, Anpu, lord of the sacred land
Keeper of mysteries
I call thee forth with dignity and honor
To aid me in my working this day/night.

Ankh Symbol

The Anubis charm is most used in response to health issues where the circumstances are serious, especially surgeries for animals or people. It can also be utilized for a crossing (funeral rite) for an animal or individual, meaning that it is employed to help the spirit pass from this lifetime to the Summerland. Cast a circle, call the quarters, and ask for the presence of Anubis. He brings great peace into the circle, and you will know that he has arrived, as there is an incredible calm that permeates everything. You can use the powder as an offering or as the calling vehicle; this is entirely up to you. The charm and powder can also be employed for protection. The ankh symbol awakens the power of Anubis. The symbol can be cut up and put directly in the powder or you can put the powder in the paper with the symbol and then twist the paper as I explained in chapter 1.

Now, I'll be honest with you: when I offered this formula in my stores, there wasn't much interest. This surprised me because when you use the ankh symbol combined with the call above, pets and people receive a very peaceful, easy passing, and you are gifted with the stability and courage you need to move forward. There will come a time when you need it, and then you will see for yourself. I've also found that if you use this symbol and the powder, the individual or animal has a clarity window where you can say goodbye. The powder and sigil can be used for healing, especially if everyone believes the person is at death's door. If this is not their intended fate, the person can recover at a faster rate. Finally, this is a good truth-finding powder for circumstances around someone's death or for information that is needed to resolve an issue around that death.

Recommended candle color: use both gold and black

Aphrodite
LOVE AND PASSION
• • •

rose, yohimbe, cinnamon, ginger, cardamom (peach
pit for inclusion in sachet bag or poppet only)

I call forth Aphrodite, goddess of sea and foam
Mother of heavenly love
I pray thee bestow your blessings upon me.

I like using this formula with pink or seafoam/light turquoise-colored candles. Carve the sigil of Venus into the candle with a clay stylus, then paint a small amount of your favorite love oil or love fluid condenser into the grooves. This is a very romantic blend that works well in a pink cloth packet with a red heart stitched on the fabric; this way you can carry it with you for as long as you like. A good mixture for a love poppet to draw love and passion to you.

Attraction

USEFUL FOR LOVE, FRIENDSHIP AND
MONEY—A MAGNET FORMULA

• • •

rose, gardenia, patchouli, marigold, cinnamon, musk

From nothing to something I will this thing to form
I know that it will manifest and to this world be born.

An Attraction Manifestation Sigil

I use both the chant and the herbal blend for drawing and manifesting a variety of objects and goals into form. To give the formula more power, add a fluid condenser of the same ingredients made on a Venus day (Friday) in a Venus hour in a waxing moon or look for when Venus is well aspected (a trine or sextile to Mercury, the moon, or Jupiter). This timing can also be used for blending the powder, empowering your mixture, or launching the magick. Works with a variety of candle colors that best vibrate with your intent. Feel free to add crushed gemstones, an attraction manifestation sigil, photos of what you desire, or your own magickal doodle.

Aura Spiritual Cleanse

• • •

rosemary, hyssop, white sage, African basil, lemongrass

I cleanse the field around me and in me of all negativity
My soul glitters with the white light of well-being
I attract joy, wisdom, harmony, and peace
Only the good remains.

This is a bright aromatic blend that can be ground into a powder, used in poppets, conjuring bags, or bath bags, and is perfect for spiritual cleansings of all kinds. When using the formula in sachets, take several deep breaths to inhale the lovely aroma, letting the sweetness travel through your whole body. Intone the sea of potential exercise and attune yourself and the field to cleansing body, mind, and soul. See your entire body filled with white light. Move this light out so that it surrounds your body to about five inches in depth. Again, activate the sea of potential. Next, move the light out farther, about ten inches from your body, and activate the sea. Finally, move the light out about fifteen inches from your body, and activate the sea. You have now cleansed the physical body and the three energy bodies that make up the core of your being.

During this exercise you may wish to rub the herbs or powder in your hands in a circular motion. See which works best for you, a clockwise motion or a counterclockwise one. You also can use this exercise with salt, rubbing the salt in the palms of your hands as you expand the light bubble around you in increments as indicated above. Thank the salt when you are finished and brush it from your hands. This is a good exercise to practice every day, particularly when you feel challenged, sick, worried, or just need a boost. If you are suspicious of someone sending you negative energy, practice three times a day.

I also use this formula in a bowl of chilled water. Once the blend is empowered, place your hands in the bowl and, while softly chanting, release the negativity you may be feeling into the water. You can do this for yourself or incorporate the process in a spiritual cleansing for others. Once the negativity has been released, dry your hands and then fill your body with feelings of joy and happiness. It is important to make an effort to change your feelings, like a train switching tracks, as leaving a void just allows the negativity to return quickly. Cleansed crystals in the water give a very empowering magickal vehicle.

Banish Problems

• • •

mistletoe, orris, sulfur, sage, sea salt

One way to use this formula is to take a large metal bowl and fill it with sea salt. Add the other herbs. Write the problem on a piece of paper, burn it, and add the ashes to the metal bowl. Sit quietly and stir the mixture with a smooth stone that you have found on a Spirit Walk. Intone your favorite banishing chant as you grind the stone in the salt and herb mixture. Allow yourself to rise above the problem. When you feel that moment of peace, release! Throw the mixture in the garbage; it is no longer of use to you.

There are several banishment formulas in this section; however, you can throw banishment powder by the ton and the process will not work if you refuse to banish the issue or person in your mind and remove both physical and energy connections you have previously built. As long as the conduits are open, the problem won't completely go away, and eventually the channel will widen and you'll have to deal with it all over again. With sickness, it is usually a major stressor that you have internalized. If you heal only the symptoms of the illness, the original root, which is based in an emotional situation that you have not processed in a healthy way, can grow again. It takes courage to walk back in time, dig deep, and choose to put the situation into the bucket of experience and go forward. Don't be ashamed if you need professional help to do this; therapy is designed to help you rise above what holds you down.

Cutting emotional ties to the issue or person leads to healing and eventual freedom. Many people swallow the pain; this pain becomes disease. Free yourself of the original wound and let go of the circumstances where you took a pounding and you know it. That was then; this is now. Time to rise.

Because people are creatures of habit, it is tough to make someone understand that "cutting ties" means exactly that. Don't sit in circle and do banishment magick for a bully you are dealing with, then stay friends with said person on social media or continue to frequent places where they go or allow their text messages or phone calls on your phone. They hit a wall. You didn't. Unfortunately, sometimes we have to let go of good people because they have made it their mission to enable harmful individuals. That is not your call. Not your problem. Celebrate the goodness in that person and move on! When you banish something, the universe doesn't take you seriously if you keep answering their texts or privately stalk them on social media. Gone is gone. Done is done.

I understand that there are situations where you must slowly disentangle yourself, balancing practical actions, therapy, magickal focus, and legal strings. In these instances, let go of what you can immediately (such as extraneous people who will tell of your business or movements to the negative person), change your daily pattern, frequently practice spiritual cleansings, etc. Keep working the four powers together: practical, therapy, magickal, and legal. Eventually, you will be able to disentangle yourself from the problem forever.

Recommended candle color: white

Banish Sickness

• • •

sea salt, pebbles

The Braucherei system has a number of diminishing chants, which are useful for banishing illness, debt, unfortunate circumstances, and ill will, removing bad habits or people from our lives, and for dieting. The Nine Weeping Sisters charm is especially useful for banishing illness, particularly fevers, tumors, odd illnesses that seem to have no diagnosis, or illnesses of a cancerous nature, or a group of people who have infiltrated your life in an unpleasant way. The chant can be used in the usual way (said nine times three times a day), added to a hypnotherapy session, or used as a working in itself.

For the working, select nine stones, buttons, or other small objects that you have cleansed in sea salt. In this example we will use stones. Do not use coins, as this will diminish your wealth. You should also have the person's name that you are trying to help written on a piece of brown paper nine times or a photograph of them to place in the center of your altar or working area. Carefully set the nine stones around the paper in a circle. You can dress the stones with a banishing magickal oil if you so desire. Say the individual's name aloud and state your petition before you begin the chanting/whispering process.

For example: "*Hail, guardian angels and angelic hosts! I call upon you to bring safe and natural healing to Amanda Jane Brubaker. Please diminish the illness trapped within her body and remove it completely. From Amanda's body to God/dess's hands, so be it!*"

The working is best done on a waning moon over a nine-day period. On the first night, anywhere from twilight to midnight, lay out the nine stones where they will not be disturbed and intone the full charm nine times. On the ninth recitation remove one stone. Ideally, you should take the stone and throw it into running water off your property. If you can't do this, wash the stone and give it back to the earth off your property.

On the next night, repeat the charm beginning at "eight weeping sisters…" nine times. The last time you repeat the charm do as before, removing the eighth stone and throwing it away, off your property, in running water.

Do this procedure every night, saying the charm nine times but only from the number of stones you have left: seven, then six, then five, etc., until you are down to the last stone.

On the last night, repeat the last four lines nine times: "*One weeping sister, left all alone, jumped from the ship and sunk like a stone. No weeping sisters stand by the lake. The evil is gone! Peace in its place!*" Remove the last stone. Return to your altar, hold your hands over the person's picture or name, and repeat the last two lines with conviction in your voice: "*No weeping sisters stand by the lake. The evil is gone! Peace in its place!*" After the last recitation, you will seal this spell in a different way. You will yell: "*So be it!*"

and then slam your hand down on the altar top as hard as you can without breaking anything.

Nine Weeping Sisters Charm

> Nine weeping sisters stood by a lake
> One was removed, and then there were eight.
> Eight weeping sisters gazed at the heavens
> One was removed, and then there were seven.
> Seven weeping sisters broke red bricks
> One was removed, and then there were six.
> Six weeping sisters ran for their lives
> One was removed, and then there were five.
> Five weeping sisters left through the door
> One was removed, and then there were four.
> Four weeping sisters put out to sea
> One was removed, and then there were three.
> Three weeping sisters left as the crew
> One was removed, and then there were two.
> Two weeping sisters shied from the sun
> One was removed, and then there was one.
> One weeping sister, left all alone
> Jumped from the ship and sank like a stone.
> No weeping sisters stand by the lake.
> The evil is gone! Peace in its place!

Note: Another variation of this spell is to write the problem on nine pieces of paper. Each night, burn one slip of paper.

Recommended candle color: white

Binding (Last Ditch)

In my magickal practice I generally go right for the banishment, feeling that binding just makes the problem hang around longer. However, there may be circumstances where you feel that a binding is necessary first, followed by the banishment. My job in this book is not to discuss the morality of the magick; I believe that by working with the plants and their spirits you will find your own way to nirvana.

You will need:

- paper with the person's photo or their name written on it nine times
- a potato (Saturn/earth)
- benzoin gum
- salt
- non-poisonous sumac
- a good spade

Make an equal-armed cross slit in the potato. Insert the paper or a photograph with the individual's name into the center of the crossed slit. Dig a small ditch at least eight inches deep. Pour salt into the ditch. Lay sumac over the salt. Place the potato on the sumac. Cover the potato with the sumac. Cover the sumac with salt. Fill in the ditch. Pour salt on the dirt. With a sharp blade, draw a circle around the ditch; this act is to cut all ties between yourself and the individual. Draw the sigil of Saturn in the salt. Place a heavy stone on top of the salt. Turn your back. Walk away. Don't look back. Please note that this spell doesn't work if someone is innocent.

> *Down in the ditch you stay*
> *Down in the ditch this day*
> *Down in the ditch cut off*
> *Down in the ditch your lot*
> *Down in the ditch you stay*
> *Ever up? No way!*

As a note, I have on more than one occasion used living vining plants to bind a problem. Both moonflower and morning glory vines work particularly well. Write the problem on a small piece of paper, then carefully twirl the vines around the paper. Tell the plant your problem and ask for assistance in this matter. Over time (about a month or two) the vine will completely cover the paper and continue to wrap itself around the problem. As summer turns to autumn and the first frost hits, the problem has always been gone.

Blessed Baby/Fertility

. . .

grains of paradise, baby powder, cornmeal,
sandalwood, mandrake, mistletoe

Bright beauty, health, and safely birth
Bring my baby to this earth
Encircle us with glowing love
And grant us blessings from above.

Designed both for fertility and safe birthing. Add the names of the parents (or intended parents) into the powder or herbal blend. Use the herbal blend to stuff into a white poppet along with a paper that has "happy, healthy, safe baby and birthing for mother and baby" written on it. Sew up the doll. Draw three Birca runes (ᛒ) on the doll with indelible marker and place the poppet under the bed.

When the woman becomes pregnant, remove from under the bed and place on its own chair in the bedroom. When it is time to go to the hospital, have the doll accompany the mother-to-be as a birthing charm.

Note: If something or someone tries to carry the poppet out from under the bed before the woman becomes pregnant, this is a sign that the parents are not in agreement or that there is an outside influence that is not in agreement with the pregnancy. Do a complete spiritual cleansing of both parents and place the doll back under the bed. Secure it to the underside of the bed if you believe a pet will try to carry the doll away.

Recommended candle color: white

Blessing

. . .

sweetgrass, rosemary, rose, lavender, salt

From head to foot, from heart to mind
I cleanse the field with three of chime
Every color is my light!
Every color is my sight!
Every color calls delight!

Red! Orange! Yellow! Green! Blue! Purple! White!
I walk in beauty, joy, and light!

This is a sweet formula that is perfect for weddings, Wiccanings, and other sacred events. I also use it to combat nightmares and encourage restful sleep. This is an excellent color spell that you may wish to use for a variety of meditations and family or personal happiness workings. As a simple charm or a full ritual, the vibratory essence of the words and herbs are filled with joy and delight.

Recommended candle color: white or all colors listed in the
  chant

Blocking

• • •

salt, rosemary, gourd seeds, pennyroyal, ivy

God/dess stands between me and thee!

Hold your hands and arms up in a crossed blocking motion with your head turned to the side (so you don't get a bloody astral nose), then turn and throw part of the powder in front of you. Turn to the right and do the same thing, then turn right again and again, turning full circle, as you intone the charm above. Mean it when you say it!

Bluebird Family Happiness

• • •

buckthorn, dandelion, sage, thistle, sunflower hulls,
celandine, white feathers, blue powder

Bucks and lions, sage and flowers
Birds of happiness at each hour
Thistledown and blended love
Always blessings from above.

Bluebird family happiness is a general wishes formula as well as a family happiness blend. This working involves your artistic creativity. Draw or use photographs of bluebirds pasted on a white or gold envelope. This envelope should be large enough to contain a family photo. You may also wish to add representations of bluebirds on your family altar. Upon each hour of the day (from dawn to dusk), intone the chant above three times. Finish by ringing a sweet bell three times and sprinkling the magickal powder on a picture of your family. At dusk take the powder outside and scatter it. Seal the photograph in a gold envelope decorated with blue-birds. If you are going through a particularly bad time, use your divination tool to determine if you should do the working for three days. If more than one day is required, adjust the working to fit your schedule.

Recommended candle color: light blue or a vibrant blue

Another blend like this one is the happy home formula, made of borage, cucumber seeds, basil, and thyme; the recommended candle color is white or gold.

Bonesetter Healing

• • •

rosemary, frankincense, cinquefoil, boneset,
goldenseal, ginger, copal, mistletoe

The Lord of Five Points rode to four corners
While the Circle of She declares what will be.
Marrow to marrow; bone to bone; joint to joint
Sinew to sinew; blood to blood; vein to vein
Hair to hair; limb to limb; flesh to flesh
The power of one will now be enmeshed![24]

This is a marvelous healing mixture that you may prefer to use as an herbal blend rather than a powder, as the boneset is hard to grind. Its purpose is to assist in the healing of wounds, bones, flesh, joints, etc. It is a splendid blend and chant to use every day after surgery or injury. To utilize the chant, add the herbal mixture to a conjuring bag along with a photograph or the name of the person who needs the healing. Each day say the individual's name aloud three times, then begin rubbing the conjuring bag while intoning the chant at least three times (nine if the situation is severe).

---

24 Adapted from Storms, *Anglo-Saxon Magic*.

Recommended candle color: white or pink (pink represents healthy internal flesh)

Boss Fix
TO REMOVE EVIL FROM THE WORKPLACE
• • •
chili peppers, orange peel, sandalwood, patchouli, tobacco, musk, name of your boss, business card with the name of the company; if the boss is lying about you, add snapdragon

I shine the light upon its face
To show the world the cruel disgrace
Unkindness, hatred, mouth of rot
Turn tail and run, the evil stops!
From in to out no place to rest
Wheel of fortune turns to west
Where water flows and gone you go
Leaving peace; I make it so!

Burn the name of your boss and the business card together. Stir the ashes. Mix the ashes with the powder. Empower with the above chant (said nine times for three days) on the waning moon. Sprinkle the powder where you know your boss will walk on it.

For added power and a better connection, take dirt from where the individual has walked immediately after they have left the area. Add that dirt to either the powder or the spell vehicle.

Recommended candle color: red

Brick Dust Protection and Warding
• • •
brick dust, dragon's blood resin

This is a good powder to lay across doorsteps or windowsills; because it is red, anyone can see it. One working begins by opening all the doors and windows in your living area. With a white candle and blessed salted water, walk around the home with the candle in the right hand and the water in the left. The candle is thought to scare the negativity into the water, where it will be dissolved. Use the following chant as you walk through the entire living space.

> I cast thee out darkness, by one, two, and three
> Ere about me the light is all that will be
> From attic to basement to that in between
> Good thoughts and great love are all to be seen.

Finish outside of the house, throwing out the water off your property. Allow the lit white candle to continue to burn in the center of the home. Lay the brick dust powder down outside all the doorways of the home so that no evil may re-enter.

Recommended candle color: white or red, depending upon the working; red is considered a battle color and is used by some practitioners when they feel that the opponent is strong and needs the vibrancy of the color to be "put down"

Brigid Creativity and Fire Healing

• • •

dandelion, sage, pumpkin, chamomile, violet
petals and flowers, wisteria leaves

> From the fire of inspiration to the hand of gentle healing
> From the well of good health flowing to the forge of fired mind
> Blessed Brigid knows what's needed, and her power now is mine.

The Brigid archetype of the exalted healer is one of the most complex of Celtic deities and a commanding figure in Irish mythology. She is the goddess of inspiration, healing, inner vitality, wisdom, skill, strength, divine justice, knowledge, hearth and home, poetry, wordsmithing, needlework, compassion, and creativity. Some believe she rules the four elements and is capable of wielding their combined power. She is the flaming arrow in the dark of night. Known by a number of names—Brighid, Bridey, Bride, Briggidda, and more—she has journeyed from Pagan roots and managed to stand strong in Christianity, a pathway blocked to many ancient gods and goddesses. In Christian lore Brigid was the midwife of Mary, present at the birth of Jesus. Brigid's colors are white, black, and red. Birthed from a triple goddess form, she is the patroness of women's rights and the safety of children.

Brigid is such a famous goddess favored by so many magickal practitioners in both her Pagan and Christian forms that I created a formula based on research of common offerings and aromas given to her. In Santería, *orishas* (deities of West African Yoruban religions) are associated with Catholic saints, in which Brigid is included. In the African diasporic religion of Voodoo, she is represented with the lwa (spirit) Maman Brigitte.[25]

Recommended candle color: white, red, and black

Buddha Smiles Good Fortune
• • •

mint, bergamot, orange peel, bamboo leaves, gold or
silver metal flakes, the largest coin of your country

Buddha smiles

Good fortune sings

Blessing life

With jeweled wings

Say you're grateful is the key

To laughter, joy, and harmony

Rich within, rich around

Rich before the sun goes down!

Create the blend and empower the largest coin of your country on a new moon. Spit on the coin. Place the blend and the coin in a prosperity bag of your choice (red, white, gold, or green) as well as a lit match, which you put out quickly in the bag. The match is the catalyst for activating the formula. Breathe into the bag three times with a feeling of joy. On the first dawn of the new moon, go outside, hold the bag up to the direction of the new moon, and repeat the above chant three times.

---

25 If you are interested in more information about Brigid, check out this excellent article written by Winter Cymres: http://www.druidry.org/library/gods -goddesses/brigid-survival-goddess. You will find many other informative articles on various deities and magick on this website as well.

Cernunnos

. . .

pine, mistletoe, woodruff, oak leaves

I invoke thee, great Cernunnos, master of the woods
Lord of the wild things, Father Herne, Hooded God
Grant me wisdom, joy, good fortune, protection, and peace
I become one in the arms of nature.

Cernunnos is the name most often used in Celtic studies about the god of the forest, the horned god. Many times the horns are depicted as antlers. He is sometimes referred to as Herne the Hunter, the Dark Lord, or the Hooded God, depending upon your course of study. He is not in any way related to Satan, as that image is a Christian construct and not associated with Celtic polytheism. Many times he is drawn in a cross-legged position surrounded by animals. He is the consciousness of the active energy of nature and therefore pervades all things. Sexuality, fertility, the hunt, and survival are all concepts of Cernunnos.

Recommended candle color: green

Cleaning House/Weekly Housework

. . .

lemon peel, sandalwood, lemon verbena, hyssop,
rosemary, basil, thyme, lemon balm, orange peel

From foundation to roof
I cleanse the field of all negativity
Joy, laughter, and happiness
Shall henceforth be my gain.

This is a general house cleansing formula that can be used as a powder, herbal blend, or added to a bucket of water for a floor wash.

Recommended candle color: white

Confusion

TO CONFUSE THE ENEMY OR SOMEONE
WHO IS TRYING TO HARM YOU

• • •

lavender, black poppy seed, crushed blueberries, galangal,
parsley, thyme, burned knotted string, blackberry
leaves, black mustard seed, the sigil of Neptune

Your vision is clouded, your mind confused
Wherever you move to harm or abuse
Thoughts and deeds of hurt and pain
Turn quickly away—you get no gain
Turner be turned, twister be twisted
The evil you wove will now be lifted!

Best cast at 3:00 a.m. on the dark of the moon. Boil all ingredients in water that just covers the bottom of the pan along with the individual or name of the business (should they have attacked you). Say the entire charm three times, then repeat the first line until the pot boils dry. Throw the paper and dried herbs in the garbage.

Recommended candle color: gray

Court Case

LEGAL VICTORY

• • •

sassafras, High John (poisonous), cascara sagrada, oregano,
galangal, buckthorn, brown sugar, a drop of honey

Three spirits came from the east
Truth, Justice, and Victory
The first one bound him/her
The second one gagged him/her
The third one dragged him/her away
I am the winner this fateful day!

Adjust the words to add the individual's name you are fighting against (if there is one) and the venue. For example, it may be a hearing, it may be "court," it may be mediation, etc. Using the right title to match the circumstances is important. The most irritating part of court cases and legal nonsense is the amount of time and energy these things eat. In Braucherei disease and trouble are thought to be energy patterns of their own, fueled by the thought of the human mind. Consider such a thing as a nonthinking entity that needs to be starved of energy.

Recommended candle color: brown, orange, and gold

Courthouse Win
FOR COURT AND LEGAL ISSUES
• • •
dirt from the steps of the courthouse where your
case will be heard, High John (poisonous), asafoetida,
devil's shoestring, celandine, galangal

Steps of the courthouse, one, two, three
Skipping over evil I win my victory!

I recommend keeping the High John whole and making the powder out of the remaining ingredients. Place in a red conjuring bag with a victory symbol of your choice. If the other party is lying about you, add snapdragon and a tiger's-eye gemstone.

Crown of Success
• • •
frankincense, vanilla, sandalwood, patchouli, orris,
petitgrain essential, and myrrh; golden sand, lodestones,
gold flakes and gold glitter can also be added

Three spirits came from the east
Bringing the field of success
The first one opened it
The second one connected it
The third one breathed it manifest.

Crown of success is a go-to formula for business, creative, and career accomplishment.

Recommended candle color: gold or yellow

Debt Reduction and Recovery

• • •

frankincense, pumpkin seeds, lavender, sweet pea, gold
glitter or gold flecks, torn bits of paper money

I breathe deep and see the beauty of all things
I breathe deep and see the beauty of all things
I breathe deep and see the beauty of all things
I breathe deep and set my mind upon the path of joy
I breathe deep and rise from what was destroyed
I breathe deep and realize the new road of joy!
It is in harmony I access the recovery I need
It is in flow that I plant the stability seed
I rise! And I know the universe will provide!

Wrap in a large maple leaf. The first charm is to be said every morning, as close to your rising as possible.

An old method to ensure food coming into the home when you are having money problems is to grind dried peas and beans together, empowering them for the abundance of food for your family. Sprinkle the powder on a piece of bread and give to nature. As the animals are drawn to the bread, so food will be brought into the home. Each year my family fills a small mason jar with a selection of dried beans and peas, a lodestone, and a petition that the gnomes of the earth bring good fortune and food into the home. We cap the jars and decorate the lids. The jars are set by the front door on top of an empowered metal trivet (to help hold the charge) to welcome good fortune into the family. At the end of the year, the jar is emptied, washed, and refilled. For us, this is often a New Year's Day activity.

Recommended candle color: green or gold

Dem Bones Uncrossing

• • •

rose, carnation petals, clove, bay, clover, myrrh,
patchouli, lemon verbena, ginger, allspice, orange peel,
3 drops white rum, chicken bones, a paper bag

I dig to the root and cast evil aside

The cross I carried no longer abides

I throw out the pain, the evil, the strife

Dem bones, they be banished from all of my life!

Keep the chicken bones whole (those from your dinner are fine, just wash them so they aren't sticky, set them in salt water for at least an hour, then allow them to dry). Mix the powder (crushed ingredients) in a bag with the bones. Shake the bag as you intone the following chant nine times. At the end of the chant, open the bag and scatter the contents and the bag in the garbage.

Recommended candle color: white

Devil's Trap

• • •

frankincense, myrrh, devil's shoestring, sandalwood, clover, eggshell, a drop of vetivert essential oil

Evil, begone; don't come back

Like a moth to a flame, enter this trap

Devil, begone; don't come back

The gate snaps shut; dissolve in a snap!

Devil's Trap Sigil

Draw the devil's trap sigil on a mirror or on the lid of a jar filled with frankincense and vinegar set upon a mirror. This symbol is used to trap and destroy negative energy. Sprinkle powder on the sigil or add the powdered herbs to the vinegar and frankincense mixture. You can also add silver glitter. Burn a white candle by the sigil for seven days or seven candles for seven days. Throw everything in the trash the seventh day, including the cold candle ends.

Recommended candle color: white

Diffusing Anger Against You/Stopping Gossip
• • •

lobelia, slippery elm, loosestrife, Pennsylvania smartweed,
snapdragon, galangal, High John (poisonous), pumpkin seed, salt

The fire recedes, the steam abates
Your tantrums die, I close the gate.
I flush you out, and out you go
Your words of hate no longer grow.
The fire recedes, the steam abates
Your own ill will will be your fate.

Write the charm on toilet paper along with the individual's name (if you know it). Place the powder in the center of the toilet paper. Ball up the paper. Hold it tightly in your right hand. Repeat the person's name three times, making the connection of the person to your words. If you don't know the person's name, simply say "You who have attacked me" or similar words that feel right to you in this circumstance. Be succinct. Say the charm three times with great gusto, then throw the paper in the toilet and flush!

Recommended candle color: red

Dirt Dauber Send It Back
• • •

eucalyptus, rue, nettles, sandalwood, skunk cabbage, red peppers,
powdered dried snakeskin (safely shed) can also be added

Any spell that you have cast
Cracks and crumbles and bites you back
Broken will is all you feel

228

Your dirty deeds are now revealed
Leaving me both clear and free
As I will, so mote it be!

Broken pieces from an organ pipe dirt dauber's nest are frequently used, particularly if someone is trying to trap you, as the primary food for a dirt dauber (or mud dauber) is the spider.

Recommended candle color: Red or red and black if they have committed a crime against you (murder of a loved one, rape, embezzlement, theft of property, etc.). The word *spell* in the first line can be changed to fit the circumstances: any lies, any action, etc.

Dreams and Visions
. . .

wintergreen, gardenia, rose, cinnamon, spearmint, anise, bay, celery seed, damiana, lavender, safflower, myrrh, vervain, eyebright

May I see the connection of all things
My mind the flight of the dragonfly
Embracing the truth of the light
Understanding my dreams and my visions.

This is a lovely blend to place in a lavender conjuring bag with the image of a dragonfly and a moonstone and tiger's-eye gemstone. Dress with aromatic lavender essential oil and hang on your bedpost for sweet divinatory dreams.

Recommended candle color: white or lavender

Egg Money/Creativity
. . .

oatmeal, dried milk powder, sassafrass, allspice, nutmeg, cinnamon, raw sugar, eggshell

I activate the field around me and within me
To enhance my gifts of creativity
Talent wakens, energy flows
Returns are great as my production grows!

This is a great formula for ritual soap to be used before any creative process that you hope to draw money to you. It can also be utilized in a purple conjuring bag along with your intent for divine creativity. Encircle around purple or gold candles that you burn while you work.

Recommended candle color: purple, gold, white, red, ivory

Evil, Begone

• • •

hot red peppers, frankincense, white sage

• • •

frankincense, sandalwood, eggshell, mistletoe, ginger

Evil, begone; do not return
The horse has run off and the bridges are burned!

I have two different formulas that I use for this working; both have worked equally well. If you are trying to make evil leave a place, add a teaspoon of dirt from that place; that way, you don't have to be at that location when you cast the spell, as you have established a connection and are keeping your work "above ground." Pets or children in bare feet should not walk on this formula. The charm also works very well when using four thieves vinegar. The chant is always intoned nine times.

Recommended candle color: red

Exorcism (General)

• • •

clove, lemon verbena, bay, horehound, black salt, dirt from
a holy place (a real holy place, not one that claims to be)

I cast thee out with light and breath
Nothing evil will be left!

Grind ingredients together and scatter over a given area or on the walkway leading to a home or establishment. If within a house, support the working with holy water, the ringing of sweet bells, drumming, or rattles, as well as a lit white candle.

Recommended candle color: white (although some practitioners
use black followed by white)

Exorcism ("You've Gotta Go")

. . .

dragon's blood, frankincense, angelica, clove, pennyroyal,
white sage, lilac flowers or lilac essential oil (if you can't
find lilac, lavender can be substituted), 1 cup sea salt

Add the powdered herb blend to the sea salt and stir well. Draw a banishing sigil of your choice into the mixture. Add other sigils as you desire that match your spell intent. If you are dealing with a negative person, place their picture in a metal bowl and cover the picture with the sea salt and herb mixture. Begin running your fingers or a pestle firmly in the bowl, pressing the herbal mixture into the face on the photograph in a circular motion. Connect with the power of the herbs, becoming one with your intent of banishment. This process is to energetically cut the conduits between you and the negative individual. The spell is not meant to harm, but, to take back control of your own energy and block all avenues of connection.

Recommended candle color: white or black

Fairy Conjure

. . .

bayberry, mistletoe, woodruff, powdered milk,
oakmoss, white sugar, heptagram symbol

Whisper magick nature hears
Ye make the bond the words be clear
Keep your promise, ye are as one
The magick of the Fey is done!

Heptagram Symbol

Draw the sigil in the dirt outside with a stick found (not cut) in the woods. Sprinkle the powder at dusk to call the fairies; add glitter to the blend if you so desire. Remember to leave an offering once you have whispered your petition.

Recommended candle color: lavender or light green

Family Protection

· · ·

African violet leaves, clove, bay, cinquefoil, dragon's blood

Family protection
Unity divine
Nothing and no one
Can harm me and mine.

This is a nice formula to powder and load into the bottom of a dark blue candle that sits on top of a family photograph. If you roll your own candles, you can craft seven or nine candles of the protective color you desire and then load with the family protection magickal powder at the bottom of the candle. Dot the bottom of each candle with your preferred magickal oil or liquid fluid condenser. Burn for the same number of days as the number of candles, as close to the same time each day as you can. Recite the charm above three times each day.

Recommended candle color: blue or red

Fast Cash

· · ·

dried cucumber seeds, chocolate mint, cedar, marigold petals, tangerine peel, bergamot, chamomile, grains of paradise

I knock three times and open the door
Welcome good fortune, fast cash, and more!

Wrap mixture in a large wildcrafted sassafras or pumpkin leaf or scatter the powder at your front door. Repeat the first line once and knock on your door from the outside. Open the door and repeat the second line nine times.

Fiery Wall of Protection

• • •

dragon's blood, frankincense, myrrh, salt

To dance, to dream the fiery scene
The flames become a sacred screen
The circle of protection firm
And I within the evil spurn.
Licking tongues of sparks and light
Will burn mine enemies day and night.

This formula and charm combination is often used to encircle a photograph or name of a person who needs protective energies. You can also choose an astrological candle (based on their birthdate) to represent the individual as the center of the working.

Fireball Motivation or Winning

• • •

cinnamon, yohimbe, dragon's blood, ginger, mace, hot peppers

Arise, O sacred salamander
I conjure thee to do my bidding!
Creature of fire, work my will by my desire!

This is a good powder to use when working all manner of fire magicks such as candle, cauldron, bonfire, etc. Sprinkle a bit of the powder on the flame and then proceed with the rest of your working.

Five Rivers Fear Breaker

• • •

rose petals, St. John's wort, horehound, yarrow flowers, ylang-ylang

Five rivers of power flow through my life
Washing away the fear and the strife.
Air flows, fire flows, water flows, earth flows
Spirit flows, I grow!
Replacing my fear with courage and light!

Add three drops of universal liquid fluid condenser. Scatter this powder in a free-flowing creek or river as you recite the charm five times. Turn and walk away. Don't look back.

If you are at home, burn a blue candle and add the powder to a glass of water. As you repeat the charm, pour the water into a second empty glass. Continue pouring the water back and forth between the two glasses until you have repeated the chant five times. Take the water outside and pour on the ground, asking that the spirits of earth and water combine to bring you peace and release.

Forgiveness

• • •

white sage, rosemary, sugar, salt

Forgiveness of the self is the most complicated pattern of all. This powder is used to work through issues of guilt, lack, and regret, and it is an excellent formula to use for meditation, spellwork, and rituals of release. Rub the powder in your hands as you verbally let go of pain, unhappiness, fears, etc. As you brush the powder from your hands, you may wish to say, "*Spirits of air, I release all that harms me, blocks me, or stands in the way of my healing. I welcome happiness and harmony into my life.*"

Four Goddess Prosperity

• • •

allspice, patchouli, peppermint, galangal, ginger,
sassafras, blue vervain, moss, yellow dock, musk

Victoria smiles upon my fate
Concordia brings it to my gate
Libertas frees me from financial strain
Abundantia blesses monetary gain
Within and without, above and below
As I will, it shall be so!

I designed this formula after reading Jason Miller's *Financial Sorcery: Magical Strategies to Create Real and Lasting Wealth*. This is a wonderful prosperity book with both magickal and practical information. In this working you are accessing the four Roman goddesses of gain and abundance. I use four candles (green, gold, blue, and red) and place the formula in the center of the working. The colors are associated with the four elements; you can choose other colors for the representations if you like.

Gede (Conjure the Dead)

* * *

myrrh, mistletoe, wormwood, lavender, seven cemetery dirt, an offering of white rum, coffee, and water in separate glasses

Spirit of the Divine

The place of the center

The vortex of the crossroads

I call the honored dead

Asking for their assistance

Empower my actions with your aid.

Add one drop of each liquid to the powder. This is a calling powder used to call forth the dead. Use carefully and wisely. Note: Wormwood is poisonous; do not inhale. However; I give the ingredient here as it is traditional, particularly if you are using poppets or making charms that use the energies of the dead.

Recommended candle color: purple and white

Goddess Caffeina

* * *

ground coffee, allspice, cocoa, ginger, universal fluid condenser (or you can create a matching fluid condenser)

I win my choice this very day

All fall back, I have my way!

A great formula to use for action, motivation, courage, to improve memory, movement, to banish nightmares, to protect the family, home, and property, and for healing. Ruled by the planet Mars. This is a super motivational formula and can be used alone or in combination with other spellwork.

Good Spirits

* * *

myrrh, allspice, rose, althea, sandalwood

Peace with the gods
Peace with nature
Peace within
Only the good remains!

This formula is designed to work with the honored dead and is scattered on the ground or altar any time you call energies from beyond the veil. It is a favorite blend for All Hallows' Eve/Samhain and All Saints' Day.

Recommended candle color: white

Granny Silver's Special
ACTION AND GOOD FORTUNE FORMULA

* * *

coffee, cinnamon, allspice, nutmeg,
vanilla, ginger, orange peel

This is a mixture that can be used for a variety of purposes. I first combined the blend for making rolled grubby candles. Later on I added hot water to stain dolls and other projects, including my runic candle board. You can save the liquid in the refrigerator for several months. Simply pour very warm water in a jar and add as much mixture as you like. The more you add, the darker the brew!

I've also used it in poppets, loaded it into candles, added it to conjuring bags and mystic packets, and used the liquid form to dress candles, talismans and ... whew! You name it!

This is an *action* formula. All items are dry, except the vanilla extract—three drops will do or use nine for a large batch.

The formula is heavily fire, and it works extremely well with gold, red, orange, or yellow candles. Very all-purpose, it can be used for luck, love, money, good fortune, success, movement, and banishing (particularly if you add red hot peppers). You can even draw runes with the blend. You can add other ingredients to suit your needs: for example, graveyard dirt for protection or banishing; lavender, mint, or cinquefoil for more money; etc. Dirt from a prosperous business can be included if you are looking to expand your income or find a job.

Once you have all your ingredients together, perform a ceremony to empower the blend. Don't forget to seal your work. And yes, it does take on more power if you bury it for three days in the earth. Keep your dry mixture in an airtight container (a coffee can works great). I clearly mark mine "Granny Silver's Special" on the top with black marker so that someone doesn't put it in the coffee maker by mistake!

Grief Relief

• • •

chamomile, bergamot, cedar, cinnamon, frankincense, celandine, vetiver, marjoram, linden, lemon peel, lavender, evening primrose liquid fluid condenser or evening primrose herb

Pain and sorrow slip away
I turn myself to a brand-new day
Where joy and light replace the dark
And peace and happiness are in my heart.

Symptoms of grief include shock, sadness, guilt, anger, or fear. Physical symptoms include fatigue, nausea, weight fluctuation, aches, pains, and insomnia. Complicated grief includes intense longing, intrusive images, searching for the deceased, extreme anger, feeling that life is meaningless, avoiding things that remind you of your loss, intense guilt, feelings of unworthiness, imagining a loved one is still alive, slow speech or body functions, and thoughts of suicide. If you are experiencing any of these symptoms, please take the time to see a grief counselor.

Hammer Down Success

• • •

allspice, dragon's blood, ginger, cinnamon, red earth clay

Hammer down I win the day
Forward motion as I say
Blip to blip and dot to dot
Skipping to the target spot!

Fashion the red clay into a flat circular piece. Use a stylus to write in the clay what you wish to banish. Allow to dry. Crumble the clay into the powdered herbs and mix thoroughly. You can also use the water tray of a clay flower pot, draw your design with red indelible marker, then break and powder the clay pot base. Use repetitive sound—drums, the banging of a stick on a pot, the slamming of a hammer on a brick, etc. , while saying the chant. Be sure to verbally announce a succinct intent before using the charm.

Healing Glow

• • •

rosemary, bergamot, white sage, basil, spray with
lemon verbena herb and water or dip conjuring bag
in a mixture of lemon juice and blessed water

I set the love of the universe upon you
Let thou be lifted from darkness and happiness be thy name
By day you are in wholeness and by night you are free of pain
The joy of Spirit surrounds you and healing be thy gain!

Caduceus Healing Sigil

Both this and the healer's touch formula (below) are excellent herbal blends for healing conjuring bags, poppets, or packets to be taken to the hospital or placed in a sick room. Lavender can also be added to either formula along with the specially designed healing sigil given above. Write the individual's name on the back of the symbol nine times covered by the words "healing is wholeness" also written nine times.

Healing Loss from Stolen Money or Property

USE WHEN YOU HAVE EXPERIENCED
FINANCIAL DISTRESS

• • •

mint, sassafras

Clear-headed and healed
The money/property regained
Success and prosperity
Are mine once again
The evil goes out
While good fortune flies in
Wise choices are made
By myself and my kin
My bank account swells
With dollars and sense
Good fortune is back
My joy heaven sent!

Choose the cycle of repetition (one, three, seven, or nine days) as it pertains to the severity of what has been lost. Give the powder back to the earth when the magickal operation is concluded.

You can also cast this spell while rubbing fresh mint and sassafras in your palms along with a string that you have soaked in your saliva each day for seven days. Give the herbs back to the earth every day. Keep the string (there will be seven total at the end of the spell) in a white envelope in a safe place. On the seventh day, tie all the strings together, repeat the spell, then burn the knotted string.

Healer's Touch

• • •

sandalwood, peppermint, eucalyptus, salt, lavender

And these signs shall follow those that believe in the power
They shall cast out demons and they shall speak in new tongues
They shall take up serpents and if they drink anything deadly
it shall not harm them
They shall lay hands upon the sick, and they shall recover.

All-purpose formula used for minor to serious health issues. The chant is a passage from the Bible (Mark 16:17–18) used by Braucherei practitioners. Different sects within the faith play with the use and the meaning of the words. Here the charm is a protection both for the healer and for the individual in need.

Recommended candle color: use the color that corresponds to the need

Hels Gate Justice

• • •

patchouli, tobacco, red pepper, grave dirt, nettle, blackthorn,
black pepper, dirt from a police station or courthouse

Three sisters came from the east
Urd, Verdandi, and Skuld
The first one found them
The second one bound them
And the third one dragged them away!

This is a poppet formula to catch criminals (real ones where the perpetrator is absolutely guilty, not a perception of guilt). Stuff the poppet with either natural stuffing and the powder or just the herbs themselves along with the name of the criminal. Bind the hands and feet. Submerge the poppet in red wine or bitters or spray with a sour apple formula. Conduct the spell, then throw the poppet in the trash. The link to the magick was already made when you did the work. By releasing the poppet to the garbage, you release the magick to do its job. I know someone who tied the poppet to the back of their car, dragged it for several miles, and cut it loose. It worked. And no, the criminal was not bodily harmed; he was, however, caught by the authorities and punished for his crimes.

Recommended candle color: gold and purple (for the highest good)

Hex Breaker

• • •

lime peel, lemon verbena, clove, bay, vetivert, wintergreen, chili pepper, hyssop, a large screw, a screwdriver, a block of wood

The nasty broken tail in a twist
May your spell travel back while I live in bliss.
Caught by the screw, twisted and tight
You're stuck with the mess while I take free flight.

Twist the screw into the wood, repeating the charm with every turn.

If you know the person who has cursed you, say their name three times and then repeat the following:

All the magick you have done
Is broken, snapped, come undone!

Honor Powder

• • •

cornmeal, crushed birdseed

Eastwards I stand for favors I pray
From Goddess Divine and Lord of the Day
Earth lends her power and breath sends the spell
Day's end will reveal that all will be well.

Honor powder was designed to be used outside as an environmentally safe offering to Spirit. It is an excellent choice for sunrise ceremonies.

House Blessing—Formal

• • •

frankincense, myrrh, rose, lemongrass, basil,
eggshell, lavender, orange peel

Bless the four corners of this house and be the lintel blest
And bless the hearth and bless the board and bless each place of rest
And bless the doors that open wide to stranger as to kin
And bless each crystal window pane that lets the moonlight in
And bless the rooftop overhead and bless each sturdy wall
And bless our hearts and bless our minds with good health
    and love for all.
Peace with the gods
Peace with nature
Peace within
Only the good remains.

The powder can be used as an incense or charcoal incense tab. Use for a complete ritual that employs a lit white candle, blessed water, the magickal powder as incense or herbs in a white conjuring bag, and sweet bells that carry light, bright sounds, not heavy gong vibrations. Open every window and every door. Carry the ritual items on a tray dressed with a white cloth and fresh white flowers such as roses or carnations. Circle the room first with the incense. Use the flower heads to sprinkle the blessed water around the room or you can use the bag of herbs for this purpose or employ both. Follow by circling the room with the lit white candle. Finish by standing in the center of the room and ringing the bell three times.

The process is usually begun by intoning the charm while standing in the very center of the home. Next, go up to the highest level of the home and proceed through the home, cleansing every room and closet down into the basement or lowest level. Come up from the basement and finish in the center of the home, reciting the blessing again. Allow the white candle to burn completely. Close all windows and doors and seal them with clove oil or other protective magickal oil of your choice.

Jinx Remove

• • •

rose, clove, wintergreen, lemongrass, cinnamon,
twitch (couch) grass, devil's shoestring, salt

Jinx, begone; I close the gate

The past is over; I rule my fate

Out and gone, pattern broken

No breath gives light to what was spoken

Out and gone, it can't come back

Jinx removed, evil sacked!

Jinx Remove Sigil

You will also need a pair of open scissors, a potato, a pot of water, vinegar, red or black thread, and a banishing fluid condenser.

Grind the powder or mix a small amount of the above-listed dried herbals in a bowl. Write what you want to remove on the back of the jinx remove sigil that you have drawn or copied. Put four equal-armed crosses on the edges of the paper, then spit on what you wrote. (Yes, I said spit.) As you spit, think of getting rid of all the garbage and negative thinking inside of yourself. Even if you think someone else is causing the problem, you are internalizing it, so spit it out! Then hold the open scissors out in front of you—between yourself and the sigil (but not too close that you are going to hurt yourself when you close them). Quickly snap the scissors open and shut three times in front of your face (the scissors should be a good foot away from your face when you do this). This is a symbolic action to cut the ties and energy threads that connect you to the negativity.

Cut a slit in the potato. Sprinkle the herbal powder in the center of the paper. Twist the paper, thinking about how good you will feel when all negativity has been removed. Shove the paper deep in the slit of the vegetable. Wrap with red or black thread.

Boil the potato in a pot of water, vinegar, and ten drops of your banishing fluid condenser. When the water reaches a rolling boil, repeat the chant as many times as you feel it will take to lift the fog of crossed conditions, moving your hands in a sweeping-away-from-you motion over the potato and boiling water (like you are sweeping a bug away from you in the air). The steam, water, and potato will become impregnated with your words. (Don't forget that—for pity's sake, *never* argue with a spouse or loved one when you are cooking and steam is rising from the stove—it ramps up the negativity!) Seal the work with three equal-armed crosses in the air.

When the potato becomes somewhat soft, remove it from the boiling water with tongs. Allow to cool. Throw the potato in the trash and make sure it goes out the door immediately. The same for the water you used—dump it outside as soon as it is cool enough to handle. Forget the working and get on with your life.

Job Find

• • •

patchouli, cinnamon, galangal, ginger, sassafras, devil's shoestring,
a tool you like that best represents the type of joy/job you desire

Dress a piece of white cloth with the powder. Wrap the powder around the tool you have chosen. Conjure the tool and the powder:

> *Spirits of Mercury, Jupiter, and Venus, I call forth your gifts of*
> *wealth, good fortune, and prosperity. Swift and golden, may the*
> *success of the sun and the silver speed of Mercury bless me this day*
> *with finding and procuring my dream job. May all my desires be*
> *met with new employment (or promotion), and may my career*
> *blossom into all that I want and need. My dream job comes easily*
> *to me.*

Recommended candle color: orange (for opportunity) or a color you feel vibrates well with your new job

Jupiter's Gain Good Fortune

• • •

coriander seeds, pumpkin pie spice, yellow dock,
nutmeg, sarsaparilla, sage, Jezebel root

Jupiter brings the best in life
On eagle's wing and lightning strike
Expansion, profits, joy, and gain
Securely linked to my good name
I seize the day and win each fight
Guided safe by Jupiter's light.

I created the Jupiter's gain powder to be used with Jupiter planetary energies. The powder is best used when Jupiter is well aspected (for example, sun trine Jupiter, or Venus trine Jupiter, or Mercury sextile Jupiter, etc.) or on a Thursday of a waxing moon in the hour of Jupiter. This is a super gain formula and works very well for business activities. Add a lodestone or a magnet to increase the attraction energy.

Recommended candle color: purple and gold

Just Judge

• • •

brown sugar, cinnamon, name of judge, a drop of honey

Fair be the judge
Bright be the mind
I win the day
My will and my way!

Place the name of the judge in a small brown envelope with the above-listed ingredients. Hold the envelope in your hands and recite the charm nine times for three consecutive days before going to court. Carry the packet with you in the courtroom, preferably in your left shoe.

Recommended candle color: brown

Kisses 'n Candy Love

. . .

crushed hard candies, rose petals, cardamom, copal,
marjoram, orange peel, yohimbe, cinnamon

Venus brings me love divine
Eros blesses me and mine
Astarte graces from above
Granting me the truest love!

This formula is nice as an herbal blend placed in a red glass container
and sprayed with rose water or your favorite perfume. Beside it put a clear
glass of water. Repeat the charm three times every evening, whispering
the words over the herbal blend and the glass of fresh water. You can
drink the water or change it each evening.

Las Madamas (Society of Spirits/House Spirits)

. . .

dried apple peel, chamomile, galangal, ginger, 3 drops
bourbon, a glass of water, red and white altar cloth

Las Madamas, lend your ear
Good fortune mine this very year
Shining apples, taste of red
Motivation in my head
Creativity lava flows
Pattern set of joy and prose
Music dances, churns the air
Success rides on the edge of dare
To know, to will the breath unfold
Silence, still point, power hold…
Sparks ignite and twist of thought
What I wish will now be wrought!

Use to bring good fortune and creativity into the home.

Legal (General)

• • •

buckthorn, slippery elm, galangal, oregano, curry, cascara sagrada,
sassafras, brown sugar, calendula, dill, vervain, abre camino

The way is open, my success is clear

I win my case; there is nothing to fear

In sync with the judge, in sync with the law

The wheel turns my way.

Love

When you get right down to it, all magick is an act of seduction—the
process of using one's energy to attract, manipulate, or charm an individual, animal, plant, place, or thing. Seduction is not necessarily sexual,
although we often look at it that way. Love, sex, and seduction are not
always the same thing, particularly when we are discussing the murky
waters of love vs. sex.

The best love spell you can ever cast is on yourself. When you rise in
self-confidence and purity of self, you are naturally attractive to others.
When you show great compassion to others—when you listen, when you
care by governing your actions so that your harmonious energy elevates
another in a positive way—these are acts of love that rebound to the self.
The following spells concentrate on yourself, opening the way for true
love to emerge in your life. For the first spell, place the herbs in a white
cotton conjuring bag. Crush the bag, reciting the following charm. Dip
the bag in blessed water and dot on your face, neck, and heart chakra each
day for seven days. (If you have skin allergies, feel free to empower the
products that are safe for your skin with the same charm.)

Love and beauty are my claim

Magick spun in Goddess's name

Joy flows forth, passions face

Grants me with adoring grace!

Recommended candle color: pink or red

CHAPTER SIX

Love Drawing Bath Soap
• • •
rose petals, patchouli, orange peel, chamomile, coriander

Follow package instructions for melt-and-pour soap base. Add herbs as the last step before pouring.

Love Drawing Body Powder
• • •
rose petals, patchouli, orange peel

Powder herbs very finely and sift to remove any large pieces, then mix with cornstarch.

Lucky Black Cat
• • •
bay, allspice, nutmeg, patchouli, cinnamon, 3 drops honey

This formula is used for all manner of luck, gambling, and good fortune workings. (There are a variety of recipes for lucky black cat; this is just one of them.) Use with a lucky black candle or a black cat statue. Place in a black cat conjuring bag (a bag with the image of a black cat on it). Carry it with you for luck and good fortune. Add your name and a lock of the hair to the bag to increase your good luck!

Lucky Louie Good Fortune
• • •
bergamot, chamomile, nutmeg, cinnamon, galangal, allspice,
3 drops apple fragrance, 3 drops bourbon, a golden key tied
to a lodestone with gold or red thread, a 3-inch stick gathered
from the woods, the symbols of Mercury and Venus

Three the stick of witness be
Gold the glitter on the key
Three the tap awaken thus
Rouse the power of Venus!
Lodestone, draw the luck to me
As I will, so mote it be!

Create the physical charm, fashioning it in the way you desire, incorporating the key, lodestone, and symbols into something you can carry. On the new moon, sprinkle with the Lucky Louie herbal powder or place your drawing charm in a red or golden bag along with the raw herbals. Empower and carry with you for luck. Renew every new moon or re-empower each month for six months with apple-scented spray.

Recommended candle color: red

Mega Money Draw

• • •

peppermint, buckwheat hull, bladderwrack, orange peel

This is a great powder to use in rolled beeswax candles or in money drawing soap.

Money Draw

• • •

allspice, patchouli, peppermint, galangal, ginger,
sassafras, sarsaparilla, blue vervain, yellow dock,
marigold petals, lavender, a magnet, 3 golden nails

Use in conjuring bags to draw money to you. Dress candles and your wallet with the powder. Place herbal formula in an earthen jar along with dirt from three profitable banks and your name. Feed the jar with coins every new moon. When the jar is full, give the change to charity or someone who needs it.

> Spirits of Venus and Jupiter, spirits of the sun and Mercury,
> I call forth your gifts of wealth, positive abundance, good fortune,
> and prosperity. Swift and golden, may the success of the sun, the
> attraction of Venus, the blessings of Jupiter, and the speed of
> Mercury encompass me this day with ever-growing success.
> May my accounts, purse, house, and wallet be full and
> overflowing with prosperity in tangible form. Money
> comes to me easily. So mote it be!

Recommended candle color: use both green and gold

Move Along

BANISHMENT OF BAD NEIGHBORS, A GOSSIP, OR THE COMMON SOCIOPATH

• • •

hot peppers, black pepper, curry, marjoram, vervain,
ginger, dill, ghost peppers, Dead Sea salt, cinnamon,
3 drops fire element fluid condenser

A better place you find today
Karma dictates which the way.
I break your claim upon my field
The pipeline closed, new way revealed
I cut your ties from me to thee
You move off and I be free.
A better place you find today
Karma dictates which the way.

The psycho neighbor who always complains about you to the authorities…the person at work who spreads gossip and tries to ruin your career…the employee who is milking the system, leaving you with all the work (that's killing you) but who is related to your boss…the person who you know isn't right in the head and the damage is causing great distress in your life: that is what this powder is all about. You don't want to hurt anyone, and you wish they would be happier somewhere else; perhaps there they will find the healing they need and not at your expense. Too often we try to micromanage spells, trying to guide the way of another's life path. This charm is for those situations where you just give it up to the universe.

You can also truncate this charm by using only the first two lines in a repetitive singsong fashion. Another way to use the blend is to encircle a citronella or lemon verbena candle with the herbs. Burn the candle in the hour of Mars for three days.

Peace

• • •

lavender, lemon peel, violet, orris, cardamom,
frankincense, bergamot, basil, copal

Peace I ask thee, O universe
I embrace the light from the heavens
I embrace the light from the earth
I embrace the light of Spirit
I accept the joy of rebirth!

Wrap the herbal formula in a small piece of white cloth and carry with you or scatter powder on both front and back doorsteps of the home.

Recommended candle color: white or light blue

Protection

• • •

cedar, rosemary, cinquefoil, marjoram, yarrow flowers,
dill, blue cohosh, African violet flowers

You can't see me
You can't find me
You can't hurt me anymore!

Scatter on the doorstep and in front (on the outside) of every window of the house on the lower level of the home. On upper levels, open window and rub against the outer sill. Turn one mirror in the house toward the wall and rub the herb formula on the back of the mirror. Leave the mirror turned inward for as long as you feel necessary; some practitioners keep it that way at all times.

Recommended candle color: dark blue

Psychic Shield

• • •

larkspur, white sage, rosemary, angelica, hyssop,
clove, lemon verbena, black salt

Designed for those who are feeling like they are under psychic attack. I originally created the formula to protect individuals who love haunted places from the unseen (whatever it may be). A friend of mine does ghost tours in Gettysburg, so I made a round bundle with the above ingredients and dressed the bag with violet essential and lemon verbena liquid fluid condenser. The bundle was tied with white cord and white feathers as well as a piece of amethyst.

Recommended candle color: white or purple

Queen of Heaven/Goddess Blessing Formula

• • •

baby powder, grapefruit seeds or dried peel, sandalwood

To be used anytime you wish to invoke the Mother Goddess.

Holy Mother, she who orchestrates the stars
Who loves unconditionally, who heals all—
Embrace my petitions with love and light
And bring grace and happiness to those who ask for thy help.
Whether bright the day or dark the night
The Mother's love will set things right.

Recommended candle color: white

Release Negativity

• • •

lavender, rose, lilac, carnation

I blend with the spirit of the universe. I release my feelings of
anxiety, hatred, insecurity, and emotional pain and attachment
from my mind, body, heart, and soul. I am one with the universe
accepting the change I desire, and I am joy!

I initially made this formula in candle form, with carnation and lilac fragrances blended with lavender essential oil, lavender herb, dried powdered rose petals, and lilac flowers and leaves. I constructed the formula so that you could let go of anything material, mental, or emotional. What I didn't expect was for it to work so well in selling things that have been difficult to unload because the person selling it had a problem releasing the object or property due to an emotional attachment. Imagine my surprise when several customers wrote to tell me that they had been able to sell a house, cars, and other home items that had before stubbornly resisted moving!

A helpful hint: take a piece of twine and wrap it one length around what you are trying to sell (yup, even a house or a car). Hey, it is actually fun doing this—you are "taking the measure" of the object. Use the charm, changing it a bit to name what you are letting go of. Cut the twine into several pieces and burn it or simply throw it in the trash, seriously indicating your release of the object.

Recommended candle color: white or light blue

Road Opener (Remove Blocks)

. . .

orange peel, chamomile, devil's shoestring, bergamot,
marigold petals, brown sugar, bay, calamus, abre
camino, honeysuckle leaves or flowers

Perfection of the universe, open the way
The sun shines bright on my path today
Doors are open, the view is clear
Forward I move with nothing to fear.
Zisa! Zisa! Zisa!

Can be used with any road opener intent. Can be utilized with the Rad and Cen runes or with Ganesha (Ganapati, Vinayaka), an elephant-headed deity in the Hindu pantheon best known for removing obstacles and who is the patron of arts and sciences. I keep a statue of an elephant on my prosperity altar surrounded with this herbal blend dressed with road opener liquid fluid condenser that I have made myself.

Recommended candle color: orange

Sekhmet

. . .

dragon's blood, cinnamon, ginger, cypress

Hear me, O great warrior queen!
She who is the eye of Ra, lady of light and terror
Sa Sekem Sahu, goddess of medicine and fire!
I call thee forth in dignity and honor
To aid me in my working this night/day.

Sekhmet is a lion-headed warrior/healing goddess in the ancient Egyptian pantheon. She will lead you when you must fight. She will bring healing when you have been stricken with disease. She protects abused women, children, and animals, and fights the good fight for honor and justice.

Recommended candle color: burgundy

Send Back (Reverse Harm)

• • •

eucalyptus, rue, nettles, sandalwood, horseradish, red
peppers wrapped in skunk cabbage leaves (or dry and grind
the skunk cabbage and use as part of the powder)

I send back the evil it cannot return
The way is closed, the bridges are burned
Your words, deeds, and thoughts retreat to your brain
By sound, herbs, and spirit, I put you to shame.

This formula is used to send back a spell or a hex. You can use the horseradish root as a poppet and roll it in the powder or you can stuff a poppet with the herbs and paint it with horseradish from the grocery store, preferably a bottled brand with additional spicy herbal additives. Add a few drops of the fire element fluid condenser by brushing it on the poppet. Intone the charm nine times over the poppet, then burn the poppet in a firesafe cauldron.

Send It to the Grave
BANISHMENT FORMULA

• • •

patchouli, devil's shoestring, twitch grass, grave dirt, coffin nail

The wicked stutter, bend, and break
Blackened ground beckons fate
Twitching shoestrings strengthen knot
Musk of grave to bury thought
Nail to fix and stone to seal
Blood to thicken and congeal

Nail to coffin, ne'er to rise
Your evil be your own demise!

I've used this formula for placing problems in small wooden coffins that you can purchase during the Halloween season. Bury the coffin in a graveyard. (If legalities are a problem—private property, rules of the cemetery, etc.—bury the coffin deep in the woods in the same way. Some practitioners prefer using the dirt edge of a deserted backcountry crossroads.) Draw the seal of Saturn over the top. Stamp on the ground three times and cover with a heavy stone. Change the wording to suit the situation. For example, if you wish to release yourself from a problem, you may choose a different charm or reword this one.

Recommended candle color: white and black (although no candles are mentioned in the spell, practitioners are encouraged to use their creativity)

Serenity
• • •
willow bark, sand from the beach, Dead Sea salt

The sea of serenity is all around me
The sea of serenity is in me
The sea of serenity is around me and in me
And I can create anything!
Peace, joy, and serenity flow in me and round me always!

You can turn this into a powder by grinding the willow bark and adding it to the sand and sea salt, or you can spread the sand and sea salt on a smooth plate and draw designs in the mixture with a willow branch while saying the charm nine times each morning for nine mornings.

Recommended candle color: white and sea green

Steady Customers
• • •
tangerine, lime, ginger, bay, sandalwood, peppermint, bladderwrack

Dress a lodestone with the herbal powder and wrap in a gold or a green cloth. Add three drops of money draw liquid fluid condenser. Spray with peppermint-scented mist (peppermint essential oil mixed with blessed water and shaken well before spraying). Carry packet with you or place in the cash register of your business.

Steady Income

· · ·

pine, ginger, moss, goldenseal, honeysuckle leaves or flowers

Dress the herbs with 3 drops jasmine essential oil. For this spell, you will need three pennies, a small toy train or ship (your ship comes in/ wealth), and a jar or conjure bag. Place herbs, toy, and pennies in the jar or conjuring bag along with 3 drops of prosperity or money draw liquid fluid condenser. Repeat "magick swell and magick flow, make my mill of money grow" for as many times as you can until you lose the thought. Follow with this daily affirmation: "I will enjoy life. I will laugh. I will find riches in harmony. I will access my full potential, and I will succeed!"

Recommended candle color: lime green

Strength and Accomplishment

· · ·

bay, saffron, tea, damiana, ginger, woodruff, pine,
cloves, olive leaf, gum mastic, mistletoe

My voice will echo loud and strong
The words the pattern magick song
My breath brings life to what will be
My thoughts create that all will see
Strength! Success! That is! In me!

Place herbs in a red conjuring bag and hold in both hands. Say loudly, "I conjure thee!" Continue with the charm, saying it three times with feeling.

Recommended candle color: red

SunLion Success

• • •

sunflower seed hulls, cinquefoil, ginger, cedar, dandelion

Mighty herbs of nature's glory
I conjure thee: success my story.

This conjuration is designed for the hour of the sun on a Sunday. It can also be used on a new moon to get projects started and works very well on midsummer or when the sun or moon is in Leo. Carry the conjuring bag with you and re-empower at each phase of the moon, from new to full (so you will be working with the conjuring bag eight times throughout the month). Charm is to be said nine times, on each moon phase.

Recommended candle color: gold or yellow

Sweet Wind Solstice/Equinox Wish Formula

• • •

sea salt, buckthorn, basil, element of air

I use this mixture on the morning of the spring equinox, summer solstice, fall equinox, and winter solstice. You can add to it, particularly if you like an unusual herb; the base, however, is simply sea salt and basil. I perform the working outdoors on my porch.

Gather your supplies—sea salt, basil, buckthorn, bowl. Utilize the sea of potential exercise.

Rub your hands together briskly in a circular motion until they become warm. Place your hands over the ingredients and intone "only the good remains" nine times.

Mix the salt and herbs together in the bowl.

Rub your fingers in a clockwise direction around the rim of the bowl, saying, "Sweet wind cometh, bringing joy" (nine times). Blow softly on the mixture (so as not to scatter it) three times. Use nice long breaths with the intent to instill joy.

Draw an equal-armed cross over the bowl to seal it.

You can bottle the mixture for later use or proceed with the next step.

Take the mixture to your doorstep, on the steps of your home, right below the steps on the ground, or on the walkway (your choice).

Straighten your shoulders. Stand up straight. Breathe deeply, then address the spirit of sweet winds:

Spirit of sweet winds, come to me now.
Bring thy joy, thy laughter, thy cleansing breath!
Circle me now and bestow the gifts of happiness, peace, and love!

Say this in a confident tone of voice. Give it a little time and you will feel the shift around you. The breezes will caress your face, and you will experience an uplifting sensation.

Scatter the sweet wind mixture on the ground, again repeating "only the good remains" for at least nine times or as long as it takes to sprinkle the mixture. In your own way, thank the universe.

Recommended candle color: white

Swift Endings
• • •

cinnamon, dill, patchouli, vervain, ginger, celery seed,
ghost peppers, 7 small dead sticks (3–4 inches in length)
collected from nature on a Spirit Walk, sea salt

Swift the closure, fast the finish
Over it! No longer in it!
Banish sadness, sever ties
I the phoenix ever rise!

Write out the problem and place the paper on the inside bottom of a small mason jar. Fill the jar halfway with the sea salt and cover with the swift endings powder. Each day insert one stick into the sand/powder mixture until it touches the bottom of the jar and the paper while reciting the charm three times. On the seventh day, cap the jar and throw it in the trash.

Recommended candle color: red

Transformation

. . .

lavender, lemon balm, lemongrass, lemon peel,
skullcap, vervain, lemon verbena

I designed this formula for people who are ready to release negativity surrounding past unfortunate circumstances and move forward. Write down what you wish to release. Spit on the paper. Allow it to dry. Cover the paper with the herbal ingredients or with the powder and burn outdoors. After the ashes are cool, release in a peaceful place.

Recommended candle color: turquoise or seafoam green

Transition

. . .

green tea, lemongrass, lemon verbena, lavender

The transition formula was originally designed to spiritually support and lessen fear for an individual who was going through the gender reassignment process. We made an herbal bath with blessed water that was used at the beginning of each stage during the two-year process, as well as a conjuring bag of the herbals for the person to carry with them. We changed the herbals every three months. This formula also works very well for ceremonies marking the change from childhood to adulthood.

Recommended candle color: white

Triple Action and Motivation

. . .

vervain, red saffron, cinnamon, calamus, galangal, vanilla

Fast and furious speeds the game
Open the road for joy and gain!
Crown of success is mine today
As I will, I win my way!

I use this formula with a centerpiece of three racing horses for all manner of business and personal success, and I have used it to stuff horse spirit dolls for totem work. This is a great formula to use as the sun rises in a dawn ceremony. I also like using the conjuration on a Tuesday during a waxing moon (best in a fire sign) in a Mars planetary hour.

Recommended candle color: red

White Owl Wisdom

. . .

white tea, spearmint, sage, horehound,
eyebright, 1 drop cypress essential oil

Like the moth, the owl is a messenger from the spirit world. To invoke owl wisdom, at dusk sprinkle the powder at your feet as you stand facing west. Whisper to the spirit of the owl with the following charm. Indicate your intent, then follow with the Call to Wisdom prayer.

> *I hear your wisdom in twilight bright*
> *And then again in dark of night*
> *Your call echoes power and tells me of death*
> *Of what must be finished and what put to rest*
> *Of where magick placed will do the most good*
> *And where I should stand in the depths of the wood.*

Call to Wisdom Prayer:

> *May the universe open the pathway*
> *To joy, wisdom, clarity, and right solutions.*
> *May I be blessed with peace of mind*
> *In my thoughts, feelings, and choices.*

Witches' Foot Hexefus Protection

• • •

black salt, yarrow, red clover, pennyroyal

Witches' Foot Blummersterne

Blummersterne means "flower star" and is also called the Hexefus Rosette. The symbol is used to ward off bad luck, accidents, illness, gossip, and general evil. It is invoked as a protective symbol and used in Braucherei magicks and healing. Write your protection request on the back of the design. Color the sigil and place the powder in the center with the colored candle you desire.

Worry Breaker

• • •

angelica, black cohosh, black-eyed Susan, chrysanthemum,
garlic, yarrow, St. John's wort, thistle

The darkness weighs upon my head
But here I conjure light instead
The joy, the love, the sweet, the peace
For on that path I find release!

This blend covers a variety of fears that lead to constant worry. The angelica provides protection given to you by your guardians, while the black cohosh dissolves the negative energy created by fear-based relationships. The black-eyed Susan is to bring light to the mind, while the chrysanthemum is thought to soothe the fear of loss of physical objects. The garlic tones down nervous energy, the yarrow keeps the individual from being overly sensitive, the St. John's wort protects from hexes and night terrors, and the thistle cuts down on the worry about bills, shelter, and food for the family. I prefer to use this blend in a white conjuring bag dressed with violet fragrance or essential oil, or I make an herb pillow, first mixing the raw herbs with several drops of the violet essential oil. Prettily decorated with ribbons and lace, this is a lovely gift for someone going through a rough time.

As you stuff the pillow or conjuring bag, remember to command the blend to work for your specific intent, then recite the charm three times. If the pillow or bag is for another person, change the wording of the charm to match the individual.

Yule Good Fortune Gift Bag Formula
• • •

ginger, lavender, chamomile, peppermint herb and candies, sassafras, crushed pine cones, cinnamon, white nutmeg, goldenseal, dressed pumpkin seeds (pumpkin seeds dried from Samhain pumpkin carving festivities and rolled in Granny Silver's special formula)

Lace mixture with pine essential oil and good fortune cornucopia fluid condenser.

I love to mix herbal sachets to give as gifts during the Yule holidays. I sew the bags myself from themed cotton material and create a ribbon drawstring closure that can be easily opened. Once I have mixed and blessed the herbal formula, I place the blend in the holiday bags. During the first healing circle in December I distribute the bags, telling the recipients that they should add their names and a lock of their hair to the bag, breathing their wishes for good fortune into the bag before they close it. Leave the bag on your altar or hang from the Yule tree. Burn on New Year's Eve as the clock strikes the first hour of the New Year!

Recommended candle color: red, green, and white

Planetary Powder Formulas

These recipes are excellent for matching the planetary hour of a working or when using the planets as the primary focus of your magick. For example, if you wish to find a solution to a problem, use the Mercury planetary powder along with a conjuration involving Mercury in the hour of Mercury. I use these formulas in my hand-rolled candles as well as other applications. These herbals were chosen by considering aroma, planetary rulership, and ease of procurement. You may wish to use other herbs in your formulas—perhaps that you have gathered yourself from your locality that share the same rulership, or unique herbals or items that can be obtained from a botanica.

Mars: allspice, basil, dragon's blood, mustard, galangal, chili, ginger, woodruff. For assertion, harnessing force, and shaping energy by will. Color: red.

Sun: sunflower hulls, tangerine, cedar, rue, marigold, chamomile, cinnamon, frankincense, oak. For power of integration, vitality, and true will. Color: yellow.

Moon: eucalyptus, myrrh, sandalwood, wintergreen, willow, lemon balm. For storage of power, instinct, and emotions. The moon is thought to collect energy and then turn it to the earth. Color: white or silver.

Venus: cardamom, rose, vervain, orris, plantain, yarrow, thyme, balm of Gilead. For attraction, strategy, beauty, abundance, and drawing energy. Color: pink or seafoam green.

Mercury: bergamot, lavender, lemon verbena, lemongrass, marjoram, horehound, peppermint, dill. For stream of consciousness, mental prowess, and the flow of energy from one point to another. Color: light blue.

Jupiter: cinquefoil, clove, sage, hyssop, sassafras, nutmeg, sarsaparilla, yellow dock, linden. For expansive nature, creativity, luck, good fortune, and grace. Color: orange/purple.

Saturn: ivy, skullcap, Solomon's seal, patchouli, lobelia, slippery elm. For limits, protection, rewards for hard work, and energy run along a particular path (guidelines). Color: brown.

The Modern Outer Planets

The modern outer planets are considered higher octaves of the classical planets, and each functions in its own way. These are considered the spiritual planets, each changing circumstances for a life more in tune with a better path. However, each of these planets is a heavy hitter; change is not necessarily so easy because we have somehow gotten stuck and refuse to see the way out. This is when the universe comes along and knocks you upside the head—usually with the energies of one of these planets. Use them wisely.

The formulas for the outer planets, Uranus, Neptune, and Pluto, are my own. In making my choices I took into consideration their modern rulership, the classical rulership of those same signs, and the type of energy these planets represent.

♅ Uranus

Electrifies energy to shatter bindings. Uranus zaps what is stuck, and therefore its energy is often seen as an unwanted shock or an unexpected bonus. Supercharged, it functions like Mercury on steroids. It is a bolt out of the blue that shakes up everything, rattling old habits and beliefs loose, allowing a pattern to be rearranged in a way that is more conducive to the practitioner. Color: electric blue.

Formula: lobelia, dill, peppermint, fenugreek, saltpeter. Please note that this formula is combustible and should be handled with care. Saltpeter is considered a toxic ingredient as it is a chemical, not a natural item.

♆ Neptune

Dissolves energy, yet in the dissolution it creates instability wherein confusion and illusion weave in and out. This is because with Neptune's ability to softly disperse, what remains is in suspension—the pattern of energy is not set and takes on a variety of images until focus is regained. Of all the planets, perhaps it is indicative of the world we really live in, one controlled only by our thoughts and actions. Since our thoughts can run rampant without a clear goal, many patterns appear and disappear until a bolstered intent is finally set. When using Neptune to dissolve a situation, it should be followed by a clear and unified goal so that the new energy pattern can be quickly set. Neptune energy can also show the many lines of possibility or breaking out of one's own illusions to see the bigger picture and therefore is favored in divination. Traditionally, Neptune energy is used in confusion spells, particularly when dealing with an enemy who has focused on you. The idea is to break that focus so that you can move away and pull the target off your back. Color: pink.

Formula: self-heal (sanicle), lemon rind, hawthorne, flax seed, poppy seed, valerian.

♇ Pluto

Transformation, death, and regeneration. Rather than electrifying or dissolving, Pluto incinerates the issue and builds something else in its place. It destroys the pattern completely so that a new pattern with different components can be constructed. It isn't interested in clearing out the clog (like Drano) or rearranging what is there (like Legos); it just makes it gone and starts with new material. This is one of the reasons why this planet was chosen to be co-ruler of Scorpio, the power down below that rises up like lava and blows everything to smithereens. Pluto sometimes stands for corruption within an organization. It is dark, it is heavy, and it erodes before it explodes. Color: burgundy.

Note: Use on the waning moon, in the last quarter (eight cycle) or at the very beginning of the balsamic (eight cycle); if you are using the quarter formula of the moon, at the beginning or middle of the fourth quarter. Use this powder or herbal blend to root out and destroy corruption.

Formula: echinacea, clove, oregano, goldenseal, garlic, hot peppers, ginger, cinnamon, tumeric, black pepper, curry, wormwood (poisonous). All of these herbs are known to kill cancer cells. This formula will work just fine without the wormwood.

Safe Herbals for Including in
Magickal Soaps or Body Powders

The following herbs or spices are considered safe for use in magickal body powders and soaps, barring personal skin allergies or other health issues; please consult your physician. These herbs can be ground into magickal powders and added to your soaps or used alone or mixed with a filler or salt if you so desire. You will find instructions for making enchanted soaps in my book *HedgeWitch*. I have included a soap base supplier in the resources section in the back of this book should you be looking for a reliable one.

Allspice: Mars/fire

Almonds: Mercury/air

Barley: Venus/earth

Basil: Mars/fire

Bergamot: Mercury/air

Bladderwrack: Moon/water

Brown Sugar: Venus/water

Calendula: Sun/fire

Cardamom: Venus/water

Chamomile: Sun/fire

Chocolate: Mars/fire

Cinnamon (use only a small amount): Sun/fire

Coffee: Mars/fire

Coriander: Mars/fire

Cornmeal: Venus/earth

Dill: Mercury/air

Eucalyptus: Moon/water

Ginger: Mars/fire

Ginseng: Sun/fire

Green Tea: Sun/fire

Juniper Berries: Sun/fire

Lavender: Mercury/air

Lemongrass: Mercury/air

Lemon Peel: Moon/water

Lemon Verbena: Mercury/air

Lime Peel: Sun/fire

Mints: Mercury/air

Nutmeg: Jupiter/fire

Oatmeal: Venus/earth

Orange: Sun/fire

Oregano: Venus/Air

Patchouli: Saturn/earth

Rosemary (finely ground): Sun/fire

Safflower: Sun/fire

Sage: Jupiter/air

Thyme: Venus/water

CONCLUSION

I would like to thank you for spending time with me! I believe that everyone deserves a life of good fortune and happiness—one where they can create and are surrounded by a tremendous atmosphere of spirituality, love, and peace. This book encourages change in yourself in unique and artistic ways based on your willingness to let go of patterns that no longer suit you. Perhaps you will look to the universal energies of love and compassion through the assistance of nature and find a new blending of personal power. It is my sincere hope that the contents of this book will help you bloom and expand your joy into the consciousness of humanity.

Commune.

Connect.

Believe!

In service,

SILVER RAVENWOLF

APPENDIX
Herbal Resources

Recommended Magickal Herb Friendly Shops

Hemlock House: 5430 Sherman-Mayville Rd. (route 430),
Mayville, NY 14757. (716) 220-2082. Open seasonally; most
days 10 a.m.–8 p.m. Feel free to call ahead if traveling through.
Stop in for a bit of that old time magic at Hemlock House, the
outpost for wayfaring wise people. Bulk herbs and essential
oils, magickally crafted objects and jewelry, bones, skins and
stones, honey produced onsite, handmade brooms and baskets,
soaps, potions, handspun alpaca and wool yarns, alpaca fiber for
spinning and felting.

Strange Brew, The Cauldron, Inc.: 2703 Elmwood Avenue,
Kenmore, NY 14217. (716) 871-0282.

Other Resources of Interest

Candle Science: http://www.candlescience.com. High-quality soy
and fragrances that indicate their ingredients. By far the best
soy candle company on the net. They also have soap base. All of
Candle Science's fragrances match their wax products.

Candlewic: http://www.candlewic.com. Beeswax sheets in a
variety of colors for rolling your own candles.

Glenbrook Farms Herbs and Such: www.glenbrookfarm.com. High-quality, good color, food-grade herbs at reasonable prices, with many organic offerings.

How to Make Your Own Loose Incense: http://www.scents-of -earth.com/makyourownna.html.

Specialty Bottle: http://www.specialtybottle.com. A wide variety of bottles, jars, and tins for your crafting and magickal needs.

Richters Herbs: http://www.richters.com. Handles a wide variety of fresh herb and vegetable plants for immediate shipment.

BIBLIOGRAPHY AND
RECOMMENDED READING

Agrippa, Henry Cornelius. *Three Books of Occult Philosophy*. St. Paul, MN: Llewellyn, 1992.

Bardon, Franz. *Initiation into Hermetics*. Salt Lake City, UT: Merkur, 1956.

Beryl, Paul. *The Master Book of Herbalism*. Ardenvoir, WA: Phoenix Publications, 1994.

Cunningham, Scott. *Cunningham's Encyclopedia of Magical Herbs*. St. Paul, MN: Llewellyn, 1985.

Dalai Lama. *The Universe in a Single Atom: The Convergence of Science and Spirituality*. New York: Harmony Books, 2005.

Daniels, Estelle. *Astrologickal Magick*. York Beach, ME: Samuel Weiser, 1995.

Davis, Owen. *America Bewitched: The Story of Witchcraft after Salem*. Oxford, UK: Oxford University Press, 2013.

Dey, Charmaine. *Facts and Fundamentals of Ritual Candle Burning*. Old Bethpage, NY: Original Publications, 1982.

Dominguez, Ivo, Jr. *Practical Astrology for Witches and Pagans*. San Francisco, CA: Red Wheel/Weiser, 2016.

Fearrington, Basil. *The New Way to Learn Astrology*. St. Paul, MN: Llewellyn, 1999.

Flowers, Stephen Edred. *Hermetic Magic: The Postmodern Magical Papyrus of Abaris*. San Francisco, CA: Red Wheel/Weiser, 1995.

Graves, Julia. *The Language of Plants: A Guide to the Doctrine of Signatures*. Great Barrington, MA: Lindisfarne Books, 2012.

Greer, John Michael, and Christopher Warnock. *The Picatrix Liber Atratus Edition*. Iowa City, IA: Adocentyn Press, 2011.

Hand, Robert. *Planets in Transit*. 1976. Algen, PA: Whitford Press, 1976.

James, Rex, and Robert James. *Essentials of the Earth*. Cascade, ID: Essentials of the Earth LLC, 2015.

Kaminski, Patricia, and Richard Katz. *Flower Essence Reparatory: A Comprehensive Guide to the Flower Essences Researched by Dr. Edward Bach and the Flower Essence Society*. Nevada City, CA: Flower Essence Society, 2004.

Kieckhefer, R. *Magic in the Middle Ages*. Cambridge, UK: Cambridge UP, 1989.

Kowalchik, Claire, and William Hylton. *Rodale's Illustrated Encyclopedia of Herbs*. 1998. Emmaus, PA: St. Martin's Press, 1998.

Leek, Sybil. *Cast Your Own Spell*. New York: Pinnacle Books/Bee-Line Books, 1970.

Makransky, Bob. *Planetary Hours*. Bournemouth, England: The Wessex Astrologer, 2015.

Miller, Jason. *Financial Sorcery: Magickal Strategies to Create Real and Lasting Wealth*. Pompton Plains, NJ: Career Press, 2012.

Paracelsus. *Paracelsus: Selected Writings*. J. Jacobi, ed. Princeton, NJ: Princeton University Press, 1951.

Rankine, David, and Sorita d'Este. *Practical Planetary Magick*. London, England: Avalonia, 2007.

RavenWolf, Silver. *Hedgewitch: Spells, Crafts, and Rituals for Natural Magick*. Woodbury, MN: Llewellyn, 2008.

———. *Solitary Witch: The Ultimate Book of Shadows for the New Generation*. St. Paul, MN: Llewellyn, 2003.

Slater, Herman. *The Magickal Formulary.* New York: Magickal Childe, 1981.

Storms, G. *Anglo-Saxon Magic.* The Hague: Nijhoff, 1948.

Three Initiates. *The Kybalion: A Study of the Hermetic Philosophy of Ancient Egypt and Greece.* Sioux Falls, SD: NuVision Publications, 2007.

Weschcke, Carl Llewellyn, and Joe H. Slate. *Clairvoyance for Psychic Empowerment.* Woodbury, MN: Llewellyn, 2015.

INDEX

To order, call 1-877-NEW-WRLD
or visit LLEWELLYN.COM

Prices subject to change without notice

Hedge Witch

Spells, Crafts & Rituals for Natural Magick

Silver RavenWolf

Get a fast and fun jumpstart on the Hedge Witch path with a little help from the immensely popular Silver RavenWolf. Arranged in an easy-to-follow format, this gifty guidebook has everything a new witch needs to practice the free-spirited, informal garden- and cottage-based witchery of Hedge Craft.

At the core of the book is a fourteen-lesson, hands-on guide that readers complete at their own pace, interacting with different aspects of nature in simple yet powerful ways, such as by performing the Night of the Starry Sky ritual. The lessons, which can be done alone or with a group, culminate in an inspiring dedication ceremony.

A handy reference section offers tips, formulas, recipes, and helpful hints on topics such as soap making, tea leaf reading, butterfly garden magick, and organically growing your own herbs.

978-0-7387-1423-3

7½ x 9⅛, 336 pp.

Secrets of Energy,
Magick & Manifestation

SILVER RAVENWOLF

MindLight

To order, call 1-877-NEW-WRLD
or visit LLEWELLYN.COM

Prices subject to change without notice

MindLight

Secrets of Energy, Magick & Manifestation

Silver RavenWolf

According to Silver RavenWolf, changing our reality is absolutely possible. The bestselling "Solitary Witch" introduces a groundbreaking system—based on quantum physics, magick, and energy—for tapping into the life-changing potential in all of us.

RavenWolf puts quantum physics theories into plain English and explains how they can be put into practice for personal fulfillment. She teaches how to achieve a special state of consciousness, including how to create and project a "mindlight," or ball of energy, through meditations, visualizations, rituals, and mind exercises. These techniques—some involving elemental energies, astrology, oils, and herbs—can be used for healing, problem solving, relaxation, banishing negative thoughts, and general well-being.

978-0-7387-0985-7

6 x 9, 288 pp.

To order, call 1-877-NEW-WRLD
or visit LLEWELLYN.COM

Prices subject to change without notice

Solitary Witch
The Ultimate Book of Shadows for the New Generation
Silver RavenWolf

This book has everything a teen witch could want and need between two covers: a magickal cookbook, encyclopedia, dictionary, and grimoire. It relates specifically to today's young adults and their concerns, yet is grounded in the magickal work of centuries past.

Information is arranged alphabetically and divided into five distinct categories: (1) Shadows of Religion and Mystery, (2) Shadows of Objects, (3) Shadows of Expertise and Proficiency, (4) Shadows of Magick and Enchantment, and (5) Shadows of Daily Life. It is organized so readers can skip over the parts they already know or read each section in alphabetical order.

978-0-7387-0319-0

8 x 10, 608 pp.

SILVER
RAVENWOLF

Angels COMPANIONS IN MAGICK

To order, call 1-877-NEW-WRLD
or visit LLEWELLYN.COM

Prices subject to change without notice

Angels

Companions in Magick

Silver RavenWolf

In this treasury of practical wisdom, magickal techniques, and fascinating angel lore you'll find out how to work with angels to create happiness, healing, and abundance; discover your true purpose for this lifetime; and make the world a better place using blessings for peace, prosperity, and protection.

978-156718-724-3

7 x 10, 360 pp.